Contents

List of figures and boxes

Figures

Box

POVERTY AND INSECURITY

Life in low-pay, no-pay Britain

Tracy Shildrick, Robert MacDonald, Colin Webster
and Kayleigh Garthwaite

First published in Great Britain in 2012 by

The Policy Press
University of Bristol
Fourth Floor
Beacon House
Queen's Road
Bristol BS8 1QU
UK
Tel +44 (0)117 331 4054
Fax +44 (0)117 331 4093
e-mail tpp-info@bristol.ac.uk
www.policypress.co.uk

North American office:
The Policy Press
c/o The University of Chicago Press
1427 East 60th Street
Chicago, IL 60637, USA
t: +1 773 702 7700
f: +1 773-702-9756
e:sales@press.uchicago.edu
www.press.uchicago.edu

British Library Cataloguing in Publication Data
A catalogue record for this book is available from the British Library.

Library of Congress Cataloging-in-Publication Data
A catalog record for this book has been requested.

ISBN 978 1 84742 910 0 paperback
ISBN 978 1 84742 911 7 hardcover

The right of Tracy Shildrick, Robert MacDonald, Colin Webster and Kayleigh Garthwaite to be identified as authors of this work has been asserted by them in accordance with the 1988 Copyright, Designs and Patents Act.

The statements and opinions contained within this publication are solely those of the authors and not of The University of Bristol or The Policy Press. The University of Bristol and The Policy Press disclaim responsibility for any injury to persons or property resulting from any material published in this publication.

The Policy Press works to counter discrimination on grounds of gender, race, disability, age and sexuality.

Cover design by Robin Hawes
Printed and bound in Great Britain by TJ International, Padstow
The Policy Press uses environmentally responsible print partners

Acknowledgements

We are indebted to the Joseph Rowntree Foundation for their support for our research and particularly to Chris Goulden who oversaw and helped us with the project. Steve Crossley kindly contributed useful reading and references at short notice. Karen Bowler at The Policy Press has helped us enormously in the development of the book and was kind enough to indulge us with our missed deadline(s). Our greatest debt and thanks, of course, is to the people who took part in this study and who gave their time to tells about their lives 'in low-pay, no-pay Britain'.

Note on cover
In Greek mythology, Sisyphus, the cunning king of Corinth, was punished by the Gods by having repeatedly to roll a huge boulder up a hill only for it to roll back down when he reached the summit (see Homer's *Odyssey*, Book XI). Cover image: 'Sisyphus', Titian, 1548.

Introduction

Work is the best route out of poverty for people who are able to work. (Blair, 1998)

Work, for the vast majority of people, is the best route out of poverty. (Duncan Smith, 2010)

"I struggle, really struggle because by the time I pay my bills, gas, electric and water rates, TV, all that I'm left with a couple of pound that's it ... I wanted to work. If I didn't work I think I'd go crazy ... I mean, to be honest, somebody in my situation, I would probably be better off on benefits." (Winnie, 44, employed as a cleaner, Middlesbrough, 2009)

"Just jumping from job to job, it's no way to go. It's a nightmare! Jack of all trades, master of none [laughs]. I just want something with a bit of job security – where maybes I can buy me own house in the future rather than just where you've got to be on a wing and a prayer type thing ... just a job that I can call me own, you know what I mean? Rather than just looking for one all the time or just jumping from job to job." (Richard, 30, currently unemployed, Middlesbrough, 2009)

This book is about the lives of individuals and families living in or near poverty – despite (or, as this book will show, because of) their enduring commitment to work and repeated engagement with jobs. We live in a period and in a country where an 'old libel' (PSE, 2011) has returned with force, is repeated as fact and is too little challenged: the poor are so because of their own failings – their weakness of morals and character, their fecklessness and idleness, their culture and ways of life. The workless are so because of their preference for 'benefit dependency' and their taking of 'unemployment as a life-style choice' (Osborne, 2010). As Polly Toynbee pointed out in her book, *Hard work* in 2003, different, more honest stories about 'the poor' are rarely heard (Toynbee, 2003). This is still, possibly even more, true now. 'The poor' are largely hidden from public view, relegated to prejudiced depictions of benefit scroungers in tabloid stories and popular television programmes that dwell on the 'titillating sins of the underclass' (2003, p 12). 'Ordinary people' who do ordinary, necessary but underpaid and undervalued jobs at the bottom of the labour market 'do not figure on the national landscape at all. They are the forgotten, the invisible' (Toynbee, 2003, p 149).

The empirical substance of this book, we hope, makes the real lives of people living in poverty a little more visible and stands as a corrective to the prejudicial modern-day myth-making so beloved of tabloid editors, social commentators and politicians. This substance consists of detailed life stories told to us by men and women, younger and older people, who live and work in Middlesbrough, the main town of Teesside in North East England. They were all poor or were so much of the time, even if this was a label now so tainted with stigma that they refused it for themselves. Drawing on their sometimes fraught experiences of juggling precarious work and meagre benefits, we show that cycling between poor work and welfare kept them in, or near, poverty. Like Sisyphus condemned by the Greek Gods to constantly roll a boulder up a hill, only for it to roll back down, theirs were life stories of repeated labour with little progress, of recurrent engagement with hard work but constant returns to unemployment. We present their stories as a cautionary tale about the meaning and implication of poor, insecure and low-waged work for an increasing number of people caught up in this low-pay, no-pay cycle in Britain. Ours is a study of the personal consequences of poor work for their lives and of the value of such work: its personal and social value to those who engage with this work; its essential contribution to the economy and society; and the value and status it is given by government and employers.

Although firmly grounded in Teesside, our descriptions and analysis are far from limited to it. Indeed, the growth and spread of precarious forms of life – centred on the sort of insecure, poor work that this book investigates – have been said to signal the emergence of a whole, new social class with a global provenance: the precariat (Standing, 2011). Although Teesside's own, in some ways unique, socioeconomic history gives a particular 'structure of feeling' to the story we tell, this story – of workers cycling between subsistence-level benefits and low-paid, low-skilled and insecure work, and circulating below and just above the poverty line as they do so – is one, we argue, that is now characteristic of working life in the flexibilised labour markets of late capitalism.

Our overall findings are that while participants moved in and out of unemployment and low-paid jobs stretching over years, most expressed enduring commitment to work. This repeated engagement in jobs failed, however, to provide routes away from poverty, largely because of there being insufficient decent job opportunities available in the local job market. A strong motivation to work coupled with the insecurity of the low-paid and low-quality jobs on offer was the main reason why shuttling between benefits and jobs had been the interviewees' predominant experience of working life. Cycling in and out of low-paid work extended to middle age and so-called 'entry-level' jobs were rarely stepping-stones to better employment in the future. Responsibilities of caring for children and other family members limited labour market participation, as did health problems, while ill health itself was sometimes the result of poor work and unemployment. Experiences beyond the labour market led interviewees to lose and leave jobs. Financial necessity, their desire to work and the lack of better opportunities led people to take poor-quality jobs that trapped them in long-term insecurity and poverty. This vicious cycle seemed as typical as it was difficult to break. We show these circumstances are likely to be an increasingly common feature of life in low-pay, no-pay Britain.

Organisation of the book and its key findings

The purpose of this chapter is solely to introduce the book. In the paragraph above we have summarised the thrust of the descriptions and its overall arguments. What follows is a description of the layout of the book, chapter by chapter, with a discussion of the main findings and arguments contained in each. Thus, for readers who want quick access to only our main findings, these are presented below.

Chapter 2, following this introduction, sets out the general theoretical and empirical terrain of the book, drawing attention to continuities and discontinuities both in the provision of welfare as an attempt to tackle or at least contain poverty and in the shape and nature of employment in the UK. It defines some of the key terms used in this book. We describe a recent turn in research to understanding the dynamics of poverty and explain the broader research programme of which the study was part. Here, too, we contend with what we regard as some important, contemporary myths about the demand for and supply of labour. In short, we sketch the broad landscape of changing employment and welfare conditions; ensuing chapters, in the middle of the book, paint a finer portrait of the consequences and reality of these changes as they are lived by people in low-pay, no-pay Britain.

Chapter 3 locates the research methodologically and geographically, describing the particular place – Middlesbrough in North East

England – in which we conducted our research, and the rapid and dramatic social and economic changes that have affected the place. These changes include, over the last 40 years, a particularly steep (and continuing) decline of relatively well-paid, skilled, standard jobs in the manufacturing industry partially off-set (in terms of total levels of employment) by a rapid increase of female participation in growing service and new manufacturing sectors of the economy. Both changes have simultaneously contributed to the lowering of wages and an increase in involuntary part-time and precarious work for men *and* women *across* employment sectors. Underemployment in non-standard, lower skilled, insecure and lower-paid jobs prevails. These changes, coupled with the persistence of high rates of unemployment, are key to the emergence of the low-pay, no-pay cycle. Picking up from Chapter 2, it argues that while persistent, structural unemployment and 'new' flexible forms of working are two well-known corollaries of economic dispossession and deindustrialisation, a third, less well reported but no less significant outcome – tied to the first two – is the emergence of patterns of work that can be characterised as the low-pay, no-pay cycle. The chapter also describes how we went about our research, the sorts of qualitative methods used and sample recruited (that is, 60 men and women, aged 30–60, all with recent experience of poor work and the low-pay no-pay cycle), and how this study builds on longer-term research, with young adults from the same neighbourhoods, about social exclusion and transitions to the labour market and adulthood.

Chapter 4 reports our investigation of the views and practices of employers and practitioners who worked for 'welfare to work' agencies in Middlesbrough, with a particular focus on the barriers they perceived as getting in the way of the unemployed getting jobs. These were predominantly seen as resting with the personal attributes and attitudes of the unemployed rather than the availability of suitable work. This focus on supposed 'supply-side' deficits in the unemployed available workforce reflects the dominant approach to tackling worklessness in national policies. Working mainly with the long-term rather than short-term unemployed compounded this view that some individuals were unable or unwilling to work.

A very significant finding is that formal qualifications and skills were notably missing from the list of personal attributes required, considered of little importance in practice by employers and agencies. In this sense the formal 'quality' of jobseekers was of far less importance than their flexibility and availability to receive low pay and poor conditions; having 'the right attitude' was key. Workers themselves have little power in this labour market – sent by agencies, hired or not by employers, only to return to agencies as jobs finish or do not start. This revolving door of employment support interventions is a function of the precarious and flexible work on offer, not the attitudes of workers, as supply-side economics has long insisted. Employers discriminated on the basis of their social understandings of the recruitment advantages of the age, gender and employment (and criminal and drug-using) records of job applicants. Some welfare to work agency staff believed that their clients belonged to inherited 'cultures of worklessness', judging their worth in derogatory terms rather than reflecting on the local history of decimated labour markets in which individuals have been placed and struggled. To conclude this chapter, we compare these perspectives briefly with what we found in practice, from interviews with recurrently unemployed people noting some strong agreement and some strong disagreement about what in reality acted as 'barriers' to employment.

In **Chapters 5**, **6** and **7** we offer a description and analysis of the low-pay, no-pay cycle from the point of view of those caught up in it. These chapters are organised with a sense of sequence in mind, moving through a discussion of the motivations informants had towards employment (in Chapter 5), how people got jobs and the support they received, or did not receive, from agencies of different sorts (in Chapter 6) to the doing and leaving of poor work (in Chapter 7).

Chapter 5 begins this discussion by first mapping the predominant pattern of work history uncovered by the research and key exceptions to it. Reflecting back on our earlier studies with young adults from the same research neighbourhoods, it examines and describes the long-term pattern of churning between low-paid jobs, ineffectual training and employability programmes and unemployment that was found previously when interviewees were in their teens and twenties – and which was found in this study to stretch into their thirties. In other words, poor work did not provide stepping-stones to better employment and security in adulthood. Exactly the same pattern of the low-pay, no-pay cycle could be found among the older people, in their forties and fifties. Thus, the study shows that these experiences are not limited to the youth stage but continue over the life course, becoming for economically marginalised groups a permanent feature of life in low-pay, no-pay Britain.

A striking finding of the research is that, despite repeated returns to unemployment and repeated engagement in only poor work, participants retained a strong commitment to employment. This is, of course, one of the most important features of debates about welfare to work (with policies informed by a view that workers need 'incentivising' and 'activating' to leave benefits). Chapter 5 locates this work motivation in working-class traditions and community and also in the social and psychological benefits of working over not working. A life outside the home in work brings the beneficial social relationships found in employment – of routines and sociability, of dignity and solidarity, of normality and activity – into play in inestimable ways. Learnt from parents, carried through family traditions, work was found to be a staple aspiration. These are not residues or nostalgia for a past age but an ongoing, active, culture of work, not worklessness. The subjective identity work brings is negated in unemployment, often damaging psychological security. Any scepticism about the personal benefits of even poor work is mostly overridden by personal and community knowledge and experience of the alternative, unemployment (and its stigma and social and psychological threats). It is for these reasons that recurrent experiences of low-status, low-waged and insecure jobs and unemployment do not diminish or discourage the commitment to work. Financial incentives alone, although necessary, are not sufficient when explaining the continuance of work motivation and commitment.

Chapter 6 explores how these motivations to work were put into practice, in searching for jobs. Economistic descriptions of labour markets offer a world of 'perfect knowledge', 'free competition' and 'equilibrium price' determinations of wage rates. The labour market we found was instituted through informal social networks and local knowledge facilitating job search, availability and offer. Chapter 6 shows that this world of association rests more on *who* you know rather than, as claimed by economic theory, *what* you know.

Supply-side economists, government and employers constantly bemoan the poor quality of workers – their lack of basic literacy, numeracy and social skills. Contrastingly, the participants in the study, while generally carrying low levels of formal qualifications, described their commitment to education and training and how they valued these as a hoped-for means of obtaining or retaining jobs. Earlier negative experiences of academic schooling were sometimes overcome later, when learning was associated with accessing and advancing jobs. For most, however, this promise of the benefits of vocational qualifications and training opportunities led to disappointment as the qualifications available were of low status, and carried little labour market purchase, not least because of the general low demand for labour. In searching for jobs, most of the costs, risks and effort were placed on jobseekers, not employers, who often made little effort to respond to individuals desperately seeking viable, geographically accessible employment. Most chose, or were forced, to stay in places of long-term investments in family, friends, social networks and housing. Chapter 6 shows what happened to a few of the interviewees who did move away and some of the difficulties they encountered.

Statutory, voluntary and private sector agencies were all used by informants in searching for jobs, with mixed outcomes and assessments. These agencies are supposed to facilitate job searches and connect the two sides of the labour market. In a benign and prosperous climate, when local and national demand for labour is high, then such agencies face an easier task. Some, in the voluntary sector in particular, were found to offer effective, welcome, practical help, perhaps because they were less driven by a targets culture and ideological assumptions about the unemployed. Private employment agencies, in particular, seemed explicitly designed to feed the offer of low-waged, precarious work, again shifting the risks and costs of employment to employees. Statutory sector agencies – Jobcentre Plus – fared badly, with plentiful evidence of negative attitudes by agency staff toward jobseekers and the unemployed generally – attitudes readily reciprocated. What should be a matching of the need and availability of jobs becomes overlaid with 'conditionality tests' for the continuation of benefits and mutual suspicion and blame, reinforced by a popular and political climate over many years that lays blame for unemployment at the feet of the unemployed rather than the failure of labour markets. Meanwhile, the informal networks in seeking and obtaining work that most often helped people into jobs only stretch so far, via an individual's immediate associations or neighbourhood, to jobs in the lower rungs of the labour market. In the context of a shrinking pool of job opportunities even these offers of casualised, low-paid work were drying up. Where these job search methods – via agencies or via informal methods – proved 'successful', they were successful in matching up flexible workers with flexible, low-waged jobs.

Chapter 7 turns more directly to the experience of these sorts of jobs, of poor work. It focuses on people's recurrent experiences of getting, doing, losing and leaving jobs. We show how much of the work now available – whether it be in the service or manufacturing sector – is typically *low-skilled*, *low-paid* and *insecure* yet usually demands uncommonly high levels of personal commitment (and sometimes social skills). These jobs were found to be typically physically and mentally demanding yet poorly valued in terms of remuneration and status. For a few, however, better quality employment meant they escaped the poverty and churning of the low-pay, no-pay cycle, and we offer these cases as simple evidence for our argument about the significance of the nature of employment opportunities in shaping patterns of recurrent poverty. Intriguingly, although able to – sometimes graphically – describe the pain and unpleasantness of poor work, interviewees would simultaneously proclaim how they 'loved' working. We explain this conundrum with reference to our findings about the intrinsic social, psychological and moral value of work to interviewees. Chapter 7 scrutinises in detail how and why workers left jobs because this is, of course, a key moment in the turning of the low-pay, no-pay cycle. Sometimes departures from jobs were voluntary, but we describe how these often appeared to be 'forced choices', sometimes connected to the pressures of work on personal health or because of wider crises in people's lives. Predominantly, the inherent insecurity of jobs, with employers who were as quick to fire as they were to hire, meant that jobs were lost.

Chapter 8 shifts attention from 'the demand side' of employment – or at least interviewees' experiences of the forms of work on offer – to 'supply-side' factors that sometimes inhibited engagement with employment, and which helped shape the low-pay, no-pay cycle. Ill health and caring responsibilities are the two empirical foci here. These apparent limits to employability in the wider aspects of individuals' lives could, however, both be the cause and *the outcome* of poor work opportunities and unemployment. Ill health had an impact on an individual's capacity for work. Yet it was also sometimes produced or exacerbated by poor work (as it was by unemployment). The chapter unravels the connections between unemployment, poor work and ill health, and speculates that long-term churning between poor work and unemployment may itself add further detriments to health. It shows how jobs often made demands of unsocial hours under unpredictable conditions. This made fulfilling caring responsibilities and accessing affordable and manageable childcare difficult. Ill health and caring responsibilities tied together in complex ways, vis-à-vis the low-pay, no-pay cycle. The chapter includes a discussion of an unpredicted finding from the study: the impact of problematic heroin use on employment, across generations. As another example: while the insecurities and costs of poor work and unemployment sometimes caused ill health, caring responsibilities for close relatives in ill health meant individuals sometimes had to leave or limit the work they did. The chapter concludes by arguing that in the long-term, lived experience of the low-pay, no-pay cycle it is not so easy to separate 'demand' from 'supply-side' factors. The pressures, constraints and demands of poor work did much to shape what, superficially, appear to be problems that reside in the situations of those looking for work (for example, ill health or difficulties with childcare).

In **Chapter 9** we examine the consequences of long-term labour market insecurity and recurrent returns to unemployment: enduring real or 'near' poverty for the interviewees, felt as the precarious 'just getting by' of day-to-day hardship. Yet informants rejected the label of poverty, preferring to distance themselves from its negative connotations that, in their minds too, spoke of the stigma and shame of the 'undeserving poor'. Unlike 'them', the interviewees professed their ability to 'manage' in tight circumstances. There was no doubting, however, that these were tight circumstances; some were surviving 'deep poverty', unable to heat their homes or clothe and feed themselves adequately. Debt was widespread and served to entrench poverty.

Here, too, we reflect on people's experience of the benefits system and its failure to provide 'social security'. Antipathy to making benefit claims coupled with the complexity, difficulty and high transaction costs of repeated moves from work to welfare served as a strong disincentive to rely on benefits. Because people in the low-pay, no-pay cycle were poorly served by welfare to work agencies that mainly catered for the long-term unemployed, and because many in it were disinclined to formally register for and claim benefits during shorter periods of unemployment, people in the study can be described as 'the missing workless'. They occupy a blind spot in current welfare to work policies.

In direct contrast to official claims that overgenerous benefits act as a barrier to seeking work, trapping the workless in dependency, participants saw claiming benefits as a sometimes necessary but mostly a costly series of obstacles, delays and loss of income. Stigmatised by officials, misinformed and disempowered, the process of claiming often meant there was a substantial gap between losing work income and receiving benefit payments, which, given the regularity by which jobs ended and benefits eventually began, recurred again and again. Taking out loans/debts became an inevitable part of this process. Participants were 'flexible' in their willingness to take up precarious work but were met with 'inflexible' responses within the benefit system when this work inevitably ended. This repeated loss or absence of income also takes an emotional toll, worsening insecurity and heightening hardship, which cuts in welfare support exacerbate.

Chapter 10 concludes the book. Its main aim is to connect the findings of the study with broader debates and research in the field (a discussion begun in Chapter 2), particularly in respect of the myth of the high skills economy, the growth of underemployment and the idea that we have witnessed the rise of a new class at the bottom of society characterised by its general insecurity and precarious work opportunities. The final part gives a critique of current political and policy approaches that bear on questions of work, welfare and poverty, highlighting their potential to seriously worsen the conditions and prospects of the sort of people whose testimonies provide the backbone of this book. It argues for policy that would tackle the insecurity and poverty of low-pay, no-pay Britain, particularly policies and strategies 'to make bad jobs better'.

Poor work, welfare and poverty

Introduction

This chapter aims to locate our particular empirical case study of the low-pay, no-pay cycle and recurrent poverty within wider debates and research about poor work, welfare and poverty. It is followed, in Chapter 3, by a discussion of the particular place of study – Middlesbrough in Teesside, North East England – and how broad-based and wide-ranging political, economic and social changes documented in this chapter have played out in Teesside.

We begin by situating the study within a wider programme and growing body of research that is interested in the dynamic study of poverty and working lives, noting that many of the findings and conclusions presented in this book are ones which, in general terms, find support in some other recent research. In the second part of the chapter we turn to the important business of defining some key terms for this discussion of, and debates about, changing forms of work. How we might define, and what we know about, trends in respect of 'low-paid work', the 'low-pay, no-pay cycle', 'precarious work' and 'poor work' in Britain are the foci. We carry this forward into the third part of the chapter by examining the idea that precariousness in work, and in people's wider lives, has risen dramatically to the point that we can now talk of a new class called 'the precariat'. Here we also begin to reflect on the extent to which the research participants, and their experiences of work and welfare, match what is claimed about this new condition and class. In the fifth part, our attention is less on the labour market and more on poverty and welfare. We provide a brief historical review of how 'the poor' and poverty have been regarded and dealt with in public policy and welfare provision. Here we show how the long history of English responses to poverty and insecurity are often unacknowledged by policy makers and politicians, in particular how the mistakes of the past have come to haunt the policy present. In the final part, and more theoretically, we debunk some important myths about how labour markets work, myths that underpin welfare to work policies and their reliance on a one-sided commitment to supply-side solutions to worklessness and poverty.

Dynamic study of poverty and the low-pay, no-pay cycle

Our study sat within a larger programme of research funded by the Joseph Rowntree Foundation (JRF) that sought to investigate 'recurrent poverty'. The impetus for the programme came from the growing recognition – confirmed in a review and discussion of relevant literature (Smith and Middleton, 2007) – that snapshot surveys did not tell the whole story and missed some people's experiences of poverty. Poverty experiences, it was felt, were recurrent and dynamic rather than fixed, one-off events in which individuals were made poor, and stayed poor (Devicienti, 2000). Substantial sections of the UK population never dip under established, objectively defined but arbitrary 'poverty lines'. At the other end of the spectrum are the 'permanently poor'. Some will have one-off experiences of poverty or, alternatively, have a transient, short-term escape from it. Of significance, however, to the JRF programme of research were those individuals and households who have *repeated* encounters with poverty across the life course. The 'recurrently poor' are those whose fluctuations in income over time swing them above and below the official poverty line (but who perhaps never move far away from it). For instance, Tomlinson and Walker (2010, p 11) find that 'recurrent poverty' affects 'around 5-7% of the population as a whole … representing around a fifth of all poverty experience.' In other words, 'about a fifth of poverty is "recurrent", where people escape from poverty only temporarily' (Goulden, 2010, p 1).

The programme contained five complimentary projects, including our own, each studying different aspects of recurrent poverty. The Tomlinson and Walker study (2010), cited above, was one of these and studied the role of family and labour market changes in shaping recurrent poverty, using a statistical analysis of a nationally representative longitudinal survey, the British Household Panel Survey (BHPS). McQuaid and colleagues (2010) examined how parents, in particular, get entrapped in cycles of recurrent poverty and low-paid jobs. Also using qualitative methods with people marginal to the labour market, Ray and colleagues (2010) examined lone parents' and unemployed people's experiences of a government programme designed to help them stay in jobs, the Employment Retention and Advancement or ERA programme (see Chapter 4). The practices and perspectives of employers in respect of the provision of different sorts of work that might shape the low-pay, no-pay cycle was the subject of the study by Metcalf and Dhudwar (2010) (see Chapter 10).

Drawing on our previous, related research (see Chapter 3) and the challenge of the wider JRF programme, our prime aim was to examine the relationship between the low-pay, no-pay cycle and recurrent poverty. We did this from the perspectives of employers, welfare to work support agencies and, most importantly, people in the middle of their working lives who were caught up in the low-pay, no-pay cycle. Within this broad aim, we were keen to see how the wider experiences of disadvantage that bear down on people living in deprived neighbourhoods might intersect with unstable employment histories and poverty, acting as barriers to labour market participation and progress. More detail and discussion of how we went about meeting these aims is presented in Chapter 3.

Goulden (2010) provides an overview and summary of the main findings and conclusions of the first four studies of the programme (ours ran longer and so was not included). Comparing his overview and the findings and conclusions presented in this book reveals a strong level of agreement. For instance, Goulden (2010, p 1) identifies as 'key points' from the programme that:

> Incomes are dynamic, with households moving in and out of poverty over time, and policy and practice needs to reflect this. Having a job, and the conditions of that job, relates strongly to recurrent poverty but other important factors included family change, qualifications, occupation, age and how the benefits system works. The issue of people moving repeatedly between work and unemployment is an endemic problem in the UK and has risen by 60 per cent since 2006, mostly as a result of the recession. Entering work cannot provide a sustainable route out of poverty if job security, low pay and lack of progression are not also addressed.

As we will see, these are also all key findings from our own study. A very significant but simple overall conclusion from the programme was that we cannot understand recurrent worklessness and recurrent poverty without also understanding opportunities on the demand side of the economy (a statement that runs counter to much prevailing practice in respect of tackling worklessness; see Chapter 4). Supply and demand in the labour market are discussed later in the chapter, and we concur with Goulden's (2010, p 2) overview of the likely future prospects for those who undertake low-waged, insecure work:

Supply and demand in the labour market are crucial factors and the issue of low-paid, insecure work is particularly pressing in the context of the recession and high levels of short- and longer-term unemployment. The downturn has decreased the security of employment and depressed wages, which is likely to make cycling between low pay and welfare more acute and widespread for those able to find work at all.

Before moving on, in the next section, to discuss more directly changes and trends that are suggestive of a rise in the sorts of precarious and poor work that are central to understanding the low-pay, no-pay cycle (and which, agreeing with Goulden above, we see as worsened by but not restricted to the recent recession), we next discuss in some detail one particular study of the dynamics of poverty and how these are linked with movements from welfare to work. Jenkins' (2011) important survey-based, longitudinal study is a good example of how we might think about poverty *processes*. Our study shares Jenkins' general approach but uses a different, qualitative method (see Chapter 3). Although complimenting the general approach, we do not necessarily agree with some of his conclusions. It does, however, offer a close national study using a contrasting methodology and discussion of it also helps paint some of the UK policy context that pertains to our study.

Pioneered by Ellwood (1988), the dynamic study of poverty and welfare is premised on the notion that poverty can never be alleviated by the payment of cash benefits alone, except as temporary support. In Ellwood's phrase, 'the long-term support system is jobs' (1988a, p 181, cited in Deacon, 2002, p 78). The problem here is that governments often wrongly assume that social and income mobility is considerable so that poor people do not stay poor and that movement into and out of poverty is essentially about significant income mobility existing. The implication is whether poverty is a short-lived event that many people experience at some time, or a long-term event concentrated among particular groups. Using data from the BHPS between 1991 and 2006, Jenkins (2011) showed that most people only make short-distance moves, whichever part of income distribution they are located in. Although 'only' 10 per cent of those stuck at the bottom stay there forever, there is a significant likelihood of returning there within a year or two years. Movements upwards and downwards are closely associated with getting a new job or higher pay and losing a job. Other 'trigger' events such as divorce, death of a partner or the birth of a child are also important in changing fortunes, usually for the worst (factors confirmed in the JRF research programme; see earlier). It is important to realise that the relationships between trigger events and poverty transitions are complex and the direction of causation is by no means clear. For example, poverty transitions may lead to a rise in stress that, in turn, results in divorce. These may be mutually reinforcing or events and changes in household income may coincide (Jenkins, 2011). One way to try to unravel this complexity is via 'close-up', qualitative and particularly biographical methods that can unpick these 'events' and the relationships between them as they happen during the course of a person's life (the approach of our own study).

Within the period Jenkins studied – 1991 to 2006 – the replacement of existing in-work benefits by Child Tax Credit and Working Tax Credit increased generosity for childcare and extended eligibility to single people and to families without children. Benefits to 'make work pay' (a policy throughout the 1990s, 2000s and currently) were supplemented by the introduction of a National Minimum Wage and active labour market programmes for specific groups, such as New Deals for unemployed young people and for lone parents, providing individualised help to improve job readiness and job search. The net impact of these interventions and reforms was to contribute towards some success of 'make work pay' policies, at least among lone parents, and to increase the incomes of working families with children, although there were also increases in the gap between incomes in work and out of work (Hills et al, 2009; Waldfogel, 2010). Persistent poverty over years – experienced by a relatively small minority of individuals – declined over the period, especially for families with children, in part explained by these policies, as well as job growth in the labour market. In all events, what happened was that changes in the tax-benefit system led to a greater cushioning of the impact of adverse life course events (Jenkins, 2011, pp 16-17). Following Jenkins' analysis, our study had a focus on whether and how the individuals we talked to were able to move out of poverty (we present a typology of their types and experiences of poverty in Chapter 3). The nature of the poverty that individuals suffer – whether persistent, recurrent or occasional – depends on poverty entries and exits over time. Jenkins showed that the longer the spells spent in poverty the lower the chances of leaving poverty, and if people managed to stay out of poverty for a couple of years, then they were unlikely to return to poverty for a very long time.

Jenkins' conclusion was that between 1991 and 2006 there was greater propulsion out of poverty among people who experienced favourable labour market, income and life events, and greater cushioning for those who experienced unfavourable events. The cause of this was, in the latter study periods at least, likely to have been the Labour government's anti-poverty focus, the continuing strength of the British economy and declining unemployment rates. This indirect evidence that New Labour's policies had a positive effect on poverty reduction – buoyed by the coincidence of an improving labour market and the introduction of more generous support for low-income working families with children – is clearly to be welcomed.

Jenkins' study confirms how national economic fortunes combined with policy interest in 'making work pay' and combating poverty can have effects on people's entries and exits from poverty. The changing political and economic context since the period of his study warns against presuming that these positive changes will be sustainable (see Chapter 10). On a different tack, and a point we return to in the next section, we wonder whether aggregate national studies, like those used by Jenkins, can really capture *geographically* determined experiences of poverty. The importance of geography, particularly in broad terms what is called the 'North–South divide' (Baker and Billinge, 2004), in differentiating *local* labour market opportunities and the *local* effects of welfare to work policies on the ground is strongly argued and evidenced by Sunley et al (2006) in their study of local labour markets and Labour's New Deal programme. They conclude that 'geographies of worklessness' are such that policies are bound to fail if they do not respond to 'local labour market problems ... and local failures in employment demand as well as in labour supply'. They conclude that:

> ... when actually implemented and grounded in different local economic contexts [of labour market distress], workfare and active labour market policies are bound to have very different practical consequences, depending on the extent and nature of local labour market opportunities. (Sunley et al, 2006, p 207)

Mapping and defining 'low-paid work', 'the low-pay, no-pay cycle', 'precarious work' and 'poor work'

So far we have defined one of the key terms used in this book, **recurrent poverty**. In the following section key terms are in bold at the point of their first use, given the definitional aim of this part of the chapter.

Let us start with **low-paid work**. Mason and colleagues note that the standard definition of low-paid work is that which is 'below two thirds of the median hourly wage for all employees' (2008, p 15). In

2005, just over 22 per cent of employees in the UK were in low-paid work, which tends to be concentrated in low skill sectors such as retail, health and hotel work (Mason et al, 2008). It is more likely to affect workers at the ends of the age spectrum, with younger and older workers being more susceptible, as are women and part-time workers. Rates of low-paid work rose dramatically until the mid-1990s, when they stabilised. Part of the explanation for this seems to rest with the New Labour policy which, because of its emphasis on promoting labour force participation, meant that more people with little employment experience entered jobs at the lower end of the labour market (which increased the proportions in low pay). At the same time, policies to 'make work pay' modified some of this impact: 'this helps explain why the rise in the incidence of low pay in the United Kingdom's economy has been halted since the mid-1990s but not forced into reverse' (Mason et al, 2008, p 33). Recent labour market analysis (Sissons, 2011) suggests that the recent recession may have seen some bifurcation in trends with growth in higher paid *and* lower paid jobs (with a hollowing out of employment in the middle, the implications of which are discussed later in this chapter). Sissons says that:

> ... at the low-wage end of the labour market elementary jobs have also begun to increase since the recession for both men and women. This may be important because although the economy has begun creating jobs, a significant number of these are in the low-wage occupations. (2011, p 30)

Regardless of the effect of these recent changes, Mason and colleagues (2008, p 33) correctly note that rates of low-paid employment in the UK remain 'far higher than thirty years ago' and are among the highest in Europe. The extent of low-paid work in the UK is discussed further in Chapter 10, when we examine claims about a shift to a high skills economy. Part of the reason for the extent of low-paid work in the UK is because of the decline of institutions and policies that once protected pay (for example, trades unions, Wages Councils and the Fair Wages Resolution where firms tendering for government contracts would only be considered if a fair wage was being paid for the work). By the end of the 1990s these had all effectively disappeared, so, as Mason and colleagues comment, there was less protection against low pay in Britain at this point than there had been at any time since the Second World War. Of course, the introduction of the National Minimum Wage in 1999 by the Labour government was a direct attempt to combat poverty, but it remains a low wage, somewhere between 17 to 18 percentage points lower than the low pay threshold (Mason et al, 2008). As described later in Chapter 5, jobs paid at the National Minimum Wage were the norm for the participants in our research.

Conveying what we mean by **the low-pay, no-pay cycle** is also relatively easy. It refers to a longitudinal pattern of employment instability and movement between low-paid jobs and unemployment, usually accompanied by claiming of welfare benefits. The concept, or term, is a relatively recent innovation (even if the experience, while argued to be increasing, is not). The term has gained some traction during the 2000s with writers who have been interested in the *instability* of low-paid work. McKnight (2002) suggests that over the past 25 years the number and proportion of low-paid jobs has increased in the UK but the relative earnings of low-paid workers has fallen. This is a theme, too, of Polly Toynbee's journalistic investigation of the realities of low-paid work in Britain (2003). She comments that:

> Low pay is fair enough if these jobs can be labelled "entry level", just a first step on the ladder ... but very few move far, few make it to the next step. They inhabit a cycle of no pay/low pay insecurity. This indeed is the end of social progress. (2003, pp 5-6)

McKnight describes a low-pay, no-pay cycle in which the low-paid are more likely than others to be unemployed in the future *and* to re-enter low-paid work. Thus, for those disadvantaged at the bottom of the labour market in societies like the UK and US, 'the precarious nature of many low-paid jobs' means that getting 'a job may only represent a turn in the cycle of poverty' (Toynbee, 2003, p 98). Thus, in this book we refer to another term, 'churning', to describe this repeated movement between jobs and welfare.

In Chapter 5 we describe how our earlier research with young adults led us to question the policy orthodoxy that insecure and low-paid 'entry-level jobs' act as 'stepping-stones' to better employment. Clearly Toynbee and McKnight would each question this too. The Trades Union Congress (TUC) Commission on Vulnerable Employment cites government research that shows that low-paid temporary work is less likely than permanent work to lead to labour market progression (TUC, 2007). Twelve per cent of benefit leavers who obtained a permanent job returned to Jobseeker's Allowance (JSA) within three months, compared with over one third (38 per cent) of benefit leavers who obtained a temporary job. The TUC report also found gender differences, with men faring worse than women as a consequence of taking fixed-term employment (in terms of later wages and chances of regular employment). Overall, their evidence is that low-paid jobs do not act as stepping-stones to higher paying work, and although fixed-term work as a whole does not create long-term disadvantage, when combined with low pay it is likely to contribute to entrapment in poor work. These are the sorts of jobs that Schmitt (2012, p 9) characterises as 'sticky state' ones, holding people in a cycle of low-pay, no-pay: 'low-wage jobs may not help, and may even hurt, the future labour-market prospects of the workers who hold low paid jobs'. He argues that low-waged jobs, like spells of unemployment, may erode workers' accumulated skills, and that for long-term earnings potential a period of education and training might be better than working in a low-wage job. Stewart (2007, p 512) confirms the general argument here, concluding that an important reason for why those who experience unemployment face a greater risk of future unemployment relates closely to the 'quality of the jobs taken by those who move into employment, which tend to be low paid and unstable'. Taking poor-quality jobs may have a 'stigmatising' effect in which employers make judgements about the employee's capabilities and likely productivity (McCormick, 1990; see Chapter 4). An important finding of Stewart's (2007) analysis of BHPS data is that:

> Low-wage jobs act as the main conduit for repeat unemployment. Those who get a better job reduce the increased risk of repeat unemployment to insignificance ... not all jobs are 'good' jobs, in the sense of improving future prospects ... low-wage jobs typically do not lead on to better things. (p 1)

UK governments have also recognised the problems of the low-pay, no-pay cycle, even if adequate policy to tackle it has not flowed from this recognition (see Chapter 10). Early in the New Labour administration, in 1997, HM Treasury commented that:

> Evidence on the dynamics of the labour market shows a clear link between unemployment and low pay. This low-pay, no-pay cycle means that, for many groups income mobility is low. Relative poverty ... is increasingly a problem through lack of work but also through low pay. (HM Treasury, 1997, p 2)

In Chapter 10 we note how a similar early but fleeting glimpse of the low-pay, no-pay cycle can be seen in analysis of poverty, welfare and worklessness undertaken by the then incoming Coalition government.

We now enter more difficult definitional territory. Let us start with **precarious work**. Obviously in common-sense terms this means work that does not last and carries the threat of its ending. Thus, perhaps the most simple, possibly simplistic, way to define this is as employment that is formally, contractually temporary or defined as being of short tenure. Definitional debates perhaps lie at the heart of a wider debate about the extent of and trends in precarious work. An important article by Fevre (2007) challenges dominant discourses about precarious work, seeing them as having their basis in social theory rather than in hard evidence. For instance, Ulrich Beck, writing in *Risk society* (1992, p 140), argued that the shift from a 'system of standardized full employment to the system of flexible and pluralized underemployment' is indicative of late modern capitalism. The current and coming conditions of the industrialised societies of the West are ones in which standard, stable, lasting, Fordist employment declines and flexible, impermanent forms of work proliferate. He declared that: 'The boundaries between work and non-work are becoming more fluid. Flexible, pluralized forms of underemployment are spreading' (1992, p 142). Precarious employment was supposed to be a central facet of this development. Fevre paraphrases this dominant discourse (2007, p 517):

> ... we're entering a new age of insecure employment in which more and more people would be forced to stitch together patchwork careers consisting of short-term spells of work. More and more of us were going to be working on fixed-term contracts, finding work through temporary agencies or relying on casual work. Continuity of employment would be a fond memory and, for many, brief spells in work would be interspersed with unemployment.

Using a range of types of survey data from the US, the UK and Europe more widely, Fevre proceeds to argue that, in fact, there is little evidence for a supposed increase in precarious working. For instance, he says that temporary employment in the UK has not increased, and in 2006 the proportion of non-permanent employees was only 5.8 per cent, lower than in the past. Auer and Cazes (2003) similarly conclude that long-term employment relationships remain the norm for most European workers and remain constant.

Other researchers come to different conclusions. Standing (2011, p 24) suggests that 'in many countries at least quarter of the adult population' could be said to be in the precariat (see later), defined as so at least in part because of insecure employment. Inui (2009) argues that since the 1980s in OECD (Organisation for Economic Co-operation and Development) countries unemployment and non-regular work has increased, and that employment and wage flexibility are key aspects of these changes. Inui also points to how part-time employment rose by a third for men between 1990 and 2004 and how temporary employment was high, at 25 per cent, for 15- to 24-year-olds in 2000 (Inui, 2009). Poor employment protection, casual work and low wages have been said to have increased work insecurity across a number of advanced industrialised countries since the 1980s (Furlong and Kelly, 2005; OECD, 2005; Furlong, 2006; Inui, 2009). The TUC Commission on Vulnerable Employment (TUC, 2007) provides some statistical estimates of 'non-standard' work. It estimates that around two million workers are in the types of 'precarious work' that place people at risk of continuing poverty. Around 40 per cent of working women and the majority of working mothers are in part-time work, compared with around 9 per cent of men. The majority of precarious workers are in the private sector, and they tend to work in smaller rather than larger companies and, with some exceptions, in lower-skilled, lower-paid and insecure occupations (Edwards, 2006; TUC, 2007; Broughton, 2010). Broughton (2010) notes that in 2007 there were around 551,500 temporary workers in the UK who were paid less than £6.50 an hour.

Even relatively inattentive readers will have noted that the passage above has introduced a range of other types of work and terms into the debate about the extent of precarious work in the UK, which, in opposition to Fevre (2007), tend to emphasise its magnitude and rise. This reflects not only the difficulties in accessing reliable data about the extent of precarious work but different definitions of what it means. Many would agree that a definition of precarious work as *contractually* temporary employment is too narrow to suitably capture real changes in the experience of work. 'Contingent', 'non-standard', 'atypical', 'non-traditional' and 'insecure' work are other terms, sometimes used to refer to an increase in precariousness and associated degradation of work conditions, but which are not limited to contractual status. Felstead and Jewson (1999, p 3) comment that 'the surge of non-standard work' in the UK in the latter part of the 20th century 'is associated with rock-bottom wages, coercive management, intensified labour processes, unsocial hours and high rates of job turnover.' Butler and Watt (2007) argue that other forms of 'non-standard' employment –

such as part-time work and self-employment – have shown markedly greater upwards trends than, for instance, temporary employment. Beynon (1997, p 31) talks of growing bands of 'hyphenated workers': 'part-time workers, temporary-workers, casual-, even self-employed workers.' Referring to Canadian research, Vosko (2006, p 3) offers a multidimensional description of precarious work in which insecurity is only one element, it 'encompasses forms of work involving limited social benefits and statutory entitlements, job insecurity, low wages, and high risks of ill-health'.

One further issue with debates about the extent of, and trends in, precarious work, beyond how we define it, is about whether precarious work might be more concentrated among some sections of the population than others. Thus, rising or extensive precariousness for some groups might be 'aggregated out' and thus hidden in the sorts of national and international survey data that seem to downplay its significance. Cam et al (2003) find, for instance, that it is among younger and less educated workers that the best evidence for increasing job insecurity is found. While Auer and Cazes (2003) were quoted above against a general rise in precariousness, they find that average job tenure for 15- to 24-year-olds has declined in several industrialised countries over the past decade. This sort of finding has also been produced in UK research that tests what, in Fenton and Dermott's case (2006), is called the 'fragmented employment' thesis. Their survey evidence from South West England showed relative stability and permanency in the labour market careers of the majority of their sample. They add, however, that there was 'a sizeable majority, mostly of low paid workers whose working lives can be described as discontinuous and fragmented ... employment fragmentation is concentrated among young adults with less education and in lower status, lower paid occupations' (2006, p 205).

If precarious work is concentrated in a social demographic way – more found among young people and those in lower-paid work – then it is more likely to appear as substantial in community-oriented or qualitative studies that focus in on such people. MacDonald (2009) argues that this methodological difference in approaches, as well as differences of definition, might help explain the apparent *insignificance* of precarious work in national surveys compared with its apparent *proliferation* in more ethnographic studies. A few examples follow. Similar to Polly Toynbee's study of low-paid work in the UK (2003), Barbara Ehrenreich (2002) worked undercover in a range of low-paid jobs in the US, pointing to how the *insecurity* of these jobs trapped people in the low-pay, no-pay cycle. David Smith's (2005, pp 195-6) ethnographic study of white, working-class residents of an outer London housing estate found that, in 'the flexible labour market of expanding peripheral work, employment is experienced as a further source of insecurity and fragmentation rather than a means to security'. His research captures the impact of a polarised labour market in which:

> Practically all those interviewed had considerable experience of entry-level jobs in the formal economy after leaving school ... few of these ... resulted in stable, reasonably paid work, the typical trajectory being into work patterns increasingly characterised by short-term, low-paid jobs. (Smith, 2005, p 95)

For his participants, 'transience' became a 'definite feature' of work for 'the irregular and low-paid workforce' (Smith, 2005, p 96). Furlong and Cartmel's (2004, p 27) examination of the labour market careers of disadvantaged young men in Scotland found that precarious jobs shaped labour market marginality:

> Their main problem was not finding work, but keeping it. This employment insecurity tended not to reflect negative attitudes ... or necessarily a lack of skills; it was almost entirely a consequence of the 'flexible' nature of low skilled employment in modern Britain.

In reflecting on questions about precarious work, it seems to us that there is good evidence that it may well be increasing in quantitative and qualitative significance for some groups of workers, and that the *feeling* of precariousness does capture the nature of jobs and working life, indeed life in general, for many workers. It certainly did for the people we talked to for this book. This more general spread of precariousness fixed on but not reduced just to labour market experiences is the subject of the next part of the chapter. We argue, however, that there is more going on at the bottom of the labour market than just this precariousness. There is also the danger that we may be mistakenly understood to be talking (only) about the formalities of an individual's contractual status. This, as we will see (particularly in Chapter 6 where we discuss the workings of private employment agencies), is important but not everything. One further practical methodological problem in sticking with 'precarious work as temporary work' as a definition and a focus is that, in the 'real life' of degraded labour markets, informants were often not clear about their contractual status, whether they were formally temporary or permanent employees (just as they were unclear sometimes about why jobs had ceased). Nevertheless, they *experienced* work as insecure and unstable. We discuss this further in Chapter 7.

We conclude this discussion with reference to a further term, **poor work**, used more widely in our book than 'precarious work' (Brown and Scase, 1991; Byrne, 1999). Interestingly, Vosko's interpretation of 'precarious work', cited earlier, is rather like our understanding of 'poor work'; as well as job insecurity it includes low wages, limited benefits and statutory entitlements and risks to health. Thus, poor work is not only low paid and insecure, it is poor-quality work, often requiring no or low formal skills or qualifications and providing little room for the expression or development of skills, often done under poor terms and conditions of employment (for example, lack of training provision, holiday, maternity and sickness entitlements, 'zero hours' work contracts and so on). Thus, critically, poor work – the sort done by most of the participants most of the time – is *low-paid, low-skilled* and *insecure work* (see Chapter 5). As argued in this book, it was the offer and acceptance of this sort of poor work that was critical to the experience of the low-pay, no-pay cycle and recurrent poverty that was characteristic of the lives of the research participants.

The rise of the precariat

Estimates of a *general* increase of 'precarious work' should be treated with caution, as the previous section has shown. There is broad agreement, however, that changes in the labour market towards more 'flexibility' and changes in macroeconomic policy towards unemployment have been influenced by the growing dominance of free market ideas and that these shifts are responsible for changes in the nature of work in Western economies, particularly the growth of poor work (see Chapter 10). Since perhaps the 1970s, and certainly the 1980s, political discourse has become increasingly colonised by an economistic idiom, which, as Collini (2012) argues, is derived not strictly from economic theory proper, but rather from the language of management schools, business consultants and financial journalism. In his ambitious book, *The precariat*, Standing (2011) argues that throughout the period from the 1980s a seemingly new category of workers emerged. Designated 'the precariat', the emergence of this new group is encapsulated by, and predicated on, the idea of 'the flexible labour market'. His argument is that as wages were driven down and work became harder to obtain and retain, employment insurance to compensate for temporary unemployment was removed, benefits were lowered and 'unemployment traps' became more widespread, since the loss of benefits entailed in taking a low paying job pushed the effective 'tax' rate to near 100 per cent. In turn, as wages fell, and as low-paid temporary jobs became more common at the lower end of labour markets, benefits were cut to 'make work pay'. The biggest change, however, has been in the image of unemployment now depicted as reflecting a lack of employability, personal failings and excessive wage or job expectations. This change in official attitudes to unemployment from the early 1980s has been particularly focused on those in the lower reaches of the labour market. In short, growing flexibility in the nature of jobs meant the number of people in insecure forms of work multiplied.

In describing these changes and their consequences for the claimed growth of precarious work, Standing's (2011) thesis raises important conceptual, definitional and evidential questions for our study. Later, in Chapter 10, we ask a more specific question about whether the research participants qualify, according to what they said about their experiences of the low-pay, no-pay cycle, as members of the precariat. At that point, too, we ask further questions about Standing's argument, on the basis of our own arguments and descriptions in this book. For now we will presume that some group like the precariat exists, and next we expand on Standing's (2011) characterisation of it. For Standing, 'flexibility' in effect meant 'transferring risks and insecurity onto workers and their families' (2011, p 1) and 'systematically making employees more insecure, claimed to be a necessary price for retaining investment and jobs' (2011, p 6). For Standing, the precariat embodies both a distinctive *class* and *status* position. It has an objective class position in the sense of being a group sharing similar objective material conditions *and* is of low status as subjectively perceived. It has minimal 'trust' relationships with employers or the welfare state as the bargain of security in exchange for subordination is removed, and its status is 'truncated' in the sense of being temporary and socially invisible. The precariat are both the working poor and the insecurely employed, but most importantly, lack a secure work-based *identity* normally associated with building a 'career' and belonging to an occupational community. This lack of control over work at a basic level combines with a lack of work security in the forms of income-earning opportunities; employment and job security giving employment protection and work progression; protection against accidents and illness at work; reduced opportunity to gain skills; assurance of an adequate stable income; and collective voice in the labour market.

Our study found that individuals cycled in and out of low-waged work and benefits because of the poor work they undertook and experienced little progression away from this cycle. Standing (2011) argues that for many, having a temporary job is a stepping-stone *down* into a lower income status, not a stepping-stone *up* into more secure employment. Later in this chapter we discuss some key myths about the labour market, where we draw attention to recent analysis of changes in the labour market using data from the BHPS which does suggest that this is occurring, but for a particular group of workers. Those losing relatively better-skilled jobs are being 'bumped down' into low-skilled, low-waged jobs at the bottom of the labour market, perhaps competing with those like the interviewees who are stuck there over their working lives. As our study shows, experience of precarious working lives is not a new phenomenon (so maybe the precariat is not so 'new' after all) but one possible reason for its new visibility is its apparent growth, in part explained by the fact that the precariat is being joined by workers displaced from higher up the income distribution. We also cast doubt on the generality of Standing's depiction of the psychological and personal consequences of precarious work. While it is the case that precarious sorts of work can undermine a *secure* work-based identity, they do not necessarily undermine work ethics. Our study found that *despite* work insecurity and a barrage of exhortations from welfare agencies and employers, individuals hold on to strong work motivation and work identity.

We do, however, concur with Standing's (2011) general depiction of changes in the labour market seen in the growth of temporary, insecure and part-time jobs concealing, among other things, the extent of underemployment. The changed features of the labour market he describes are: first, the labour relationship has been made more responsive to demand and supply, eroding labour security and making it easier to sack workers ('boosting jobs'), and making more work temporary (witnessed by a growth of employment agencies). Second, stagnant earnings and economic insecurity have been concealed by cheap credit (that is, debt), subsidised by governments. Third, precarious incomes are a direct result of 'moving in and out of short-term low paid jobs and dealing with the unfriendly complexities of the welfare system, [and] easily drift into chronic debt' (Standing, 2011, p 44). Fourth, individuals caught in 'a labour market based on precarious labour produces high transaction costs for those on the margins' (2011, p 48). These costs were particularly apparent from the accounts given by the interviewees, which are: the time it takes to apply for benefits if they become unemployed; the lack of income in that period; the time and cost associated with searching for jobs; the time and cost in learning new labour routines; and the time and cost involved in adjusting activities outside jobs to accommodate the demands of new temporary jobs. When jobs end there are few if any savings to fall back on. Waiting for benefits, a person may have to borrow or go into debt by delaying payment for rent and bills (see Chapters 8 and 9). As our study shows, people doing poor work sometimes do not rush to apply for benefits, so debts and obligations to relatives, neighbours and friends mount. Eventually, the benefits obtained are insufficient to repay debt, while the offer of further insecure work presents the prospect of that ending, beginning the whole cycle of facing daunting transaction costs again.

A point of departure for us, from Standing's general depiction, concerns his claim that the disincentive to work implied by the precarity trap is much greater than the conventional poverty trap. We did not find this to be the case and the issue of insecure, poor work *not* creating disincentives to work is discussed further in Chapter 5 and 7. Note here that it is our belief that the strong culture of work found in the sort of place we studied, and in other traditional working-class places in Britain, seems highly resistant to the discouragement and demoralisation of work ethics. And yet, we found little evidence of interviewees strongly identifying with, or belonging to, a specific class- or status-based group work identity which, of course, has implications for the extent to which we might regard the informants as representatives of a new class called the precariat (see Chapter 10).

In the next section we turn our attention to a discussion of welfare, and politics and policies that encourage the movement from 'welfare to work', providing some historical backdrop to the way that 'the poor' and poverty are now – and long have been – regarded and dealt with in public policy.

'Setting the poor on work': a brief historical sketch of poverty and welfare

Left with a copiously documented historical legacy obsessed by invidious comparisons between groups deserving of welfare support at times of hardship and those 'undeserving' of such support (see PSE, 2011), politicians and policy makers pointedly ignore this legacy. We are compelled therefore to remind readers that the English system of welfare, going back to the Elizabethan old Poor Laws, has relied almost exclusively on separating the 'deserving' from the 'undeserving' poor in terms of their 'eligibility' for support. We briefly document some of the nuances of this legacy for the purposes of challenging the often ahistorical amnesia found in political and policy circles. To evoke the well-known saying by the Spanish philosopher George Santayana

(1905): 'those who cannot remember the past are condemned to repeat it'. This, as we shall see, has been particularly the case in recent and current policies towards moving people from welfare to work.

The common themes that mark the English system are first, the dangers that welfare support is said to present to the ability and willingness among the poor to work; and second, the problem of cutting welfare support in times of its greatest need, in times of recession and poor demand for labour. This historical legacy at various times demonised the working class, returned in the 1980s and early 1990s recessions, and can be observed in the current recession (Jones, 2011). (Perhaps what is novel about the recent period is the extent that welfare to work gained traction in *the boom years* of the New Labour administration, to which we shall return shortly.) The very repetition and recurrence of this ideological trope, nevertheless, seemed to make it even more immune to any nuanced correction in terms of historical or contemporary facts about the workings of the labour market or experiences of poverty and worklessness.

Historical changes and continuities in the English system of welfare illustrate how contemporary welfare to work policy relies on unexamined and unacknowledged ideas and assumptions inherited over centuries. Each successive reform was rationalised by contemporaneous reformers as humane and progressive, rejecting the supposed ineffectiveness, cruelty and repressiveness of its predecessor. Thus, the Victorians restricted the scope, cost and eligibility of poor relief inherited from the Elizabethan Poor Laws while rejecting the basic insight of the Poor Law Act of 1601 that the 'causes of unemployment beyond the idle whim of the vagrant' meant 'distinguishing between those who would work and could not and those who could work but would not ...' (Fraser, 2009, p 39). Indeed the Old Poor Laws inherited from the 1601 Act were in many ways more generous than those that superseded them after 1834. For example, a meticulous study of contemporaneous parish records in the 18th and early 19th centuries established that the Old Poor Law could often provide the destitute with over 60 and up to 78 per cent of income from employment enjoyed by typical neighbouring households – a higher proportion than that under today's welfare state (Williams, 2011, p 16). Any acknowledgement that people might be unemployed because there were no jobs was absent from the assumptions of the 1834 Poor Law. Although the 1601 Act was meant to 'set the poor on work' it did at least acknowledge some responsibility for those unable to work. Whatever else may be said about it, Elizabethan poor relief did not have the social stigma it was later to acquire, nor were the poor regarded as a species apart, never mind an 'underclass' (Fraser, 2009, pp 38-45). Both the Elizabethan and Victorian Acts assumed the route out of poverty was via paid work so poor relief would encourage the 'undeserving poor' to return to full-time employment. Such encouragement took the form of the principle of 'less eligibility', that is, the position of the unemployed person dependent on welfare must be made lower than that of the lowest paid worker in order to provide a clear incentive to seek paid work. This principle remains a core feature of social security protection in the UK in the 21st century (Alcock, 2003).

The principle of less eligibility implied then, just as welfare does today, that the allowance system not only depressed wages but offered an open invitation to idleness, encouraged pauperism by its generosity, and that public poor relief then, as now, made many low-wage earners with large families better off on relief than in work (Fraser, 2009). From the 1834 Act onwards the perennial problem of expenditure on poor relief and disincentives to work was to be met with doctrines of *laissez-faire* economics that defined the key problem as the over-generous Poor Law allowance system, which unfairly competed with free labour, demoralised and discouraged its offer, and interfered with and depressed wages. These perceived problems of incentives define the field of welfare to work today. The 1834 critique of the old Elizabethan Poor Law was that it gave relief to labourers in work suffering poverty (that is, low wages) rather than restricting itself to a properly sole concern with destitution (pauperism). The new Victorian Poor Law assumed men were masters of their own fate and unemployment was 'voluntary', while the real nature of industrial poverty was ignored as mass unemployment grew. The target population – as always – was able-bodied adults, especially men encouraged into pauperism 'by what Mrs Thatcher was later to call perverse incentives' (Fraser, 2009, p 67). These blind spots in policy, we would argue, are legacies of a long history of 'poor relief' that continues to inform current thinking (see Chapter 10).

Much of the logic and thinking behind welfare to work policy has rested on crude economistic assumptions about human behaviour reduced to a bundle of 'incentives'. John Cassidy's (2009, p 285) history of the baleful effects of economic thought is surely correct when he states 'economics, when you strip away the guff and the mathematical sophistry, is largely about incentives'. Offe (1984, p 149) conceptualises the contradictions of the welfare state in terms of how it is attacked from the Right and defended on the Left of the political spectrum, neither of which, he believes, really address these contradictions. The sharp economic recession of the mid-1970s was said to give rise to a powerful renaissance of free market and monetarist economic doctrines obsessed with incentives. The Right argued that,

> First, the welfare state apparatus imposes a burden of taxation and regulation on capital which amounts to a *disincentive to invest*. Second, at the same time, the welfare state grants claims, entitlements and collective power positions to workers and unions which amount to a *disincentive to work*, or at least to work as hard and productively as they would be forced to under the reign of unfettered market forces. Taken together, these two effects lead into a dynamic of declining growth and increased expectations, of economic ... inflation ... as well as ... 'ungovernability' ... which can be satisfied less and less by the available [economic] output.

This quote succinctly captures the thinking behind welfare to work policy as one of trade-offs between investment and work incentives, which underlie the purpose of the welfare state to 'balance the asymmetrical power relation of labour and capital' (Offe, 1984, p 147). Both 'demand-side' (Left) and 'supply-side' (Right) perspectives, motivated more by political than economic considerations, nevertheless assumed that the design and development of welfare should operate within competitive labour markets. Then, with the election of the New Labour government in 1997, the supposedly 'novel' and utterly banal belief that work is the best route out of poverty (circa 1601!) became central to 'welfare to work' (who would disagree, who had ever disagreed with this nostrum?). As ever, *what mattered was whether there was work*. Fortunately for New Labour, there was work as the 1990s boom began to once again increase the number of jobs being offered. As argued earlier, however, it was the nature and type of some of these jobs that is of issue here. In practice, the policy was about encouraging work incentives and the work ethic rather than providing work (although new public sector employment rose substantially; see Chapter 3). Just as New Labour's introduction of a National Minimum Wage was reminiscent of Liberal Britain, its new wage subsidies were reminiscent of Hanoverian Britain! Plus ça change, plus c'est la même chose?

The New Poor Law nostrum of 'low wage discipline of "less eligibility"' (Alcock, 2003, p 73) also seemed part and parcel of New Labour's supply-side interventions at a time of employment growth, perhaps more through benign neglect of the nature of low-waged labour markets than any conscious policy to maintain people in poverty.

Against previous Conservative administrations, New Labour's version of welfare to work was that any attempt to solve the problems of welfare had to start with the working poor – those who could not earn enough to keep themselves or their families out of poverty, and received little help from the welfare system. By definition, the working poor did not conform to previous Conservative stereotypes of a dysfunctional underclass. New Labour's solution, progressively introduced from quite early in its administration, was to bring in and then increase the Minimum Wage and expand Tax Credits to lower-paid workers, enforce child support from estranged fathers, offer incentives to working lone mothers, offer more worthwhile training and educational programmes for those without work, and childcare and in-work benefits for those in low-paid jobs, all with full and active government support. By and large, this was the position taken by New Labour, impressed by the impact of not completely dissimilar welfare reforms in the US. New Labour's New Deal implied that 'if work is to be enforced, then it must be rewarded' (Deacon, 2002, p 109).

New Labour was 'very confident that the problem lies entirely on the supply side of the labour market. In other words it is caused by the characteristics or motivation of workless people and not by any shortage of demand for labour' (Webster, 2006, p 107, cited in Dorling, 2012, p 37). This confidence, in our view, is misplaced, as this chapter and the rest of the book will argue. The social geographer Danny Dorling (2012) recently asked the question why New Labour had failed in its aims to significantly reduce poverty. He also asked whether current Coalition government policy is better or worse than what preceded it. He notes that JSA and Income Support benefit recipients have been channelled mostly into low pay work, under various initiatives in those areas of highest uptake. Dorling (2012), in a comparison of cities and towns using various indicators of long-term trends in inequality and deprivation, argues that it is *the shortage of demand for labour* that keeps places like Middlesbrough down, at or near the bottom of league tables of prosperity and growth, not the fecklessness of those who still live there. His verdict on New Labour's policies to reduce poverty through its welfare to work policies is that there are no signs of a reduction in the overall national level of poverty in Britain, despite absolute but not relative reductions in child poverty compared to European countries. There have been welcome, if somewhat modest, improvements in health inequalities – the unemployment rate fell to an unprecedented low before the recession of 2008, and over half the poor were in work (but still poor). Some of the poorest were better off – materially, subjectively and in income – but wealth inequalities widened and debt grew, creating new inequalities and poverty. According to Dorling (2012), the current danger, for any progress in reducing or alleviating poverty – even before the new Coalition government's welfare reforms gain traction (see Chapter 10) – was already beginning to be seen at the end of New Labour's period in office. If the government keeps benefits so low (JSA is just £9 a day) or reduces them further, and allows unemployment to rise rather than reducing wages at the top, we can expect to see rapidly rising poverty. Social security rights were already being rapidly curtailed: starting late in 2010, 'clients' were to be compelled to undertake 'meaningful activity' after spending 12 months on JSA. This is now escalating to benefits being conditional on the acceptance of 'work experience' (see Chapter 10).

This section argues that the English system of welfare to work was never aimed at alleviating or abolishing poverty as a whole, only alleviating the pressure welfare was said to pose to the low-waged economy if welfare support was made too 'generous'. The existence of the low-waged economy itself was, of course, simply the outcome of the 'natural' demand and supply of work. As policy makers came to believe that their reforms were an inevitable improvement on their predecessors' policies, there emerged a policy cycle only temporarily punctuated by any real progress in the conditions of the poor – notably in the postwar period to the 1970s and very selectively under New Labour in the 1990s and 2000s. New Labour struggled to alleviate poverty among lone parents and working couples with children ('the deserving poor'), but failed to tackle wider sources of poverty found in low-pay, no-pay Britain (of the sort described earlier in the chapter in our discussion of 'poor' and 'precarious' work).

In the next and final part of the chapter we build on and extend the discussion so far by describing and seeking to debunk some popular ways of thinking about how labour markets work, showing the ramifications of this for the orthodox, supply-side approach of welfare to work policy.

Some important labour market myths

Polanyi (1944, p 76) famously condemned crude economistic understandings of work as a 'commodity' the same as other goods and services:

> To allow the market mechanism to be director of the
> fate of human beings and their natural environment,

indeed, even of the amount and use of purchasing power, would result in the demolition of society. For the alleged commodity 'labour power' cannot be shoved about, used indiscriminately, or even left unused, without effecting also the human individual who happens to be the bearer of this peculiar commodity.... Finally, the market administration of purchasing power would periodically liquidate business enterprise, for shortages and surfeits of money would prove as disastrous to business as floods and droughts in primitive society ... no society could stand the effects of such a system of crude fictions even for the shortest stretch of time unless its human and natural substance as well as its business organization was protected against the ravages of this satanic mill.

Against free market economic perspectives, Polanyi (1944, p 75) argues that:

Labor is only another name for a human activity which goes with life itself, which in its turn is not produced for sale but for entirely different reasons, nor can that activity be detached from the rest of life, be stored or mobilized.... The commodity description of labor is entirely fictitious.

According to popular views, and conservative orthodoxy, however, competitive free markets in labour exist, and the function of welfare is to channel or coerce workers to accept the prevailing conditions and wages available to them, while markets do the rest. In this view, disparities between low pay and high pay are the product of different contributions to society, so both the rich and the poor deserve what they get. The intersection of demand with supply explains why particular workers or groups of workers get much higher wages than others. This model is used to emphasise the futility of Minimum Wage legislation, or other interference with the free working of the market mechanism, which is said to increase unemployment because it will reduce the demand from employers by creating an artificially high wage level. Trying to boost demand to increase employment will also fail, because this can only be done by raising the productivity of labour on the supply side, and will in any case merely cause wage inflation, without increasing profits. Moreover, market outcomes will be fair because they reflect individual productivity on the one hand, and the labour–leisure preferences of individuals on the other (Keen, 2011).

Debunking this model, Keen (2011, p 130) argues that in the labour market, households supply labour, and labour demand decisions are made by employers and firms. The demand for labour is determined by producers, while the supply of labour is determined by consumers (households), which inverts the usual situation of demand and supply found in other markets. This should tell us that there is something different about labour markets and the nature of labour. Unlike other 'commodities', workers are not produced for profit or turned out according to demand. Their availability is constrained by a 24-hour cycle, because workers have to attend to sleep, family, personal life and recreation and other necessities of life. They cannot very easily work longer if wages fall or even work less if wages rise. This should not, however, ignore the fact that low-waged, precarious workers are under unusual pressure to work unsocial hours and work a number of part-time jobs in an attempt to receive a living wage (see Chapter 7). In any case, employers and firms decide demand, and *involuntary* unemployment exists in the real world when the employment offered by firms is less than the labour offered by workers, regardless of whether wages are reduced. In the overall economy, wages are determined by the relative bargaining power of firms and workers, which cannot be determined by the market. Workers cannot freely choose between work and leisure as leisure cannot be enjoyed without income. In reality, the only 'leisure activity' which one can devote more time to with less income is sleeping. Work is not an option for most but a necessity, at least in the absence of a very generous social security system, and Keen's (2011, p 139) conclusion about labour market economics is that:

> ... economists are forever opposing 'market interventions' which might raise the wages of the poor, while defending astronomical salary levels for top executives on the basis that if the market is willing to pay them that much, they must be worth it.

This is consistent with Offe's (1985, p 37) analysis of marginal labour markets, that those who are exempted or excluded from the labour market are not in a position to place 'excessive demands' and 'expectations' on work offers. He goes on to argue that 'the labour market cannot absorb "everyone"; that would only lead to its self destruction'. By this he means the loss of the capacity of employers to recruit and select among competing jobseekers. Every hiring of an employee entails fixed costs of recruitment, training and the risks entail whether the employee performs. These costs are considerably lowered when processes of familiarisation and qualification are shortened or dispensed with, substitution or sacking at short notice and turnover high, the wages low, the chances of advancement slim and working conditions restrictive (that is, the exact sort of processes and conditions that confronted many people in our study). This leads employers to actively target and recruit marginal categories of workers as a 'marginal workforce' to which employers return again and again, subsidised by the welfare system. In other words, welfare subsidises and encourages poor work (see Chapter 10). Offe's analysis pre-empts New Labour's battery of welfare to work interventions of the 1990s and 2000s (described earlier) but well describes its effects:

> ... a thoroughly 'counter-intuitive' but none the less rational exploitation of welfare-state protection guarantees becomes evident in the hiring policy of employers. The firm's employment policies anticipate (and, at least implicitly, refer employees to) the availability of social and political 'safety nets' outside the labour market for certain employees.... The more options there are provided by the welfare state, the more a firm can afford to impose rigorous demands upon the beneficiaries of such options. For the firm, this has the advantage of creating a more-or-less sizeable group of 'bad' jobs that can be terminated or refilled without difficulty in case of fluctuating demand ... such that the burden of unemployment is predominantly imposed upon the marginal workers. (1985, pp 40-1)

Thus, welfare policies assist in the production of 'bad jobs'. Recent labour market analysis shows that this has been the case in the UK of late. Using estimates from the BHPS, Sissons (2011) shows how the last decade has seen a period of considerable change in the labour market, in particular the growth in lower-wage service occupations combined with a reduction in middle-wage occupations, leading to concerns about employment polarisation. This hollowing-out of the middle and *growth at the top and bottom of the labour market* suggests to Sissons that the labour market is coming to resemble an hourglass, increasingly polarised into 'lovely' and 'lousy' jobs. Consistent with Offe's (1985) earlier observation about the creation of 'bad jobs', in the 2000s the growth in employment share was solely among the highest wage and the lowest wage occupations among men, and a strong growth in personal service occupations among women. There are complex patterns here; in the recent recession the large-scale job losses were in routine manual and non-manual occupations but the early recovery (now stalled) saw a growth in the numbers of unskilled and low-wage jobs. Sissons (2011) makes the important point that those who lose jobs in relatively better-paid and more skilled occupations may have to take work at a lower wage and skill level. As these workers are 'bumped down' in the labour market, competition for 'entry-level' work has become intense, further disadvantaging those least able to compete for jobs. The employment rate for those with no qualifications fell markedly during the recession, with those leaving relatively more skilled jobs (and, even more recently, with wide-scale redundancies, jobs in the public sector) competing for those jobs which are available. An implication of this is, of course, that labour market opportunities (and competition for what is there) are likely to have worsened substantially for the research participants, since the fieldwork in 2008–09 (see Chapter 3). One of the potentially damaging aspects of growing polarisation in the labour market is that it may further create additional barriers to improving work income and moves out of poverty (Sissons, 2011, p 5):

> Estimates from the British Household Panel Survey (BHPS) suggest that around a third of those in the bottom ten per cent of earners in 2001/2 were still there in 2008/9, and that more than 60 per cent remained in the bottom three deciles. The BHPS also shows that women and those with no qualifications were significantly more likely to remain stuck at the bottom of the earnings distribution. There is therefore concern that in many cases low wage work is not acting as an 'escalator' into employment which offers better wages and prospects, but is instead a dead-end.

Thus, there is a growing body of research that suggests that labour markets in the US, the UK and other European countries are becoming increasingly polarised into high-quality and low-quality jobs, with declines in the middle but growth at the top and bottom. Between 2001 and 2007 there was a growth of some quarter of a million jobs at the bottom end of the wage distribution in the UK, trapping individuals in poor-quality, low-paid work, while unskilled workers are displaced by relatively greater-skilled workers losing jobs and competing for the pool of lower-wage, lower-skilled jobs that are available.

To conclude, the total demand for labour determines employment, and *that is essentially the entire story*. If companies are not hiring, job training is irrelevant (and welfare to work policy illogical; see Chapter 10): 'training and even education are no substitute … for ensuring that good jobs at decent wages are actually available when needed' (Galbraith, 2008, p 156). There are two main underlying structural reasons for the growth of a low pay economy and the growth of job insecurity in Britain. First, we see the push from the 1970s to restore generally falling profit rates by, in part, reducing the costs and conditions of labour (Glyn, 2006), under the imperative of 'flexibility'. Second, the shift away from full employment to the control of inflation as a primary goal of macroeconomic policy has resulted in a reassertion of the prerogatives of capital and a decline in workers' ability to control both the supply and demand for their labour, exacerbated by increasing global competition (Ingham, 2008). The means by which labour controls its supply – 'collective bargaining' through trades unions across an industry or sector of the economy – has sharply declined over the past three decades. A defence against management strategies of flexibility – and the associated growth of low-paid and insecure employment in Britain – has been severely weakened with the collapse of (private sector) trades union membership to half what it was in 1980. This decline was the result of an active political strategy by governments in Britain and the US from the late 1970s to change the central power relationship between employers and employees in liberal capitalist societies in favour of the former at the expense of the latter, and to deregulate the labour market in the cause of flexibility (Ingham, 2008; Brady, 2009).

As a consequence, income inequality has increased as real wages have stagnated, and the security of employment has diminished as employers impose 'flexible' poor work on those outside the elite of educated knowledge workers (see Glyn, 2006). Remembering Standing's account of the growing precariat (2011), an important debate remains, however, about the extent to which underemployment and precarious work has now extended from its working-class base to the middle-class 'knowledge workers' of the 21st century (Ross, 2009; Brown et al, 2011; MacDonald, 2011). This is a debate we continue in Chapter 10.

Conclusion

This chapter has sought to introduce theoretical debates and empirical research about: poverty (and how we might better understand it dynamically so as to reveal and understand, for instance, experiences of recurrent poverty); changing forms of work in Britain and elsewhere (and particularly the spread of low-paid, precarious, poor work that entraps people in the low-pay, no-pay cycle); how increasing insecurity in work and more widely has led to a claimed new class in many advanced capitalist societies (the precariat); the long-run tendency to limit welfare and to 'set the poor on work' as the method of dealing with 'the poor' and poverty (and its replication in contemporary politics and welfare to work policy); and, finally, about supply and demand in the labour market (pointing up some key myths and current trends).

All of this acts as a precursor and introduction to what follows in the rest of the book. Our study will show that the offer of poor work has significant implications for welfare and poverty and for welfare to work policy that is dominated by supply-side labour market views about the personal attributes that jobseekers bring to the labour market. Jobseekers are variously said to lack work motivation, qualifications, basic and social skills. Supply-side policy – from the provision of childcare, good schooling and training, to effective employment agencies and reform of the benefit system – aims to match suitable jobseekers to the needs of employers. Policy has been less concerned with the intrinsic personal and social *value* of work and more with its purported devaluing and avoidance by certain groups said to inhabit a 'culture of worklessness'. It says even less about the work's remuneration and availability, which are best left, it is argued, to what turns out to be a fictitious market, the demand from employers and the vicissitudes of private investment.

We argue, contrary to claims made for welfare to work, that such policies channel jobseekers into low-waged, low-skilled poor work, insecure work that keeps people in poverty, undermines the purpose of welfare as temporary respite and denies prosperity. Employers and welfare to work agencies have often assumed that 'barriers to employment' are exclusively found in the availability, reliability and quality of workers without seeking answers in the general availability of decent work, which depends on demand, investment and growth. Welfare to work policy encourages doubts about unemployed people's commitment to work and feeds poor people into poor work; it stresses that work is the best route out of poverty but does little to alleviate 'in-work poverty' or the problems of churning between low-paid work and benefits. For us, the fundamental problem is not lack of work motivation but the mismatch between the availability of decent jobs and the desire for such jobs. In short, our study will show, and Chapter 10 will set suggestions out more fully, that we must instead concentrate on the other side of 'the employability equation': demand-side opportunities for work rather than the supposed deficiencies among the supply of workers (McQuaid and Lindsay, 2005).

Researching the low-pay, no-pay cycle and recurrent poverty

Introduction

Our study was conducted in Teesside, North East England. The participants came from Middlesbrough, the main town of this large, industrial conurbation. Anecdotally, Teesside has been described variously as both a 'research laboratory' and a 'policy laboratory'. It has had a fascination for research because of the speed and scope of social and economic changes as they have affected this locality, and the social problems that these have generated have been met with a multitude of successive policy interventions geared toward tackling them, as described later.

This chapter has the following aims and parts. First, we sketch the remarkable social and economic transformations of the 19th century that created Teesside as a place famous for its industry and how later, during the latter part of the 20th century, it went 'from boom to bust in quick time' (Foord et al, 1985). Second, we examine changing patterns and forms of employment and, particularly, how precarious work has spread where once there were better-paid, higher-skilled and more secure jobs. Third, we describe briefly the previous research projects that we have undertaken in this locality and how they are linked to this one. This helps explain the choice of the specific research sites from which we recruited participants; these neighbourhoods are described in the fourth part of the chapter. Fifth, the methods for the research are outlined, as is the sample we recruited.

Brief socioeconomic history of Teesside: the metamorphoses of a place

Understanding the birth and development of Teesside, in particular its main town of Middlesbrough, is, we think, significant in understanding its current economic fortunes and the sociological character of working-class community and lives in this place. In part, we wish to show some continuities and discontinuities in the historical development of the town.

In the 19th century Middlesbrough was the fastest-growing town in England, mushrooming from a rural hamlet with a population of 40 people in 1820 to a bustling industrial town with a population of over 90,000 residents by the end of the 19th century (it had around 140,000 residents at the time of writing, in 2012). The historian Asa Briggs, writing in *Victorian cities* (1963, p 279), commented:

> ... the real interest of Middlesbrough's nineteenth century history lies ... not so much in the newness of the community that was created there as in the speed with which an intricate and complex economic, social and political sequence was unfolded.

The shift from rural backwater to industrial powerhouse, and the consequent population boom supplied by incoming migrant workers from other parts of the British Isles, rested primarily on the development of the local iron and then steel making industries during the mid-1900s (pre-empted in earlier decades by the development of the port trade, and railways, to serve the Durham coalfields). By 1871, 90 steel blast furnaces ringed the River Tees. By 1929, the Dorman Long Company alone employed 33,000 workers in steel production. Teesside really 'came of age', as Beynon et al (1994) put it, with development of chemical production around the River Tees following the First World War. By 1945 the Billingham ICI plant was the single biggest chemical plant in the world and, by 1965, ICI was employing 29,000 people in its Teesside plants.

Of course, this brief resumé should not be taken to imply that Middlesbrough's economic history has been a straightforward, uniform story of economic growth and success. Just as with other local economies, during the 19th and 20th centuries it reflected the booms and troughs of the national and, increasingly, international economy. Nor should we think that, prior to economic collapse in the 1980s, industrial work on Teesside was always well paid and secure. Commenting on Middlesbrough's iron workers in 1907, for example, Lady Bell (1907, p 47) stated:

> The dire need of the people who cannot find employment has been so ever-present to our minds in recent days that we are apt to believe that once employment is secured, once what seems like regular work is obtained, all must be well

> ... we forget how terribly near the margin of disaster the man, even the thrifty man, walks ... the spectre of illness and disability is always confronting the working man.

Nicholas's (1986) study of the devastating social effects of unemployment on Teesside between 1919 and 1939 shows how deeply precarious work or complete worklessness brought everyday hardships (effects compounded by the repeated reduction of the scale of 'able-bodied' poor relief during the 1920s in accordance with the less eligibility principle; see Chapter 2).

Nevertheless, the *overall* trend for Middlesbrough was upward, to the point that by the 1960s it was a place renowned for the rapid development and success of its steel, chemical and heavy engineering industries, which together granted relative prosperity. Teesside's economic growth and success assumed special importance, supposedly capable of absorbing workers from declining industries like coalmining, and playing the lead in the 'modernisation' (centred on petrochemicals) of the North East economy. Chemicals and steel industries benefited from massive capital investment due to the recognition of the strategic *national* importance of these industries on Teesside. Indeed, plans to develop car production (to benefit from good transport links, local steel production and the skilled workforce) were opposed by central government because of the fear that this would threaten the supply of skilled labour to the chemical and steel industry (Hudson, 1989a). Nationally and locally driven government strategic plans to expand key industries meant the 1960s was, therefore, a period of great optimism in and for Teesside (Beynon et al, 1994). Gross value added (GVA) statistics are a key indicator of the wealth of an area, reflecting industrial and occupational structure, levels of employment and unemployment, company profitability and earnings. Chiefly owing to its low levels of unemployment, the success of its core industries and the relatively high wages paid to the skilled workforce, in the early 1970s GVA in Teesside was well above the national average (and third highest in the country, after London and Aberdeen) (Tees Valley Unlimited, 2010a).

If Teesside's rise was remarkable, the scope and speed of its economic collapse was equally so (Foord et al, 1985). Following the global economic crises of the early 1970s, increased global competition in Teesside's main industries, shifting national policy in respect of support for the steel industry and a failure of regional policy to diversify and develop other industry all came together to presage massive restructuring and redundancy (Hudson, 1989a). Previous state regulation of Teesside, particularly of the steel industry, changed as energy prices increased and a slump in the demand for manufactured goods in 1973 and 1974 led to chronic over-capacity. Although state involvement continued during this period of crisis, the crisis of profitability now greatly worsened. With the UK economy in deep crisis and cuts in public expenditure, the policy of expansion was switched to one of retrenchment. British Steel followed many of its customers and competitors in moving its centres of production out of the UK. Teesside increasingly suffered from the internationalisation of its industries, including chemicals. The limit to the state's capacity to manage a national economy under conditions of intense international competition was cruelly exposed on Teesside.

From the 1980s, central government chose to define its industrial policy as actively embracing the pressures of international competition 'as *the* mechanism through which to restructure the UK's productive base' (Beynon et al, 1994, p 99). Because Teesside's core industries were so narrow in scope and so key to local employment, the hasty retrenchment of chemicals, steel and heavy engineering had enormous effects for the local populace. Writing in 1989, Hudson summarised these shifts in fortunes and the processes that led to Teesside's economic vulnerability:

> What had seemed in the 1960s to be the great advantages conferred by Teesside's unique location in corporate, national and regional modernisation policies now rendered it uniquely vulnerable to changes in UK state policies ... and the 'new' international division of labour in the late 1970s and 1980s. The vulnerability of chemicals, oil and steel to pressures of international competition led to serious cuts in capacity and jobs on Teesside (and still threatens more), leading to the prospect of still further increases in unemployment. (1989a, p 352)

Hudson's worries were confirmed. In 1965 the unemployment rate in Middlesbrough stood at less than 2 per cent. By 1987 it reached over 21 per cent and, overall, close to 100,000 manufacturing jobs were lost in Teesside between 1971 and 2008.

Local unemployment has reduced markedly since the nadir of the 1980s partly as a result of the growth of service sector employment. Jobs lost in steel, chemicals and engineering were gradually replaced by jobs in the service sector (92,000 were created in the same period that 100,000 manufacturing jobs were lost), mainly located in the public sector (local government, health and education), call centres and leisure services. As a consequence, jobs became less 'masculine' and less likely to be full time and permanent. They also became relatively less well paid. These changes in the structure, organisation and composition of Teesside's labour market reflected the national labour market since the 1960s. They were, however, more dramatic because of the proportional dominance of manufacturing compared to the service sector, male compared to female employment, and full-time and permanent compared to part-time and temporary employment found elsewhere. Nationally, part-time and temporary employment has sharply increased for women, men, younger and older workers, particularly in the 1980s and 1990s. In other words, employment became de-standardised and less stable (see Chapter 2).

Even these service sector employment gains have not been able to overcome the aftermath of the deindustrialisation of Teesside. It is a place that has still not recovered from the structural decline of the local economy set in train in the 1970s and 1980s and, over the past 30 years, Middlesbrough has typically had significantly higher unemployment rates than the national average (usually at least double the rate). Cleveland County Council Research and Intelligent Unit (1988) reported that in 1988 there were 22 unemployed people for every notified vacancy in the then county of Cleveland. Nearly 25 years later, in February 2012, central government statistics state that there were nearly 24 people on JSA in Middlesbrough chasing every vacancy reported by Jobcentre Plus (ONS, 2012) (with the Great Britain average being 5.7 jobseekers for every notified vacancy). In the early 1970s Teesside was the third 'most prosperous' sub-region in the UK economy, but recent figures show Teesside's GVA now to be only 75 per cent of the national average. This not only reflects the stubborn persistence of unemployment in Teesside, but the replacement of relatively skilled, well-paid production employment with relatively less-skilled, lower-paid service jobs (Tees Valley Unlimited, 2010a).

Emergence of a 'flexible', low-pay, no-pay economy on Teesside

The impact of unemployment and other changes in the Teesside labour market was to introduce new forms of work and flexible labour markets into the 'very heart' of the Teesside economy in the 1980s and since (Beynon et al, 1994). Beynon and colleagues undertook incisive and extensive studies of Teesside during the 1980s and 1990s which we draw heavily on in this section. These are invaluable in uncovering the processes of change in the nature of employment locally, in demonstrating the transformation from a comparatively high-skilled, high-waged and secure, to a predominantly low-waged, 'flexible' labour market. They point out, for instance, how a collective emphasis on modernisation in the 1960s was replaced by local employers' search for flexibility during the 1980s. Unlike in the earlier period, the effect was to create a predominantly low-waged local economy and to cut wages. Across all sectors the rationale remained the same – cutting costs and/or boosting profits. The growth of unemployment (both its reality and threat) in the 1980s, the rupturing of the notion of 'jobs for life' formerly associated with the chemicals and steel industries, now joined by offshore oil industry construction, ineffective resistance from compliant trades unions and little resistance in weakly unionised sectors, all filtered through to create an increasingly flexible and lower-paying labour market.

Key manifestations of these changes were felt and enacted across Teesside's core steel, chemical and engineering industries. Short-term contracts and new working conditions and practices were introduced and sub-contracted labour with poorer employment conditions grew exponentially as employers sought to reduce the size of their core workforce. Job cuts and labour flexibility was offered as an alternative to total closure, while non-union agreements flourished. Local pay deals increasingly replaced nationally agreed ones. As Beynon et al (1994) point out, not all workers saw increased flexibility as a 'bad thing'. It could offer more autonomy and control to some workers, at least for a time. Although the chemicals and steel industries were implicated in this process of increasing flexibility, the impact was greatest in the 'new' manufacturing economy and the growing service sector.

Attracted by Teesside's pool of unemployed skilled workers, new types of manufacturing industry grew in Teesside during the 1980s and 1990s, such as textiles, electronic components and food processing. These industries sought to impose flexibility on workers from the outset. Significantly, food processing, for instance, had never sought formally qualified or skilled workers, but selected employees on the basis of physique, manual dexterity, health and personal hygiene (and age and gender). Attitudes not aptitudes were the criteria for recruiting workers into this 'new' manufacturing economy on Teesside (see Chapter 4). High local unemployment, weakened trades unions and government legislation to deregulate the labour market (see Chapter 2) enabled employers to adopt a much more flexible approach to the hiring and firing of workers, subject to fluctuations in the demand for products or services. The flexible quantity rather than the quality of labour became important. As a consequence, there was an increase in part-time, temporary and casual working, once again reducing wage costs and workers' employment benefits. This was particularly achieved through the employment of female workers, but what was also noticeable was the replacement of permanent with temporary and sub-contracted workers through redundancies. As Beynon et al (1994, p 149) describe, sub-contracting was just:

> ... one element in a wider picture which depicts the 'new' manufacturing economy as predominantly a low-wage one, in which pressures to decrease wages further (or at least to contain wage increases) were strongly evident.

During the 1980s low wages, especially for women, became common across both smaller and larger firms in Teesside (although usually higher in manufacturing than, say, retailing, and in any case lower than in Teesside's traditional heavy industries). And it was in non-unionised workplaces that work conditions were worse and wages lowest. In private service sector activities such as retailing, employment on Teesside was subject to the same sorts of pressures as seen elsewhere, with its substitution of part-time for full-time jobs in a low wage sector. Areas such as low-end financial services (customer services and routine data entry) benefited from Teesside's history of low female activity rates in formal waged employment. Describing the influx of private service sector jobs to Teesside in the 1980s, Beynon et al (1994, p 155) conclude:

> Much of it consisted of low-skilled routine work taken by women eager for a wage, despite the conditions ... the route to such limited private service sector employment growth as there had been was ... precarious and partial.

Following close on the heels of the news that one of Teesside's last remaining steel processing plants was facing shutdown with the loss of 1,600 jobs, the shock closure of the Teesside-based Garlands call centre received far less national publicity. In 2010 it went into administration with the loss of 1,000 jobs in the North East, over 300 of which were in Middlesbrough. The case of Garlands shows that service-based employment in the private sector has not been immune to the same global competition that has so impacted on Teesside's core manufacturing industries. A statement released by the company at the time said: 'the appointment of an administrator follows decisions by a number of Garlands' largest clients to move their outsourced customer service activity to other centres, many in low wage countries [sic] including Asia and Africa' (BBC News, 2010b). Interestingly, unlike with the Redcar steel plant, no political and trades union campaign was launched to save these jobs, local people did not parade in the streets in their hundreds and no national press stories were posted. The story was big news locally, not only because of the severe impact on employment in an already struggling locality but also because of the casual *way* in which workers were released. With no prior warning redundancies were announced over the company's in-house radio station, giving staff one hour to collect their belongings and leave the building. Subsequently ex-employees brought a successful legal case against Garlands (claiming for unpaid wages and redundancy payments), arguing that the company had deliberately concealed its dire commercial circumstances and had announced that it was going into administration with immediate effect, so as to avoid being liable for redundancy payments. Giving the tribunal bench's verdict, chair Pamela Arullendran said the company had shown a 'complete failure to provide required information and consult affected employees' (*Evening Gazette*, 2010).

The public sector, however, had been the main source of growth in services employment in the Teesside economy in the postwar period, in health and education. Even here, changed employment conditions and levels in the 1980s led to contracting out and closures through competitive tendering of services and the growth of part-time work and casualisation at the margins.

Beynon et al (1994) sketch out some of the responses made by local people during the 1980s to the radical changes to opportunities for employment and the nature of the jobs available in the local labour market (see also Hudson, 1989b). As we will see, they describe many similarities with our own study, for instance, of residents in Middlesbrough facing severe social stress under the impact of repeated rounds of redundancy and their desperation to find work in a context of mass unemployment. In many households where men were unemployed, women's wages took on new significance, without unseating deep-rooted assumptions of work roles for men and women, making the loss of a job keenly felt by many men. In the fierce competition for jobs – any jobs – 'contacts and reputation become almost as important as qualifications and experience, at least in some segments of the labour market' (Beynon et al, 1994, p 124; see Chapter 6). Some sought employment in the south of England or in the international labour market by competing with other migrants. Moving to find work was fraught with the problem of affording higher housing costs. Encouraged by the Thatcher government's espousal of an enterprise culture, others created small businesses (MacDonald and Coffield, 1991). And still others joined the informal economy, increasingly with the active collusion of employers (MacDonald, 1994). Many of these alternatives were intensely self-exploitative, low waged, insecure and temporary (MacDonald, 1996). The implications of industrial decline permeated all aspects of Teesside's labour market and yet still people were 'desperate for work at practically any price' (Beynon et al, 1994, p 126). By the early 1990s well-established peripheral employment on the margins of the formal sector through temporary contract work and sub-contracting completed this picture of a transformed labour market.

Scrolling forward from the 1980s and 1990s to now, the increased reliance on the public sector for local employment – amounting to 42 per cent of the local workforce in 2010 – has made the locality particularly susceptible to the public spending cuts enacted by the Coalition government since its election. Indeed, research in 2010 by Experian, commissioned by the BBC, identified Middlesbrough as being 'the least resilient' to planned government cut-backs. Middlesbrough was placed 324th out of 324 local authorities in respect of its predicted ability to successfully weather the cuts (BBC News, 2010a). In 2011, Middlesbrough Council set its budget to face this new austerity, aiming to cater for £50 million cuts over four years with a predicted loss of 500 council jobs (BBC News, 2011a). Middlesbrough Council (nd; our emphasis) comments that the Experian research 'exposes the overall vulnerability of the town' but emphasises the significance of 'the *state-dependent* nature of Middlesbrough' because of its high proportions of people employed in public sector jobs or living on state welfare benefits.

MacDonald and Coffield (1991) describe how, in the early 1990s, a similar discourse of 'dependency' was employed by politicians and policy makers to explain the doleful state of the local economy. Then, the dependency was said to be on large employers. In a context of high unemployment and long-term dependency on the fortunes of big companies such as ICI and British Steel for prosperity and jobs, local people were encouraged to embrace 'the enterprise culture' and to form their own small business and to become self-employed. Despite the burgeoning of a local 'enterprise industry' of support agencies, this did not happen in any substantial way (MacDonald and Coffield, 1991). Teesside still has comparatively low rates of new business start-ups, self-employment and employment in small firms. Following on its research about 'the least resilient' local authorities, more recent research by Experian (2012, p i) for the BBC has presented a more positive of Middlesbrough's economic situation, eagerly and understandably seized on by local media keen to run 'better news' stories about the town. The research argues that there 'is significant evidence and potential for growth, especially in some of the country's most deprived areas', placing Middlesbrough in the top five local authorities in England for its relatively high proportion of newer, small, growing and entrepreneurial firms.

Over the past three decades and to date, newer, private sector service-based or manufacturing firms have, however, been unable to provide sufficient employment of sufficient quality to fill 'the jobs gap' left in the wake of the failure of large employers in Teesside's core industries. This has meant that the locality has seen subjected to a multitude of state-supported regeneration interventions (which perhaps represent another facet or form of 'dependency'). Albeit with different remits, funding schemes and spheres of operation, since the 1980s these area-based programmes have included: an Urban Development Corporation, the City Challenge programme, the Single Regeneration Budget, Education, Health and Enterprise Action Zones, a Working Neighbourhoods Pilot, the New Deal for Communities programme and, most recently, a Local Enterprise Partnership (LEP) designed to 'drive sustainable private sector growth and job creation' (Bellis et al, 2011a). There is no intention to offer any evaluation of these programmes here. Undoubtedly each will have had successes and undoubtedly conditions in Teesside would have been worse for their absence, but that levels and local mappings of contemporary deprivation so closely match those before the onset of these interventions caused one local regeneration manager to remark candidly to us that "sometimes it feels like we've tipped an awful lot of money down a very wide drain".

Teesside Studies of Youth Transitions and Social Exclusion

These social and economic changes formed the background to our previous studies of youth transitions and social exclusion on Teesside (see Box 3.1). It is important to discuss these here because their findings not only relate to those presented in this book but earlier research provoked questions we wished to explore in this study. Thus, because a central aim of *this* study was to understand the potential for and dynamics of long-term patterns of churning between low-paid jobs and unemployment, one of its key methodological features was the re-interviewing of people who had participated in our earlier studies of youth transitions and social exclusion. This section therefore provides some necessary description of these earlier research projects.

Our first two studies – *Snakes and ladders* (Johnston et al, 2000) and *Disconnected youth?* (MacDonald and Marsh, 2005) – each investigated the transitions to adulthood of young people, aged 15–25, who were growing up in neighbourhoods of multiple deprivation. Theoretically, they aimed to critique underclass theory and assess and add to conceptualisations of social exclusion. Methodologically, they incorporated some participant observation, and when the samples were combined, semi-structured interviews with over 50 practitioners who worked locally and with 186 young people (82 females and 104 males) from the predominantly white, manual working-class population resident in Middlesbrough. For the first two studies, sample recruitment was a mixture of purposive, theoretical and convenience sampling so as to allow as broad an analysis of youth transitions and social exclusion as possible. Thus, we interviewed young people from the research neighbourhoods who were young offenders, college students, youth trainees, single parents, unemployed people as well as those in jobs. Because of our recruitment methods (chiefly via agencies and via 'snowballing') we cannot claim that this combined sample of 186 people from the *Snakes and ladders* and *Disconnected youth?* studies was statistically representative of young adults in these neighbourhoods; we do believe, however, that we achieved a sample that was representative of the range of transitions typical of young adults in these neighbourhoods (see MacDonald et al, 2011).

The third study – *Poor transitions* (Webster et al, 2004) – was designed as a follow-up to the two earlier ones. The key research question was where earlier youth transitions *led* individuals in their mid to late twenties. Fieldwork was undertaken in 2003, between two and four years after our first interviews. We re-interviewed 34 people (18 females and 16 males), now aged 23–29, from the two original samples. We sampled theoretically so as to understand key experiences in longer-term transitions, including of prolonged labour market marginality. Again, we make no claim that these 34 individuals were strictly representative of the larger samples of the first studies. Our knowledge of the research site and of *potential* re-interviewees makes us think that those we did speak to were broadly representative of the initial, larger samples (see Webster et al, 2004).

Box 3.1: Teesside Studies of Youth Transitions and Social Exclusion: research design

Study 1 (*Snakes and ladders*, Johnston et al, 2000)
- Funded by the Joseph Rowntree Foundation
- Fieldwork in 1998–99, in one very deprived ward in Teesside
- 20 interviews with practitioners
- Some limited observational work in the research site
- 98 one-off, qualitative interviews with young adults, aged 15–25

Study 2 (*Disconnected youth?*, MacDonald and Marsh, 2005)
- Funded by the Economic and Social Research Council (ESRC)
- Fieldwork in 1999–2001, in five neighbouring, very deprived wards in Teesside
- 30 interviews with practitioners
- Participation/observation with young people in three sites over a year
- 88 qualitative interviews (some repeated) with young adults, aged 15–25

Study 3 (*Poor transitions*, Webster et al, 2004)
- Funded by the Joseph Rowntree Foundation
- Fieldwork in 2003
- 34 qualitative interviews with young adults, aged 23–29, drawn from the samples of studies 1 and 2, exploring three sub-themes:
  - Young parenthood (*n* = 11)
  - Persistent 'poor work' (*n* = 11)
  - Long-term criminal and drug-using careers (*n* = 12)

Longitudinal qualitative youth research (particularly with so-called 'hard to reach' young people), as comprised in these first three Teesside studies, is relatively rare in British social science (see MacDonald, 2010). The study we report in this book was able to extend this long view of youth transitions for some of these interviewees into their thirties, as we describe shortly. Space precludes anything but the briefest discussion of one or two general findings about the nature of youth transitions as revealed by these projects. Despite the heavy burden of social and economic pressures bearing down on these lives, virtually all clung tight to traditional working-class values, practices and goals (in respect of employment and family and community life). Unemployment was a common, recurrent experience but so was employment. 'Economic marginality', rather than exclusion, characterised their churning, non-progressive movement around low-level jobs, training places and time on 'the dole'. Economic marginality was the preserve of virtually all and determining of the overall shape of transitions but at the individual level, contingency, flux, indeterminacy and the power of unpredictable 'critical moments' reigned (see Thomson et al, 2002). Overall, we concluded, that for these individuals in these locales at this time, broad sweep socioeconomic processes of deindustrialisation, the economic dispossession of the traditional working class, the dismantling of previously effective routes to working-class adulthood, the new vagaries of 'getting by' in the lack of these and the concentration of the hardships of poverty onto these lives did most to explain young people's biographies.

Research neighbourhoods

At the time of the fieldwork for these youth studies in the late 1990s and early 2000s, the seven wards that comprised our research sites all featured in the top five per cent most deprived nationally (DETR, 2000), and two were in the worst five – of 8,414 – in England. As is common in qualitative research, we used pseudonyms for research participants and particular neighbourhoods (and do so again in this study). We called our two research neighbourhoods 'East Kelby' and 'Willowdene' in order to help preserve the anonymity of individuals who took part and to protect these places from the potential for negative labelling as a consequence of the project. We recruited our sample for *this* study from the same neighbourhoods.

Both are in many ways typical of UK estates of social housing (away from the metropolitan South East England), built in the mid-20th century to house working-class families as the result of 'slum clearance' in inner-urban areas. One was built as a 'garden suburb' not far from the town centre. The other is a larger locale of five, interlinked estates on the outskirts of town, and was originally constructed to house skilled workers in nearby heavy industry and their families. Both are predominantly white, working-class areas (circa 98 per cent White British, according to the 2001 Census) with relative stability in residence, with many extended families having lived here over decades. These neighbourhoods remain heavily working-class places, not only in terms of their history but also by measures of the occupational class status of residents.

By the 1990s and 2000s, the period of our fieldwork across the earlier projects described above, these areas had undergone serious decline and dereliction as a result of processes typical of the decline of 'poor neighbourhoods' in the North of England (Lupton and Power, 2002). Built for and sought after by Teesside's skilled working class (and, in the case of Willowdene, lower middle-class families as well) in the postwar hey-day, several of these Teesside residential neighbourhoods had become classic examples of residualised housing of last resort.

There was some socioeconomic improvement locally during the 2000s reflecting an economic upturn nationally. Local unemployment rates dipped and began to converge with national ones (for example, in July 2007, national unemployment stood at 4.2 per cent and in Middlesbrough at 5.9 per cent). Economic prospects for Middlesbrough's residents were improving. As described earlier, however, opportunities for employment on Teesside have long reflected the vicissitudes of the national and international economy. Global economic crises ushered in national recession in 2008 and harder times again for Teesside, demonstrated vividly by the decision of Corus (the Indian-owned inheritor of many of the previously nationalised British Steel foundries) in 2010 to 'mothball' its remaining Teesside plant with the loss of 1,600 jobs. (The plant, bought by the Thai steel firm SSI, was re-opened in late 2011, with over 4,500 applications for the 1,000 jobs on offer; BBC News, 2011b.)

At the time of this study, with fieldwork beginning in autumn 2008, unemployment was increasing rapidly, again heading towards twice the national average. Our research neighbourhoods have experienced higher rates of worklessness than Middlesbrough as a whole. In August 2008, nationally around 12 per cent of the population were claiming 'key out-of-work benefits' (for example, JSA, Incapacity Benefit, Lone Parent Benefit). The figure for Middlesbrough was just over 20 per cent and for the wards in our research neighbourhoods it ranged from 25 to 37 per cent. Thus, these neighbourhoods – which we have been researching in since the end of the 1990s – remained very deprived ones at the end of the 2000s. They featured in the top 3 per cent most deprived wards in the country, reflecting high rates of worklessness, low income, low educational achievement, poor health and disability, crime, inadequate housing and services (Tees Valley Joint Strategy Unit, 2010; Tees Valley Unlimited, 2010b).

Research design and participants

We researched the low-pay, no-pay cycle against the background of this social and economic history and in a context of rising unemployment in Teesside's local labour market. Our fieldwork had two elements to it: interviews with local employers and staff from agencies that aim to support local workless people into jobs; and – the main component of our research – interviews with people from the research neighbourhoods who were engaged in the 'low-pay, no-pay cycle'.

Employer and agency interviews

The research with local employers and 'welfare to work' agency practitioners was undertaken to gain their perspectives on our key research questions and, importantly, to explore the extent to which their understandings of the causes of local worklessness, and their perspectives on the experiences of their 'clients' (or employees), matched with those described by people who were looking for work, using their services or employed in the sort of jobs they offered (see Chapter 4).

Thirteen interviews were undertaken with staff from statutory and voluntary sector agencies in Middlesbrough that sought to help people into jobs (for example, Jobcentre Plus, welfare to work agencies, community-based employability schemes, local regeneration programmes). We interviewed representatives of 10 employers that offer jobs to local residents. These were large organisations (for example, the local university, a major supermarket) and small ones (for example, a corner shop, a hair salon, a care home). All participants in the study were assured that all information given would be treated confidentially. Appropriate research ethics, following the British Sociological Association's guidelines, were approved by Teesside University's Research Ethics Committee. All identifying features, such as the real names of individuals, organisations and employers, have been omitted and pseudonyms used throughout.

Interviewing people in the low-pay, no-pay cycle

The sample for this main part of the research comprised 60 people, aged 30–60, who were resident in the research neighbourhoods and who had experience of the low-pay, no-pay cycle. The sample was equally divided between men and women, all could be categorised as working class (on the basis of their occupational histories) and all were ethnically White British, reflecting the sociodemographic profile of these neighbourhoods. This sample can, however, be understood as consisting of two sub-groups: 30 people aged 30–40 who we had interviewed previously as young adults in the Teesside Studies of Youth Transitions and Social Exclusion (see above) and 30 people aged 41–60 (older workers who we had not met before this study).

The key theoretical aim of following up people interviewed in our previous studies in Teesside, and of providing such a long view of youth transitions, was to see whether the low-pay, no-pay cycle, typical of young people and young adults in their teens and twenties, extended into their mid working lives and if so, how it was experienced and what drove it. Sample recruitment involved identifying from our previous combined samples of 186 people (for the *Snakes and ladders* and *Disconnected youth?* studies) those now aged over 30 and who, at previous contact, had had the predominant labour market 'churning' experience of the earlier studies (see Figure 3.1). We were also keen to include equal numbers of men and women. If interviewees had been included among the 34 followed up in *Poor transitions*, in their mid to late twenties, this would have given three waves of interviews over a 10-year period (four in some cases, because *Disconnected youth?* interviewed most participants twice).

Figure 3.1: The Teesside studies and sample recruitment

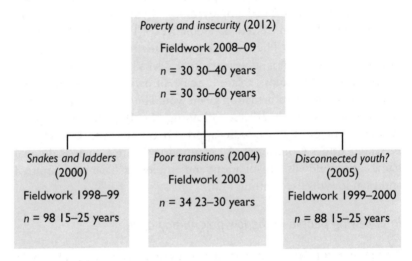

We drew up a list of all those previous research participants who would fit the age profile chosen for this study and worked through the list using a variety of techniques to re-contact and recruit them. These included using previous contact details and, where this did not work, we searched the electoral register and the Facebook social networking site. Neighbourhood contacts also helped us, as did interviewees who we successfully re-contacted (sometimes they were able to tell us the current whereabouts of people who had moved). There were several people we could not find and a small handful who did not wish to participate again, but approximately nine out of ten of those we did re-contact agreed to take part in this study. Meeting again people we had interviewed previously as young adults, several times over the past 10 years, provided further insight into how lives unfold in sometimes unpredictable ways. For this younger group, many, but not all, seemed to be further along a transition of 'settling down' into adulthood: of more stable partnerships, life organised around the demands of parenthood and moving to more secure housing situations in 'quieter' parts of town.

The theoretical aim of interviewing a new sample of 30 people, aged 41–60, was to explore the dynamics and experience of the low-pay, no-pay cycle for older workers. As such, we specifically sought to recruit individuals who we knew to have had recent experience of the low-pay, no-pay cycle. It is important to stress that this was not the case with our younger interviewees – we *did* know that their earlier work histories had been ones in which churning between jobs and unemployment had been the norm but we did *not* know when we recruited them for interview that this would still be the case. Part of the aim was to see if and how this pattern continued for them. As it turned out, virtually all were still caught up in the low-pay, no-pay cycle, but a small handful were not, which provided valuable insight into the processes whereby a person may be able to escape this sort of labour market situation (see Chapter 7).

One self-criticism of our previous youth studies has been that we have not been able to properly explore processes of social and economic change across and between generations. The inclusion here of an older age group remedies that, to some extent. It also allowed us to ask important social scientific questions about, for instance, the extent to which the low-pay, no-pay cycle is a relatively novel working-class experience and/or limited to younger workers.

We also used a variety of techniques to recruit this new sample of older interviewees. We began with enquiries to the range of 'welfare to work' agencies we interviewed (see above) but suitable recommendations were virtually never forthcoming. These agencies primarily worked with the longer-term jobless, rather than those who churned more quickly between jobs and unemployment (see Chapter 4). Advertising in local newsletters and putting posters in shop windows, church halls, libraries and schools in the research neighbourhoods, to our surprise, generated some interviewees. This had not worked well as a recruitment strategy in our earlier studies or in other research with socially excluded groups (Sixsmith et al, 2003). For some, the £20 'out of pocket expenses' that we gave to people for participating in the research was an important incentive. As described in Chapter 9, material hardship was an everyday reality for the participants and we should not underestimate the value of this unexpected income to household budgets. One man, 54-year-old Colin, told us how he was planning to spend the £20 on a present for his son (whose birthday it happened to be on the day of the interview) and Debbie, 43, said she would use it to buy new pairs of jeans for her and her daughter. Most often interviewees appeared to respond out of interest rather than for solely pecuniary reasons, wanting to express their views about our research topics in the hope that this might help improve things (for example, services in their local area or to how the benefit system worked). Others pointed to the attraction of having something to do in what were often long and boring days if they were unemployed.

What the Chicago School sociologist Robert Park called 'shoe-leather ethnography' (Park et al, 1925) also helped enormously in recruitment: 'hanging around' the estates, public libraries and the neighbourhood Jobcentre Plus office, and approaching members of the public to see if they were willing to participate and fitted our recruitment criteria (aged 41–60, long-term resident in the research locales and having had recent periods on unemployment benefits and in jobs). Some initial questions helped to screen out those with very limited employment careers and/or near permanent joblessness (in favour of those with low-pay, no-pay work histories). Despite our efforts it still transpired that a handful of interviewees had job histories that did not fit our research brief exactly. These few have been retained in the research sample nonetheless because they still provided some valuable insights on our research questions.

In total we talked to 30 men and 30 women, aged between 30 and 60, who were able to relate their biographies to us with generosity, candour and detail. Biographically focused, qualitative interviews were held with both sub-samples and shared common features. They were audio-recorded, lasted between one and two hours, were conducted in people's homes or at the university and were organised around a set of thematic headings yet flexible enough to allow exploration of issues that might not have been expected. In short, interviews enquired widely and in-depth about interviewees' lives, but with the main focus being on people's history of engagement with the labour market and with the welfare system and personal and household experiences of poverty. The interview transcripts were analysed qualitatively, by comparing key themes, to search for common (and unusual) patterns of experience and commentary on those experiences. This analysis provides the empirical core of the book (Chapters 5–9). The interviews were also subjected to some basic quantitative analysis in the sense that the frequency of key experiences (such as numbers and types of jobs, spells of unemployment, training programmes undertaken and so on) were counted and compared. This aspect of our method also contained an analysis and mapping of individual and household experiences of poverty over time that we present next.

Profiling the interviewees' experiences of poverty

Despite the challenges of sample recruitment, we believe that the 60 interviews provided for a rare, qualitative account of long-term, changing experiences of poverty, mapped against experiences of the labour market and wider aspects of social disadvantage (see Chapter 8). While prioritising subjective understanding and definition, because of the lack of research evidence of this sort in the extant literature we felt it useful to simultaneously seek a more objective classification of poverty experiences among our sample. As far as possible, we mapped interviewees' descriptions of personal and household income over their complete working lives against standard measures of poverty, that is, the most often used government measure of 'less than 60 per cent of median income after housing costs' and the Joseph Rowntree Foundation's 'Minimum Income Standard' (MIS) (Bradshaw et al, 2008).

We also sought interviewees' own accounts of their experiences and their self-definitions (as we will show in Chapter 9, these often were at odds with objective measures). It was difficult to find out about variations in household and personal income over lengthy periods of time, and to situate these against changing, external measures of poverty. Informants were sometimes only able to provide rough details of changing financial circumstances. Estimating changing housing costs proved particularly difficult. We have sometimes used their 'best guesses'. Acknowledging these limitations, and that this is not a study that seeks to measure prevalence of forms of poverty, we can say that, using the 60 per cent median measure, *three fifths* of the sample were *recurrently poor*. That is, they had experienced at least two separate periods in poverty over their working life (and the majority had several more such episodes). *One fifth* were *permanently poor* in that they had never risen above either the 60 per cent poverty or MIS poverty line, even when they managed to access jobs. The remaining *fifth* were comprised of people who had had only one spell of poverty, one spell of not being in poverty and a small number who were 'never poor' according to these measures.

Moving away from this technical description, we can say that regardless of any differences between the younger and older people in our sample, regardless of the differences of particular biography between each interviewee and regardless of whether interviewees were currently in work or on benefits, what most shared was poverty. None were 'well-off'; a loose and non-technical term, but we doubt that any UK-based observer would regard any participant as such. One or two had 'escaped poverty' by finding more stable employment positions (that is, they now occupied 'ordinary', relatively secure jobs with average levels of pay) (see Chapter 7). While most interviewees shied away from the self-label of 'poor', some appeared to be very poor, in deep poverty; they were unable to clothe, feed themselves or furnish and heat their homes adequately on the income they received (Chapter 9). Between was the majority experience of living close to, usually under, sometimes just above, official poverty lines. As we will see, this was the lasting, precarious experience of poor work, unemployment and recurrent poverty – one to be expected and 'accepted', but told in the resiliency of 'things being tight' but 'surviving' and 'getting by'.

Conclusions

Teesside is not a place that is typical of the processes of socioeconomic change in the UK; it is just the speed and scope of change – first prolific rise, then disastrous fall – that makes it highly unusual. Nor are the causes of its deindustrialisation the usual ones. The problem of overconcentration and heavy investment in the then successful but narrow triumvirate of steel, chemicals and heavy engineering was at the root of Teesside's economic growth and prosperity in the immediate postwar period, and of its decline since the latter part of the 1970s (Hudson, 1989b). Although the *reasons* for its decline may be 'most untypical' (Hudson, 1986, p 13), nevertheless, it is a place that 'displays the socio-economic *consequences* of de-industrialisation in ways that will be familiar to students of the failure of "old industrial regions" and "rust-belt" cities of Britain and elsewhere' (MacDonald and Marsh, 2005, p 39). Our story of low-pay, no-pay and recurrent poverty is not special to Teesside (see Chapters 2 and 10).

As described in this chapter, first among these consequences has been the stubborn persistence of unemployment. Since the waning of Teesside's traditional core industries in the 1970s and 1980s, neither new service-based employment growth in the private or public sector, nor a host of special area policy interventions has been able to reduce local unemployment rates below, usually, twice the national average. Some neighbourhoods, like those studied, have displayed much higher levels of worklessness than even this. Prolonged, spatially concentrated worklessness has served to impoverish residents of these neighbourhoods. During this period of decline, sought-after neighbourhoods *constructed* to house industrial workers and their families have metamorphosed into 'hard-to-let' estates of residualised social housing marked by poverty, worklessness and all the other indicators of severe social deprivation that accompany economic redundancy and that signal our research neighbourhoods to be some of the most deprived in the country.

A second key consequence of Teesside's deindustrialisation has been not only reduced opportunities for employment and consequently high unemployment but changes in the nature of the sort of work on offer. In broad terms we have seen manual working-class jobs (for men) in manufacturing industry that were, typically, full-time, skilled, unionised, long-lasting and relatively well-paid become replaced by service sector and 'new' manufacturing jobs that were more likely to be undertaken by women and to be non-standard (for example, temporary or part-time jobs), non-unionised, low skilled and relatively poorly paid. Contemporary forms of employment have been driven by employers' search for greater flexibility which, as previous studies of this locality have shown, has seriously degraded the conditions of employment for many of Teesside's workers.

These socioeconomic trends and conditions provided the backdrop to our study, conducted with younger and older workers, with men and men, who sought to make their living in this impoverished economic landscape. Building on research carried out in earlier studies, we undertook detailed qualitative interviews in order to explore the dynamics and experience of recurrent poverty and the low-pay, no-pay cycle. Their experiences, we suggest in this book, stand as testimony to a third major consequence of the deindustrialisation of places like Teesside (and one that has not previously been sketched out to any extent by previous studies of this place). The combined legacies of persistent unemployment and more flexible, insecure employment left in the wake of deindustrialisation mean that the biographies of many working-class people are not usually characterised now by complete worklessness, or by a life in steady work, but by the insecurities of churning between unemployment and low-paid and low-skilled jobs. Moving in and out of jobs, and above and below the poverty line, over a working life is, we argue, now the normal experience for many working-class people. It is the experience and dynamics of this that we investigate in the following chapters.

The low-pay, no-pay cycle: the perspectives and practices of employers and 'welfare to work' agencies

Introduction

The prime aim of the study was to understand recurrent poverty and its connection to the low-pay, no-pay cycle on the basis of accounts gathered from those engaged in this cycle. We also, however, sought to investigate the perspectives and practices of, first, local employers in Teesside who might offer jobs to people such as the interviewees and, second, of those agencies that seek to help people from 'welfare to work'. We were interested in exploring their views about local worklessness and what might cause people to become caught up in the low-pay, no-pay cycle. As noted in Chapter 3, we interviewed 10 employers, representing larger (for example, the local university and a major supermarket chain) and smaller organisations (for example, a corner shop, a hair salon, a care home). We interviewed 13 people who worked for statutory or voluntary sector agencies whose remit included assisting unemployed people into jobs in Middlesbrough (for example, Jobcentre Plus, employment support agencies, housing associations).

There was a strong level of agreement between employers and welfare to work agencies in respect of their perspectives on what might explain local worklessness and the low-pay, no-pay cycle. For this reason we have presented their comments together in this chapter. Using the terminology that is common in policy and practice in respect of worklessness, the bulk of the chapter is organised around what these interviewees perceived as the 'barriers' to employment for local people. After this we briefly discuss the extent to which the 'barriers' perceived by employers and support agencies matched the experiences and perspectives of local people who were in or looking for jobs, as revealed by interviews with those in the low-pay, no-pay cycle. We begin, however, with a discussion of the role and situation of welfare to work agencies.

Activities of welfare to work agencies

It is an understatement to note that welfare to work agencies face a substantial challenge in seeking to help people into jobs in a local economy that has undergone severe deindustrialisation – and at a time of national economic recession and high and rising local unemployment. By definition, their activities are almost wholly geared towards the supply side of the labour market (that is, improving people's 'employability' and overcoming perceived 'barriers' to employment that individuals might have in their lives). In trying to tackle worklessness, their attention is predominantly on the characteristics and failings of workless people rather than the characteristics of the labour market or the lack of available work (see Chapter 2).

There were instances of exceptions to this prevailing pattern. Some welfare to work agencies we interviewed had been more involved with employers in trying to create opportunities for clients, via the New Labour government's Local Employment Partnership programme. Introduced in 2007, their purpose was to encourage employers to recruit disadvantaged people into work, and a formal commitment to achieve 250,000 'job outcomes' for them through the partnerships by the end of 2010 was put in place. They were part of a broader effort to connect workless individuals with vacancies, overcoming barriers to work and improving the job matching services offered by Jobcentre Plus and its partners. Originally aimed at disadvantaged jobseekers who had been out of work for six months or more and who fell into a Jobcentre Plus priority customer group (for example, lone parents, Incapacity Benefit claimants, people out of work for six months or more), the recession in 2008 saw the inclusion of newly unemployed JSA customers (Bellis et al, 2011b, p 2). A recent evaluation (Bellis et al, 2011b) found that employers, Jobcentre Plus and training providers have worked closely together on the partnerships and services provided, and organisational understanding between these stakeholders had improved. Many employers reported positively on the service they received and the quality of candidates coming through for vacancies. Some support service staff in our study said they had been able to make progress with some local employers, encouraging them, for instance, to recruit people who were single parents or long-term unemployed.

The Local Employment Partnership programme was discontinued in summer 2010 by the incoming Coalition government.

Schemes like this are inevitably going to be more successful in tight labour markets with low unemployment. Shelley, who worked for a welfare to work organisation, told us that, since the onset of national economic recession in 2008, and rapidly rising local unemployment, Local Employment Partnership policy as originally conceived had been "watered down" and that despite some progress, many local employers were still not fully aware of what it was about. Daniel, a marketing manager from a welfare to work agency, added that, in this context of local joblessness, it had become harder to engage employers and that the Local Employment Partnership had become "an elusive beast". (It should be pointed out that in June 2010 the Coalition government introduced Local Enterprise Partnerships [LEPs], organisations that connect local authorities with employers in order to support local economic development.)

Putting aside this example, the activities of the agencies we talked to were wholly directed towards the 'supply side' of the labour market. The scale and history of unemployment in Teesside, and government resolution to tackle worklessness over the New Labour period (see Chapters 2 and 3), has meant that the locality has had a thriving 'welfare to work industry' (albeit one that, since the advent of austerity-driven cuts to public and voluntary sector funding under the Coalition government, has faced serious retrenchment).

Ironically one potential barrier to successful (re)engagement with the labour market that we observed first hand was the profusion, and confusion, of agencies and support services. In one cluster of streets alone in Middlesbrough we found almost a dozen statutory, private and voluntary sector agencies (with sometimes similar names), often in uninviting buildings and some appearing to be closed. Indeed, as researchers we once arrived for an interview appointment at the wrong office because of the similarity of the agencies' names. This lack of clarity and openness could potentially discourage jobseekers, particularly if they have low confidence or are wary of seeking help to begin with. Similarly, this confusion and profusion of agencies meant that there is the potential for better-quality services to be lost amidst poorer-quality ones (see Chapter 5, where we describe the apparently uneven quality of employment support services from the point of view of their clients). When it is sometimes difficult to tell the difference between agencies and interventions, it is possible that all become 'tarred with the same brush' of negative experience.

A second issue related to this multiplicity of agencies and their programmes, is a 'revolving door' scenario, described by some of those in the low-pay, no-pay cycle, wherein the same 'client' circulates through 'the system' repeatedly in an attempt to find work. Clients can find themselves on a merry-go-round of interventions, repeatedly returning to a previous (or new) agency in their search for employment (see Chapter 5). There are three explanations for this.

First, these agencies are in competition and are paid via government contracts for the number of clients on their books (and *private* employment agencies obviously have a direct commercial imperative to have a ready supply of available workers to supply to employers; see Chapter 6). It is in their financial interests to register as many clients as possible even if this means that the support jobseekers receive becomes confused. Wright (2003) found that much of the behaviour of employment support service staff could be explained by the need to meet targets and to fill quotas.

Second, these 'revolving doors' are explained by the simple fact of the relative absence of jobs compared with the relative availability of jobseekers. Progressing through 'interventions' – for example, completing courses that aim to increase motivation, hone interview skills, polish CVs and application letters, improve basic skills and so on – that do not then lead to employment has the result that the client is 'returned' to unemployment (in reality, he or she has never left it) and then, in time, back to a similar employability course with the same or different agency. Melanie, a manager in a voluntary sector regeneration programme, expressed her exasperation at her role in this respect: "what's the point in aspirating [sic] people if the jobs aren't there?" Most of the welfare to work agencies we interviewed were primarily or completely focused on the initial movement of clients from welfare to employment, that is, their work with jobseekers tended to conclude once a person got a job. For others, more emphasis was placed on helping to ensure that a person remained in a job (for at least a minimum of 13 weeks, after which the agency received a greater funding payment because the client had been officially classed as being 'retained' in employment). Even if their own agency was not providing this service, many interviewees agreed that more effort, including from employers, needed to be put into helping people stay in jobs once initial barriers to labour market entry had been overcome. Melanie, for instance, commented that "it's not just about shoving people into work"; she felt that the longer-term, 'after care' service that her voluntary sector agency supplied helped retain people in jobs. In Chapter 7 we discuss examples of better-quality employment that help explain why a handful of people in our study were able to stay and make progress in the jobs they got. Dorsett and colleagues' evaluation (2007) of the government's ERA programme – which was a rare example of a government scheme that purposefully sought to address the insecurity of employment, not just the movement from welfare to work – found that people can be helped to stay in jobs and that a variety of factors, including training, communication skills, attitude, and also, critically, the nature of the work people managed to get, affected retention in jobs. Three groups traditionally characterised by a weak labour market position and low 'job attachment' were eligible for ERA: long-term unemployed people over the age of 25 who were mandated to start the New Deal 25 Plus programme, lone parents who had volunteered for the New Deal for Lone Parents programme, and lone parents who were already working part time and receiving Working Tax Credits. Sianesi's evaluation of the scheme (2011, p 3) found, however, that ERA had no impact on the New Deal for Lone Parents or Working Tax Credit workers' employment retention (as measured by the share of the five follow-up years spent in employment). For both lone parent groups, ERA had no impact on hourly wages either during or after the programme and an insubstantial impact on the number of hours worked by lone parents (which might then have led to increased earnings). There was no evidence of improved job quality as a result of ERA for New Deal for Lone Parents workers, both during and after the programme. For Working Tax Credit workers, the overall impression is that ERA did not affect job quality in any dimension except for a sustained increase in sick pay eligibility. The ERA scheme officially ended in 2007 (Hendra et al, 2011).

Third, and highlighting Dorsett and colleagues' point about the importance of the nature of employment to questions of job retention (Dorsett et al, 2007), in our study not only were jobs in short supply overall, but many of the jobs that *were* available to people on completion of agency interventions were short-term and insecure (Clayton and Brinkley, 2011). Precarious employment not only drives the low-pay, no-pay cycle but it is also implicated in the merry-go-round of agency interventions that the unemployed are now increasingly required to undertake (see Chapter 10).

'Barriers to work' for the unemployed

Danziger and colleagues (2002) describe how individuals may face multiple barriers to employment, such as a lack of job-relevant skills and experience and problems accessing the work environment (often relating to transport and carer costs). Often people face multiple and overlapping barriers, which means that policy or practice that focus only on one of these is unlikely to be successful in moving people from welfare to work (Gardiner, 1997; Bambra et al, 2005; Ritchie et al, 2005). In this section we review how local welfare practitioners and employers described these barriers.

Inadequate services for the unemployed: childcare and transport

Problems with services commonly featured in the barriers listed by support agencies. Foremost were problems with childcare, this being discussed virtually exclusively in respect of women who were mothers, rather than men who were fathers. Childcare was reported to be expensive and often unaffordable, given the part-time and low-paid jobs that might be available. Lack of availability of childcare places, especially ones local enough to the places where the clients of agencies lived, was another aspect of this problem, as was the inflexibility of provision. Even where childcare might be available locally, and potentially affordable, very often it only operated hours fixed to the standard working day. Childcare that fitted well with the *non-standard* (for example, evenings, nights, early mornings, weekends) and *variable* working hours (and wages) (for example, available from 'zero hours' contracts) that came with the sorts of employment often available was rare (see Chapter 8). For older workers, informal childcare of their families' children was sometimes considered to be a barrier, according to Nigel, a local partnership manager for a welfare to work organisation.

The other aspect of inadequate services that was referred to by welfare practitioners was public transport. A lack of accessible public transport was often raised, echoed by Lucas et al (2008), who found transport was a crucial barrier for people seeking a job. Transport issues were also linked to the confidence of unemployed people by Kelly, a performance manager for a welfare to work organisation. She stated that most of the people she dealt with were keen to find jobs "on their doorstep" as it could be daunting travelling further afield to find work. Later in this chapter we suggest that some employers in the lower sectors of the UK labour market actually prefer to employ local workers (throwing into question this problem of transport), and in Chapter 6 we discuss the geographical scope of the job search parameters of those engaged in the low-pay, no-pay cycle and the extent to which this was shaped by the possibilities of public transport.

Personal skills and attributes, not levels of qualification

More frequently – and more fully discussed – than inadequate services, welfare to work agencies described the personal attributes of the unemployed as the main barrier to them getting work. These included low self-confidence and self-esteem (which were widely mentioned), poor personal hygiene and limited basic skills in literacy and numeracy. Bellis et al (2011a) validate our finding here in that Jobcentre Plus advisers in their study often referred to claimants' lack of self-confidence as a potential barrier to work. They also report that some claimants had poor body language and were unable to hold eye contact with advisers, and advisers, overall, spoke very negatively about clients' abilities and skills (see Chapter 9). In particular, our welfare to work agency interviews stressed the importance of clients possessing 'the right attitude' to employment. By this they meant that people needed to be well motivated towards job opportunities, keen to take them up and do the job well, be punctual and reliable and flexible and responsive to the demands of employers.

There was a strong correspondence between what welfare to work agencies and what employers saw as the main barriers to employment for the local unemployed. Employers told us that basic skills and personal qualities were on the whole more important to them than formal qualifications or more specialist, advanced skills (Nickson et al, 2012). Newton et al undertook original research and a wide literature review (2005) to investigate what employers look for when recruiting from the unemployed and the economically inactive. While acknowledging that different sectors, occupations and regions will have different requirements (and that some occupations are legislated to require certain qualifications), a key finding from Newton et al's study is that if candidates 'exhibit employability' and soft skills (such as interpersonal and communication skills), then employers do not demand technical skills or job-related qualifications. The key personal characteristics that employers look for are motivation and flexibility: 'qualifications do not appear to be important for a large number of employers and jobs, consistently ranking beneath characteristics and soft skills in recruitment frameworks' (Newton et al, 2005, p 2). 'Motivation' and 'flexibility' might be indicated by an apparent 'willingness to work and learn, and appearance, behaviour, confidence, and positive gestures and mannerisms' (Bunt et al, 2005, cited in Newton et al, 2005, p 2). Canny's (2004) study of the recruitment of younger workers revealed that employers emphasised enthusiasm for the work, work discipline and a positive attitude. Atkinson and Williams (2003) looked more particularly at employer requirements for low-status, low-paid work. They, too, found that, in respect of the recruitment of staff, employers prioritised perceived personal characteristics (for example, reliability and work motivation). These authors cite US research (Holzer, 1998) that surveyed a large sample of employers' recruitment practices and found that technical job skills were ranked the least important characteristic of jobseekers (with information about absenteeism, attitude and substance use being substantially more relevant to them and, interestingly for our findings, as we show later, criminal records being relatively less of a deterrent to employment).

We believe these to be very important findings. Given policy orthodoxy about joblessness as an effect of the possession of low skills/qualifications in 'a high-skills economy' (MacDonald, 2011; see Chapters 2 and 10), neither employers nor support agencies described poor formal qualifications as a significant barrier to getting a job. The 'skills agenda' was notable for its absence from our interviews. For instance, Kevin, a manager of a care home for elderly people, commented that: "qualifications aren't important as long as they [applicants] are interested in the job, flexible and committed to working in care". When questioned about what he looked for in a potential employee, Brian, a cafe owner, stated he "wasn't asking for Cambridge" but did seek staff that had "a bit of intelligence". Brian was most impressed by a clean and tidy appearance and a friendly and enthusiastic manner. Sandra, a personnel manager for the local branch of a large supermarket chain, said that she "looks at people's qualifications because it's polite but I don't take much notice of them".

Keep (2004, cited in Newton et al, 2005) argues that despite the alleged growth of the knowledge economy there has been a decline in the value of qualifications to employers because of the relative growth of service sector work in the economy (which relies more on softer, social skills which are less easy to certify). There is certainly some support for this in our study but we would also argue that this finding reflects the sort of low-skilled work that still exists in some abundance locally (see Chapter 5). The absence of 'the skills agenda' in commentaries from welfare to work practitioners also reflects this fact and, we think, their imperative to support entry to (any) employment rather than what might be needed for gaining sustained jobs (for example, better qualifications that might give access to better-quality jobs higher up in the labour market).

Fear of insecurity and entrapment in welfare?

Also significant was that the low pay offered by many jobs was not mentioned as a barrier to employment (in any straightforward sense) by welfare practitioners or by employers. In fact, we were struck by the number of times in these interviews (and in interviews with people who took them) that jobs offering the National Minimum Wage were described as offering not 'low pay' but 'good' or 'fair' pay, a point that will be explored in greater depth in Chapter 5. This was not a straightforward finding because several welfare to work agency interviewees commented that one barrier to employment was a sense of security that people might feel when claiming welfare benefits (which might be taken to imply that jobs on offer were not perceived as paying enough comparatively). Usually, however, they did not mean that over-generous benefit payments dissipated a willingness to work but that the 'security' of welfare benefits in meeting living costs (particularly for housing) was greater than that available from the sort of employment that was available. People were often not able to find work that enabled them as easily and securely to meet basic living costs, they said. Thus, attempting to leave unemployment by moving into employment involved risks and a greater sense of insecurity. For example, Leslie, an employment coach with a recruitment partnership, spoke about how people can feel "safe" while receiving benefits, as they are "getting their rent paid", they do not have "to worry about paying their council tax" and they have a notion of a daily routine that structures their lives, which they are wary of altering. Leslie stated: "if they haven't got anything, nobody can take it away". (In Chapter 9 we discuss the realities of this from the perspective of people who do, recurrently, attempt to leave benefits for employment and the extent to which the 'security of benefits' was a barrier for them.)

Practitioners spoke of the potential benefits of working with a client to tackle this perceived barrier. One of the techniques they used – and which they saw as being helpful in encouraging people into or back into work – was the Better Off Calculation (BOC). This is a nationally used tool, which calculates income in work (including any benefits and credits to which the individual would be entitled) and how much this differs from income from welfare payments (although costs associated with employment, such as travel costs, are not included) (Dorsett et al, 2007). One Jobcentre Plus adviser, Carol, viewed it as the "best tool" for getting people back into work because it showed people that "working can be worthwhile and it turns their lives around". Knight and Kasparova's study of lone parents (2006) was less conclusive in showing the positive effects of its use in encouraging them to enter work or leave benefits.

The complexities of the benefits system were also mentioned frequently by support agencies as a barrier to employment. The bureaucratic difficulties of re-establishing benefit claims after the loss of a job meant some agencies saw the benefits system as a barrier to employment as being one of the key risks jobseekers faced. Unemployed people were reported as fearing the risk of losing income from employment, when a prospective job ended, and then facing a potentially significant period with no income before benefit claims could be processed and payments resumed (see Chapter 9). The importance, and also the complexity, of the Tax Credits system was often cited by welfare agency interviewees as being both a source of help and a barrier for those seeking work. Chzhen and Middleton (2007, pp 43-4) report how the experience of applying for and receiving Child Tax Credits was not 'hassle free', and some of the interviewees, such as Charlie, a welfare to work adviser, and Kelly, a performance manager for a welfare to work organisation, both pointed to the difficulties that they had encountered with the administration of this welfare payment in respect of their customers.

Discriminatory practices?

Interviews with agency staff and with employers revealed the potential for unemployed people to be discriminated against in different ways.

It was suggested that, sometimes, a chequered employment history could act as a barrier to getting a job. Agency practitioners said that employers might be reluctant to recruit somebody who had been long-term unemployed because that person may not possess the necessary habits, routines and expectations for employment. Similarly, Devins and Hogarth (2005) conclude that lengthy unemployment (or inactivity) is an important factor in some employers' recruitment preferences because it may signify that candidates are not 'ready for work' and may quit jobs at short notice. In our research, a record of *recurrent* unemployment interspersed with jobs was perceived by practitioners as potentially suggesting (to an employer) that that individual was unreliable or did not possess the sort of attitude and motivation necessary to hold down a job. We enquired about the potential for employers to discriminate against applicants with criminal records or those with problems with drug dependency. Agency practitioners felt that sometimes employers did discriminate against applicants in these categories but that this was not uniform. According to Peter, an employment adviser, employers tended to take each case on its merits and Leslie, also an employment adviser, advised clients to reserve discussion of their criminal records for interviews (rather than mention them on application forms).

These were questions we put directly to local employers. In the main, they stated that they would potentially offer a job to someone who had been long-term unemployed but that they would need to be convinced of the applicant's trustworthiness and reliability. Most also claimed that they were open to employing someone with a criminal record, but this was always dependent on the 'nature and circumstances' of the offence or offences. For example, Martha, a local shop owner, said she would employ someone with a criminal record but acknowledged that if the offence was theft or involved violence she would be "reluctant" to do this. Interestingly, for this study of the low-pay, no-pay cycle, employers said they would be more likely to discriminate against someone who had moved in and out of jobs repeatedly than they would in respect of someone with a criminal record (see Holzer, 1998). Helen, a hotel manager, explained that she would be tempted to see such a chequered employment career as indicating a lack of reliability and, overall, as the fault of the potential employee. Larger employers (such as the university and a major supermarket chain), on the other hand, described relatively progressive staffing policies that allowed for recruitment from those with criminal records and the local unemployed. We suspect this reflects, to some extent, the truth of the matter and not just more politically and legally attuned understandings of what to say in research interviews about employment practices. Klee et al (2002, p ix) also found that there were differences between companies' recruitment practices depending on the size of the business. The larger companies that had occupational health departments were more likely to have standard recruitment and disciplinary procedures that dealt with the employment of drug users and ex-offenders. In our study, larger firms could also be distinguished from smaller ones by the emphasis they placed (in interviews) on their positive terms and conditions of employment (for example, 'family-friendly' working hours, staff training) compared with the negative ones sometimes admitted by small firms (for example, long hours for low pay).

In Chapter 3 we described the changes to the Teesside labour market, drawing attention to the increasingly 'feminised' nature of local employment opportunities. This theme featured strongly in employer and agency interviews, with both sets of interviewees remarking how job vacancies were now more concentrated in what they saw as female-dominated sectors such as retail, call centre and care work. For example, Charlie, a welfare to work adviser, suggested that women "have a greater sense of responsibility" and valued certain jobs, such as cleaning and care work, more than men (see Chapter 5). Some of the smaller employers, who did not have politically polished rhetoric on staffing, were open about their discrimination in favour of female, and older, workers. Brian, the cafe manager, noted that: "all the staff are women, obviously ... they're better at cleaning and cooking". A range of studies have also shown that service sector jobs, now dominating the lower reaches of the labour market, are often perceived (by both jobseekers and employers) to require attributes typically thought of as 'feminine', such as care, deference and sensitivity, leading to their rejection among working-class men who follow traditional understandings of what constitutes 'men's work' (Lindsay and McQuaid, 2004; Nixon, 2006; see Chapter 5 for a critical discussion).

Age discrimination was also present in welfare practitioner and employer interviews. Middle-aged and older workers were preferred because they were deemed to be more reliable and more used to the disciplines of working life. Falling in line with a pejorative perception of young workers, Martha, the owner of a local corner shop, explained her preference for middle-aged workers with the blunt statement: "young people are thick and not interested in working". Like Martha, Brian (the cafe manager) ignored the possible sensitivities of his 23-year-old interviewer when he stated that "people under the age of 25 are completely useless when it comes to working". Other employers displayed prejudicial attitudes towards young women in particular, suggesting that they were more likely "to go out and get pregnant" than persist with the job (according to Martha, the shop owner).

Several small-scale employers stressed a strong preference for local – sometimes very local – workers. Kevin, the care home manager, typically employed people who lived "within half a mile" as he believed they would be likely to be more reliable, in terms of attendance and punctuality, if they "lived on the doorstep". For similar reasons, Dawn, the manager of a social club, said she preferred to give jobs serving at the bar to people who lived on "this part of the estate". Like Brian above, she only ever considered employing women for these roles.

One aspect of discrimination – by neighbourhood (the so-called 'postcode effect') – was only mentioned as a barrier to employment by one welfare to work practitioner. It was not mentioned at all by employers. Hard evidence of discrimination by area of residence is relatively difficult to come by in the research literature. On a broader theme than recruitment to jobs, Lupton (2003) provides evidence showing how residents of deprived areas can be become excluded from consumption (that is, they were unable to get credit to buy household goods or to purchase items from catalogues) on the basis of their postcode. Nunn et al (2010, p 3) found that statements made by some of their respondents suggested that postcode discrimination could be occurring. Both Lawless (1995) and Speak (2000) uncovered some implicit discrimination by employers against jobseekers (the long-term unemployed and lone parents, in the respective studies) because of the negative reputations of the localities they came from. Syrett (nd) implies that the problem of postcode discrimination, however, might be more imagined than real, citing research that showed that a large proportion of young adults from a deprived part of London *thought* employers discriminated against them. Lupton's (2012) recent empirical testing of this question in three urban local labour markets in England and Wales also found that, while the public perceived this to be a problem, the research uncovered no evidence, other things being equal, that employers actively discriminate against applicants on the basis of their address. Our study suggested little evidence of this being perceived as a problem among employers, support agencies, or local jobseekers (see Chapter 5). It is not impossible that this finding in part reflects the multiplicity of deprived neighbourhoods in this town (MacDonald et al, 2005). In other words, deprived neighbourhoods are not few in number in Middlesbrough, perhaps lessening the potential for postcode discrimination.

Finally, we note that neither agency staff nor the employers we interviewed believed that indigenous, white working-class jobseekers were likely to be discriminated against in favour of migrant workers. Migrant workers were not perceived as a threat to those who were seeking low-skilled, National Minimum Wage jobs as the former were said to tend to move into more highly skilled positions, ensuring that the jobs at the lower end of the labour market remain. Lemos and Portes (2008) confirm this and state that, despite assertions to the contrary, there is no necessary presumption that recent economic migration has had an adverse impact on the labour market outcomes for lower-skilled, indigenous workers. We discuss this question in more detail in Chapter 5.

A culture of worklessness, or the curious case of 'the young man who woke his parents'

Practitioners who implement policy directives are of key importance in trying to understand the effects of any policy agenda. Lipsky (1980) and Wirth (1991) argue that it is not policy makers per se, but the providers of services or 'street-level bureaucrats' who are the most important in determining how policy works 'on the ground' because they have the power to decide access to services and benefits, often by providing immediate, face-to-face decisions. Faced with high workloads, limited resources and organisational targets, discretion and quick decisions must be utilised by practitioners. For instance, welfare to work providers ultimately decide on whether a claimant is seriously seeking work and consequently have significant, unavoidable discretion (Grant, 2011). In Chapter 5, where we discuss the encounters the interviewees had with agencies in their search for jobs, and in Chapter 9, where we describe experiences of claiming welfare benefits, we will see evidence of this decision making by 'street-level bureaucrats' as it affected people caught up in the low-pay, no-pay cycle.

How the unemployed are perceived and how 'street-level bureaucrats' explain unemployment will influence how the unemployed are treated by them. For example, in our study, Kelly, who worked for a welfare to work agency, told us that her "pet hate" was customers who possessed no desire to work and were 'wasting her time'. This was one example of a broader view shared by many agency staff, and employers, that a local *culture* of worklessness was a serious barrier to people getting jobs. Popular folk theories of worklessness were abundant in these interviews (as they have been in our previous studies in Teesside; see MacDonald and Marsh, 2005). Common refrains were that unemployment might be a 'lifestyle choice' (Osborne, 2010) and a life on benefits preferred to a life in work, as was the idea that an antipathy to working for a living and a preference for idleness was passed down from generation to generation in benefit-dependent families. For welfare to work staff, working with benefits recipients could result in distinct categories of 'us' and 'them'. Foster and Hoggett (1999) found that benefits agency frontline staff (some of whom would now be advisers within Jobcentre Plus) felt that many of their clientele were not deserving of welfare support. Staff strongly identified themselves as different from the claimants they dealt with. Moral judgements are also important for Lipsky (1980), who found that practitioners would afford some clients more time and resources if they were judged to be more deserving. This is not simply a UK phenomenon; research on benefit administrators in the US found similar negative views of claimants, including them being labelled as dishonest (Kingfisher, 1998). This suggests an implicit moral hierarchy in which advisers view themselves as more worthy or deserving than claimants. Wright (2003) identifies the derogatory terms used by advisers when discussing claimants who challenged the workings of the job centre bureaucracy, with terms such as 'nutters' and 'numpties' used to describe claimants. Behind the scenes, they were referred to by staff using such terms as 'wee bastard', 'pain in the arse' or 'arsehole' (Wright, 2003, p 238).

Curiously, as evidence for alleged 'cultures of worklessness', we heard the same anecdote several times from different practitioner interviewees (who worked for *different* agencies). Two of these were Melanie (a manager in a voluntary sector regeneration programme) and Shelley (a performance manager from a welfare to work organisation). They each spoke confidently about a case they said their agency (not them personally) had dealt with. An unemployed young man had eventually, after the successful intervention of his agency, managed to get a job that he enjoyed. Both his parents were unemployed and liked to lie in bed in the morning. Because the young man, in getting ready for work, would wake his parents, they insisted he pack in the job, which he did. Melanie, Shelley and others recited this story as a prime example of the effect of family cultures of unemployment and benefit dependency as a barrier to employment and of the difficulties they faced in helping people from welfare to work. Shildrick et al (2012) discuss a more recent research project, about the idea of 'intergenerational cultures of worklessness', with a research and policy manager of a national welfare to work provider who acknowledged that she did not know much in detail about the subject. She helpfully added, however, that she *did* know that her office, this time in London, had recently dealt with a young man who had recently got a job but had had to surrender it on his parents' insistence because he kept waking them in the morning when he went off to work.

Of course, it is not impossible that such a story is true. The fact, however, that it has been repeated to us on several occasions, by different interviewees working from different offices for different agencies (and in different cities) suggests this story has the quality of an urban myth. It is testament to the power of this particular ideological stance on worklessness and how deeply embedded it is within practitioners' interpretations of the problems of worklessness. A similar sentiment can be found in the work of Garthwaite (2012) on practitioners' perspectives of long-term Incapacity Benefit recipients. Such ideas rehearse discredited cultural underclass and culture of poverty theories (see Shildrick et al, 2012) and oddly jar with, and contradict, the other explanations of local unemployment given by the same practitioner interviewees.

Barriers to employment: comparing the perspectives of agencies, employers and 'clients'

Thus, employers and welfare to work practitioners identified many 'barriers' that they felt stood in the way of unemployed people getting or keeping jobs. One of the purposes of conducting these interviews was to explore the correspondence between their viewpoints and practices and the experiences, views and practices of people who were recurrently employed and unemployed. There was certainly some agreement. For instance, we found that those caught up in the low-pay, no-pay cycle also reported that difficulty in accessing suitable, affordable childcare (see Chapter 8), the time, costs and awkwardness of public transport (Chapter 6), the complexities of the benefit systems (see Chapter 9) and for some, low self-confidence about getting employment (Chapter 7), were sometimes 'barriers' to them getting jobs (even if they did not use this policy terminology). It is not impossible that some had also suffered discrimination (because of their gender or age) in seeking jobs but this was rarely mentioned, perhaps because it would be very difficult for job applicants to know they had been discriminated against – applicants for jobs very rarely got a response from employers, never mind an explanation of why they had been unsuccessful (Chapter 6). Some did agree, however, that a biography that included offending and/or drug dependency had been a 'barrier' to employment (Chapter 5). The low pay of potential jobs was virtually never commented on, across all interviews in the study, as a barrier to employment (Chapter 5). A very significant finding was that employers, support agencies and the local people we interviewed agreed about the relative importance of skills and qualifications versus personal attributes (in particular, possessing 'the right attitude', meaning being well motivated towards the job and flexible to the needs of employers). Confirming existing research on the topic, all parties agreed that the latter 'characteristics' carried much more weight in the search for jobs (Chapter 6).

There was some fit but not a perfect match between interviewees quoted in this chapter and those in forthcoming chapters about perceived barriers to employment. A fear of leaving the 'security' of a life on benefits was rarely mentioned by those in the low-pay, no-pay cycle (and by definition, they were recurrently leaving benefits for jobs) (Chapter 9). The most glaring difference, however, centred on a key explanation given by welfare to work agencies and employers about the causes of local unemployment. We have seen that many argued that this could be explained by 'intergenerational unemployment' wherein 'a culture of worklessness' was learned by families and passed down through generations. These negative views of the unemployed, we suggest, are likely to have an impact to some extent on the way that policies are put into practice by 'street-level bureaucrats' in their day-to-day dealings with jobseekers and benefit claimants (see Chapter 9). Our study was not designed to test the ideas about cultures of worklessness or intergenerational unemployment (see Shildrick et al, 2012, for research that was). Nevertheless, the story we begin to tell in the next chapter, of how an enduring motivation towards work in the face of radically worsened local opportunities for decent jobs caught working-class people up in a cycle of recurrent poverty and labour market churning, certainly stands at odds with, and provides an empirical corrective to, these powerful, popular depictions of the workless.

Conclusions

Enduring, high unemployment in Teesside over the past three decades is the backdrop to the growth of a profusion of local agencies, in the private, voluntary and statutory sector, that seek to assist unemployed people in finding jobs. Overall, these can be understood as operating within a 'weak' conception of social exclusion (Veit-Wilson, 1998). In other words, social exclusion can be understood as a consequence of, and is responded to in respect of, the *characteristics* of socially excluded people, in this case the workless. Attending to the deficits that they possess (for example, by improving basic skills, some training, work experience, help with job applications etc) will help them get jobs. Predominantly these agencies do not work to address the *deficit of jobs* that under a 'strong' conceptualisation of social exclusion might be understood to generate unemployment (see Byrne, 1999). This is one explanation for the 'revolving door' of repeated engagement with agencies that was reported by interviewees.

Reflecting government funding, the main 'client group' for statutory and voluntary sector agencies has been the longer-term unemployed (rather than those with shorter and/or intermittent periods of worklessness), and the main focus of activity has been on the initial movement from 'welfare to work' rather than retention or advancement in jobs (although more recent changes to welfare policy has targeted funding so as to encourage greater effort by agencies to keep people in jobs; see Chapter 10). These two facets of support services for the unemployed are very important for our discussion of the low-pay, no-pay cycle, as the following chapters will reveal. First, many in the low-pay, no-pay cycle were simply ineligible for much of the support on offer because they frequently did not remain unemployed long enough (Chapter 5) or did not formally register as unemployed (Chapter 9). Indeed, some of the welfare to work agency interviewees recognised this problem, acknowledging that they might rarely work with the sort of people we interviewed for the basis of this book. Liam, a partnership and development manager for a local welfare to work scheme, described people in the "revolving door" of jobs and benefits as "the missing workless" (see Chapters 6 and 9). Second, one of the problems of employment support services has been that they focus too heavily on the movement of people from welfare to work, closing client files when this has been achieved. As the next chapter shows, the movement into a job was rarely, for our informants, a movement into a secure job that lasted.

The low-pay, no-pay cycle: its pattern and people's commitment to work

Introduction

In this chapter we begin telling the story of life in low-pay, no-pay Britain, as revealed to us by those caught up in it. It has two main purposes: first, to describe the predominant shape of the low-pay, no-pay cycle and how this differed slightly for some participants; and second, to discuss commitment to employment. Thus, this chapter seeks to illustrate the overall shape of the work histories we uncovered and then, with a feel for the processes that underpin it, to describe the sort and level of motivations that those engaged in it had towards jobs. It begins with a reflection on what we learned of the earlier labour market experiences of the younger participants from previous research in Teesside.

The longer-term labour market careers of young adults: 'stepping-stones to something better' or 'roads to nowhere'?

It has been well documented that youth transitions to the labour market in the UK have undergone radical restructuring (see, for example, Furlong and Cartmel, 2007). The movement from youth to adulthood is now understood to be more extended, fragmented, complex and individualised than was the case in the postwar decades, albeit that youth researchers often understate *continuity* in the experience of youth transitions (MacDonald, 2011). Vickerstaff (2003) and Goodwin and O'Connor (2005), for instance, have argued that in the 'golden age' of the 1960s and 1970s transitions could also be complicated and 'non-linear' and that we should not presume that the difficulties working-class young people have in making smooth transitions to employment is a new phenomena. Nevertheless, Gill Jones (2002) reviews extensive research to describe how youth transitions have become polarised, with a widening 'youth divide' between a growing proportion of often more advantaged young people who now follow longer but successful 'slow track' transitions through further and higher education and those disadvantaged young people who leave school 'early', making 'fast track' transitions into the labour market, independent living and parenthood. Such transitions, typical of many working-class young people, are said to reflect and to add to social and economic disadvantage.

The Teesside Studies of Youth Transitions and Social Exclusion (see Chapter 3) have provided one of main empirical investigations of these sorts of 'fast track' transitions among particularly disadvantaged working-class young people in the UK. Although they had a broad approach to defining and analysing transitions (for example, looking at changing housing and family situations), they have paid close attention to young people's labour market experiences. Churning employment careers comprised of government-sponsored 'work readiness' and training programmes, unemployment and insecure poor work were the dominant labour market experience for young people in our earlier studies as they left school and moved through their late teens and early twenties (Johnston et al, 2000; MacDonald and Marsh, 2005).

MacDonald (2009) argues that the research and policy orthodoxy sees unstable early labour market careers – wherein young people move between low-quality, 'entry-level' jobs – as part of the process of settling into the labour market, prior to advancement to more secure, better jobs. Quintini and colleagues provide a useful summary of youth transitions in OECD countries and side with this 'stepping-stones thesis' (2007, p 7):

> Unsurprisingly, youth represent a high proportion of new hires and job changers [and job quits] ... youth tend to change jobs more frequently at the beginning of their career in search for the best possible match between their skills and those required by employers ... this is just part of the natural dynamics of settling into the world of work.

Our earlier studies questioned this orthodoxy (see Chapters 2 and 10), and *Poor transitions* allowed us to test it further (see Chapter 3). One of the prime motivations for that follow-up study (Webster et al, 2004) was to see whether early economic marginality was lasting or whether individuals were able to make better progress in employment after a faltering start. Labour market insecurity and poverty, however, remained constant (hence the title of that study) (see Webster et al, 2004). At age 27 people tended to be employed in the same sorts of low-level employment, and experienced the same churning between jobs and unemployment and training schemes, as at age 17. While we agree that youth researchers can sometimes forget how transitions were complicated and difficult in the supposed 'golden age' of earlier decades, we would argue that the very *prolonged* churning and job insecurity of virtually all the informants, and the fact that this was a *shared* experience, signifies a real difference in the labour market transitions of disadvantaged working-class youth (see Chapter 2).

Our studies question the explanatory reach of the 'stepping-stones thesis' rather than seek to dispense with it completely. They were small-scale studies of young people in particularly deprived contexts. It is undoubtedly the case that many young people will follow circuitous steps through the labour market before establishing themselves in more secure employment. More generally, in Chapter 2 we discussed existing evidence on trends in precarious employment. We made the point, for instance, that Fevre's (2007) *critique* of the idea of increasing insecurity is based on national, aggregate-level data that is unable to take sufficient account of the geographies and social class concentrations of precarious work (see also MacDonald, 2009).

In a different vein, influential research by Arnett (2004, 2006), based on large-scale quantitative surveying in North America and Europe, has suggested that a new life phase has appeared in advanced industrialised societies which is in part defined by young adults' unsettled labour market careers. The point of Arnett's 'emerging adulthood' theory for this discussion is that the flux in the employment patterns he observes is argued primarily to be a reflection of *the active choice making of young adults* – of experimentation with different jobs in an 'age of explorations' – before settling down later into more stable careers.

John Bynner (2005) has criticised Arnett's argument. His main point is simple. He argues that Arnett has downplayed the role of institutional and social structural factors that differentiate and shape patterns of transitions in young adulthood. In Jones' (2002) discussion of the *Youth divide*, for example, the insecure employment patterns of those on 'fast track' transitions are understood to be not a reflection of inquisitive engagement with career possibilities but of the lack of possibilities for more secure jobs. Thus, some better-off young people may opt for 'non-standard employment to help maintain leisure focused lifestyles and as part of a strategy to avoid long-term commitment' (Furlong and Cartmel, 2007, p 43). These may be middle-class students 'paying their way' through university by doing lower-quality jobs to finance study and leisure, knowing that this employment is neither enduring nor constitutive of their transitions. For less advantaged young adults, precarious employment can be more serious and lasting, *defining* their labour market transitions and outcomes. This was what we found in our earlier Teesside studies. Jobs as, for example, care assistants, factory workers, labourers or shop assistants did not act as 'stepping-stones' to better employment.

A key question for the research for this book was whether the low-pay, no-pay cycle that had entrapped young adults in 'poor transitions' continued. In short, it did – as we describe in this chapter. We give one brief example here that encapsulates the sort of longer-term work history – and the types of jobs – described by the younger sub-sample of re-interviewees. Simon is discussed again in Chapter 8 in some detail when we describe the reasons people left jobs. We talked to him for the *Disconnected youth* study aged 19, and he was re-interviewed for *Poor transitions* at age 23. Simon was 30 years old when we met him again for this study and currently unemployed. Since leaving school at 16 with a handful of low-level qualifications he had taken part in four training courses (for example, in computer repairs, motor mechanics). Over the previous 14 years he had had nine episodes of unemployment and 12 different jobs, the majority of which had been temporary contract positions (for example, working in food processing and electrical assembly factories, as a shop assistant, driver and cleaner, in a fast food restaurant and call centre). The pattern of Simon's work history is archetypal of those of the younger interviewees in our study – a history of churning around low-paid, low-skilled, insecure jobs, ineffectual training schemes and unemployment.

Next we map the predominant types of work history – for younger and older workers – that we found across the study.

Low-pay, no-pay work histories

With the older interviewees, aged 41–60, our purpose was not to prove the existence or otherwise of the low-pay, no-pay cycle among this age group – we purposefully recruited individuals who seemed to fit this pattern (see Chapter 3) – but to better understand its dynamics and complexities. Nevertheless, it is worth noting that the relative ease with which we were able to recruit white working-class participants of this age with this sort of working life stands at odds with media and academic discourses that tend to see this sort of insecure work as typical of young people's 'entry-level' employment (as described earlier). Alternatively, it is sometimes argued that this sort of work is reserved largely for new economic migrants. McDowell et al (2009) describe the way that new economic migrants have been positioned in media and political debates about immigration and employment, documenting their increasing contribution to the UK economy's precarious work. A recent study of the conditions for workers in the food processing industry (EHRC, 2010) found that 70 per cent of workers supplied to these firms by employment agencies could be classed as 'migrant workers'. Similarly, a study by Wills et al (2008, p 30) concludes that there is:

> ... a striking migrant division of labour in London's low paid occupations. Well over half of all workers in occupations like catering, cleaning and care are foreign-born. It is clear that migrants are filling gaps in the labour market and taking jobs that the British born and British naturalised populations are increasingly unwilling to do.

The impact of recent migration on the composition of the workforce in the lower reaches of the UK economy is, however, most 'clear' in the London labour market, as Wills et al acknowledge: 'the foreign-born proportion of total employment in the UK increased from just 7 per cent in 1993/4 to 10 per cent in 2004/5, rates in London for the same period increased from 25 per cent to 34 per cent' (Wills et al, 2008, p 17). The impact is less clear elsewhere and little research has been conducted on this question outside of London, for instance, in North East England. It is likely – compared with the time of our fieldwork in 2008–09 – that greater numbers of migrant workers will now be engaged in lower-level jobs in sub-regions like Teesside. All we are able to report on this topic, given the nature of our research design, is that first, we had no difficulty in recruiting for our research British-born, white working-class men and women who *were* willing to engage in poor work at the bottom of the labour market and, second, according to our interviews with them, nor did local employers face problems recruiting such people for low-level jobs (see Chapter 4).

In sum, then, the predominant pattern of work career for this older age – and for the younger re-interviewees – was one of shuttling between low-paid work and unemployment recurrently over their working lives – classic 'low-pay "careers"' (McKnight, 2002, p 97). Even for many of the older interviewees (those aged over 40), this had been a long-lasting pattern, stretching back to when they first entered the labour market after they left school. Looking back on his working life, Don, at age 40, said: "I was probably out of work on and off, like job here, job there, job here, job there."

If we pictured these working lives as a line over time we would see quickly repeated peaks (jobs) and troughs (unemployment), like a series of waves (see Figure 5.1). For most interviewees these movements in and out of employment also equated with moves above and below the poverty line (using the 'less than 60 per cent of median income' measure; see Chapter 3). Getting jobs, even low-paid jobs, usually improved household income to the extent that it carried interviewees over official poverty thresholds, albeit usually only marginally. A fuller discussion of the experience of recurrent poverty is presented in Chapter 9.

Figure 5.1: Typical low-pay, no-pay work history

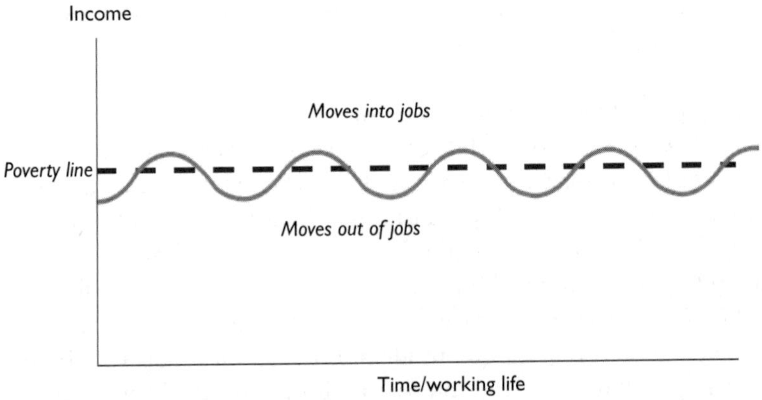

There were three noteworthy variations to this pattern.

First, we found work histories to be strongly influenced by gender. Unsurprisingly, women in the study were much more likely to have periods of their lives where patterns of employment were complicated by childbearing and childcare (not just relating to their own children, as we see in Chapter 8) to a far greater extent than most of the men in the study. Childcare responsibilities often shaped women's pattern of engagement with the low-pay, no-pay cycle, with longer periods out of the labour market. Linda, 33, was now very keen to return to a job and sometimes regretted not doing sooner after having children:

> "… once I had kids I thought 'this is the job for me; staying at home with the kids' and then I had Alex and I think you just get into a routine … and you're busy when you have kids. I'm not sat down all the time. I couldn't. I'd be like a cabbage. But I think you get into a routine of getting up, taking the kids to school, coming home. It gets so boring."

Thus, for these interviewees, presented graphically the wave pattern of the predominant low-pay, no-pay cycle would be interspersed with 'troughs' stretched out over time. For some women these spells away from employment could be long, with the troughs drawn out over years, depending on the nature of their caring commitments (see Figure 5.2).

Figure 5.2: Less typical low-pay, no-pay work history (1)

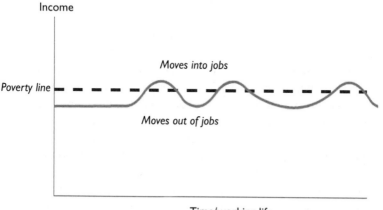

Second, a very similar pattern to this was found among a small number of interviewees (predominantly younger men) although the causation was quite different. These were people who had histories of serious offending motivated by problematic drug use. Struggling with drug dependency and the social, health and legal problems it brought, with time in drug treatment programmes and imprisoned for drug-related offending, meant that labour market engagement was difficult to maintain for lengthy periods (see Chapter 8). Intriguingly, however, even those with lengthy records of offending, criminal convictions and drug dependency were not completely excluded from the labour market (see MacDonald et al, 2011). Even if engagement with it was suspended, it was not abandoned completely, and nor were those with such life histories excluded from employment. Richard, 30, for instance had, from his mid-teens, been embroiled in heroin dependency that motivated a career of acquisitive offending (chiefly shoplifting to raise funds to purchase drugs). He received numerous convictions, spent time in Young Offenders Institutions on remand, served time on probation and participated in several, failed drug rehabilitation programmes. This had an impact on an already faltering post-school labour market career.

From 16 to 18 he had participated in a few training programmes and had one low-skilled job, interspersed with unemployment. Between the ages of 19 and 23, in the full throes of his drug crime career, Richard spent no time in jobs or in training. Revisiting him for this study, now aged 30, revealed how Richard had managed to overcome his drug dependency, and associated offending. For the previous seven years, he had been engaged in the sort of low-pay, no-pay cycle typical of the interviewees in general. Despite his lengthy period away from the labour market, by this point his work history comprised 15 separate periods of unemployment, time on five training schemes of different sorts and nine episodes of low-paid employment (the longest of which had lasted 18 months) (see Chapter 8).

Third, a handful of interviewees, typically skilled tradespeople, had a slightly different pattern of work history from the general one. Their occasional ability to secure better-paid, skilled jobs lifted them further away from poverty than was true of most interviewees' moves into employment. While some of these had lengthier stretches of employment in their earlier working lives, more recently they had the typical wave pattern of churning between jobs and unemployment – the jobs they got remained insecure – but the 'peaks' in their pattern were higher because they were sometimes better paid (see Figure 5.3). For instance, Mark, 36, was a time-served joiner who reported being able to earn considerably more than most of the sample when he was able to find work (on occasions as much as £1,200 per week). Because

Figure 5.3: Less typical low-pay, no-pay work history (2)

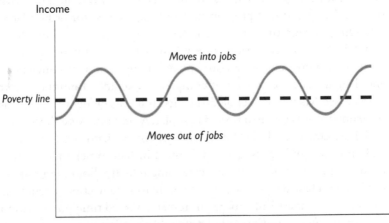

his wife worked part time, however, when he was unemployed he was only able to claim £19 per week JSA.

To begin to explain the patterns of work history that we have described we move next to investigate interviewees' personal orientations to employment – what work meant to them and their motivations for doing it.

Work motivations

Perhaps one of the strongest, single findings of the study was that interviewees, who had been caught up in the low-pay, no-pay cycle over years, expressed great personal commitment to employment. Our earlier studies with young adults found the same. Deeply embedded class cultural expectations and attitudes about the necessity and value of working for a living drove earlier, post-school transitions and led young people quickly into the labour market (in preference to extended education) (MacDonald and Marsh, 2005). In doing so they replicated the early work histories of the older interviewees and followed a class-based transition to adulthood traditional in working-class communities like this one (Willis, 1977). This remained true for those we re-interviewed and was also true for our new, older interviewees. Typically, most interviewees gave several reasons for their motivation towards employment and, in identifying different aspects of its appeal, it should be borne in mind that most interviewees agreed with most of these explanations. We focus in this section on the social, cultural and psychological values of working. In Chapter 9 we make clear the financial value of employment to people when we turn to their experiences of unemployment, welfare and poverty.

A life outside the home

A common response from interviewees was that work was valued because it linked them into activities and social networks beyond the immediate sphere of family and home. John was 40 and had been struggling to free himself of heroin dependency. He was unemployed and had lived alone since splitting up with his girlfriend. For him the attraction of a job was in large part to escape his loneliness and social isolation:

> "Some of the time I start getting depressed about it – but when I'm out working it's alright. I don't mind [living alone]. If I had a job I'd have to start mixing with people.

If I get the right job I might start talking to people and mixing more, making mates and that … I'd like to have a social life that but at the moment I haven't got that. Over the last six years [since the last interview] I haven't had a social life; I'd like to go out drinking and that with people."

Debbie, aged 43, had been on benefits for a long period after leaving school and while bringing up children. After returning to employment, subsequent to college courses, she had had a series of jobs and was currently employed part time working with young people. Her husband, Sean, was self-employed. The way she describes the appeal of work is in striking contrast to the lack of social contact experienced by John above:

"I couldn't do it any more [be unemployed]. I enjoy going to work. I enjoy having summat to come home from. Sean telling me what's happened at work. Me telling him what's happened at work and both having like an interest outside of here … you come back with all sorts of stories; people at work and what have you. So what would you have to talk about without all that, really? Apart from the kids driving you nuts."

Janice, aged 56 and unemployed for several years, said:

"I think you all need an interest outside your home really … you just get in a rut and you can't get out. That's how I feel sometimes, not all the time. My husband is a big help, he does most of the work in here [in the house] … there's very little I do."

The loss of employment seemed to weigh particularly heavily on the older participants in the study, particularly those who now, like Janice, had been out of work for several years. Ronnie was 57 and had been unemployed for five years, his most recent employment being as a bus driver. Asked about how it felt to be without work, he emphasised the loss of the daily routines of working life:

"I found it hard to begin with, you know? Because I'm used to getting up early … I still get up early … five o'clock I was up this morning, because I have to feed and look after the dog … I've never been short of money because me Mam used to help us out, and then when I was married, you know, I used to give Carol me wages. I kept a couple of pound and that would do. I used to go out on a Friday night and me wife would go out on a Saturday night so it was a good combination….A job's more than about money. It determines how your life leads and how your health feels. If you've got a job I think you're happier in a job … like the weather, if you get a bit of sunshine it brightens up the day."

Melvyn, aged 60, described how the voluntary work he now did for a local tenants' group helped fill the space left by the loss of employment:

"I did miss working, so I do voluntary work … we don't get paid for that. I'm on the residents' panel and there are quite a lot of meetings, probably four or five in a month. We got to different places. Went to Blackpool, they paid for all of this. I think it is good. It keeps you active. I like to get out. I couldn't just sit."

Dignity in labour

Often interviews that stressed the personal importance of life outside the home would be instilled with a sense of pride of working for a living (rather then being reliant on welfare payments; see Chapter 9). Again, these themes were bound up with others too, as we see in the next extract. Mary, aged 30, had two children, and was currently unemployed:

"I don't know what it's like now but I was much better off on my own working than I was on benefits, and it was nice to earn my own money and not have to go and queue up in the post office. It was nice to do that. It was the money … and it was the pride. Like the pride of working, earning your own money and actually going to work every day and having something to do. I would drop Dylan off at school and I would go to work. It was just nice to actually go to work. It made a nice difference from sitting at home with the kids. I'm looking for work at the minute. I really need to go back to work now just for the financial reason of it and Ruby's full time [at school] now so I've got all day to myself so your brain turns to mush a little bit!"

Mark was 36 and a trained joiner. He said this about the times he had had in employment:

> "Yeah, I enjoyed doing it. I like my work when I've done it. I like to see what I've done. I can say to the kids when we're driving about, 'Look at all the roofs on that estate. I've done them'. There's a lot of houses around here I have done."

John, 40, who we quoted earlier in respect of his lack of social contact in the absence of employment, also described the sense of fulfilment and pride that came with a job:

> "Oh, it is important to work to support me kids and that. Yeah, I can start feeling proud about myself then if I come off it [heroin], clean myself up. I'd start feeling better about myself and get more confident to mix with people and that. Definitely, I think if I got a job I could start picking me life up and getting better, yeah. I did warehouse work in the past. I loved it; just the whole thing, really. Just busy all the time, the atmosphere, and always moving, being busy. The social side, and that."

Work as an alternative to drugs and crime

For some men who had been caught up in crime or drug use (or both) – and the personal troubles and relative detachment from the labour market that that brought – employment often had a quite particular appeal.

Max, 34, lived with his girlfriend (an ex-heroin user). They were about to become parents. Despite a criminal record, Max had managed to get a manual job working at the local docks (which was relatively well paid, in comparison to most of the jobs people did). Max had been involved in crime but was staunchly critical of heroin use (and heroin dealers):

> "Heroin and crack have done a lot of damage to this area.... If I went on the dole and I couldn't handle it, it'd do my fucking head in. I couldn't be on the dole. I have to work, simple as that. So, yes, work is very, very important: an important thing in my life, my job, absolutely. I mean – touch wood – but if it did happen [lose his job at the docks] I'd have to work away [from Teesside]. And if I couldn't get

a job working away, I'd have to do fucking crime. I'd hate to do it. It would kill me doing it but I really would have to do it because there's no way I could go on that dole. There's fucking no chance. I'd be suicidal. It'd fucking do me in. I wouldn't be able to do it. I mean I see some lads now and like they can't even afford to just go out and have a couple of pints."

For Max work was valued because it provided enough income to provide for his family and to enjoy a normal, basic social life (the sort his unemployed peers could not afford). Although only implied in this extract, the risk of the unstructured time and purposelessness of unemployment was well understood by those seeking to maintain a process of desistance from crime (and for some, from heroin use). Boring, empty days jeopardised attempts to 'go straight' (MacDonald et al, 2011). Max, in emphasising that he would have to return to crime if he became unemployed, was not just describing his wish to avoid the financial hardship of being reliant on welfare. In addition, for him, the activity and purposefulness of the daily routines of offending was *psychologically* preferable to the idleness and stigma of 'the dole'.

Micky had been less successful than Max in finding employment. Now aged 31, he had desisted from heroin use for several years. He had been released from prison a year earlier, was living with his girlfriend and was desperate to get a job:

"No, getting a job wasn't really much on mind when you last talked to me [an interview with him six years previously]. Just, like, obviously, like, you know, I've been in and out of jail all me life. I'm getting older and I've just come to the stage where I think I need a life now. It's like 'life's too short', isn't it? That's all it is. I just wanna get a job and just live a normal life because in my eyes I'd say I've had a really bad past so that's what made me think, like, 'get settled down'. While I was in jail I thought I'll get as many certificates as I can and then when I go home I might be able to make something of 'em. But what made me see sense, like, to get work and that really is boredom. It is pure boredom. Because when I'm sat bored, I drink. It'd be nice to have a job."

For Micky, like many ex-offenders trying to go straight, a job offered the prospect of 'a normal life' (a phrase we heard repeatedly in our discussions with such interviewees across our earlier studies; see

MacDonald and Marsh, 2005). Criminological research literature tells us that gaining employment is one key aid to desistance from crime (see, for example, Farrall and Calverley, 2006; see also Chapter 8). It provides a new, socially condoned purpose in life, legitimate income, structure and activities with which to fill days and to deflect the temptations of crime and a new social and self-identity through which ex-offenders can tell new narratives to others, and to themselves, about who they are and will be (Maruna, 2001). Achieving employment – as a biographical turning point – is, of course, very difficult for individuals like Micky, especially in the restricted labour market of Teesside in the 2000s (Webster et al, 2004).

Work as a family tradition

> Interviewer: "Do you think that was important for you once you did come out of prison, to get work?"
>
> Angus: "It was, yeah. Me Dad and Mum always worked and it was a strain on them visiting me in prison, having to come to Manchester and all over but, yeah, they were a good influence, me parents, and I hope I am to my two [children], that they don't get in bother."

Here Angus, now aged 47, refers back to a period in his twenties when he had a series of criminal convictions – and spells in prison – for burglary. Since then his work history has been typical of the wider sample: churning between jobs, unemployment and various training schemes. While his parents may not have *succeeded* completely in being a 'good influence', Angus's comments here were reflective of a strong theme in interviews: the importance of employment had been learned from parents. Working for a living was reported as a family tradition among participants. Richard, 30, also an ex-offender, commented: "yeah, they've always worked and yes of course if influences you. I'm only ever happy when I'm in work. It focuses me time."

Other interviewees would refer directly to how they had learned from their parents the value of working *in contrast to* the effects of poverty and unemployment. For instance, Carol Anne (34, a part-time teaching assistant and mother to a young son) said:

> "My Dad always worked and my Mum did. I think that influenced me. I saw the difference between when my Dad worked and when he didn't, you know? The money

situation: I seen how they struggled when he wasn't working ... like they felt awful at Christmas when they can't buy you the stuff that they want and it really doesn't matter what you get but ... that made me want to work and do the best for Ben [her son] really."

As well as learning from their parents, interviewees would often emphasise how they wished to set a good example for their own children – and to improve their lives, particularly materially, by being in employment. We mentioned Linda, 33, earlier in the chapter, as an example of women's longer spells away from the labour market because of parenting and childcare. Here she emphasises the appeal of employment for her, stressing many of the themes discussed so far, including the provision of a better life for her children (specifically, the dream of a family holiday; see Chapter 9):

"It is very important for me to get a job. They're going to grow up and leave home and, I'm sorry, but I couldn't live on the benefit that they give you. It sounds daft when they say life begins at 40 but mine is definitely going to because I wanna be out there working and being very independent. I'd be out this house. I'd have a life. I could make more friends. I think that's a part of it really, like I say, having something for myself like 'I've done that. I've been out to work today. I've put some money into the house'. That's my ideal situation: 'Right we're going to Disneyland Paris in six weeks!' That'd be absolutely brilliant to say to them instead of just sat here thinking I'll never go on holiday with the kids, do you know what I mean?"

As with our earlier studies in these neighbourhoods, we heard repeatedly how, in academic language, interviewees had inherited intergenerationally a cultural predisposition *toward* work: they talked of how a work ethic was learned from parents and interviewees attempted to instil this in their own children. In Chapter 3 we described, briefly, the remarkable history of Teesside as a place, how it transformed from a small, rural hamlet into a powerful site of industrial production in a very quick time and of how a thoroughly working-class town was built. Teesside was, and is, a place whose essential character and working-class culture has been shaped by the demands of hard, manual labour (Beynon et al, 1994). In documenting the motivations towards employment held by the interviewees, especially but not only when thinking about work as a family tradition, it is hard not to see strong traces of this working-class culture and history playing out, even in the aftermath of massive deindustrialisation. This class cultural valuing of employment – of 'real jobs' (Willis, 1977) – remains even when traditional opportunities to put these motivations into practice have withered. In other words, what we still hear, in participants' talk of the dignity of labour and how they have learned in their families that working is the right thing to do, are expressions of a culture of work, not of a culture of worklessness. This finding, and this argument, reverses common assumptions and stereotypes – that are widespread in political, policy and popular discourse (and among support agencies we interviewed; see Chapter 4) – that explain unemployment in terms of the intergenerational transmission of cultures of worklessness (Murray, 1994; see Shildrick et al, 2012).

Work as the opposite of unemployment

Behind *all* the various motivations towards employment discussed so far, at the back of interviewees' statements about the value of work stands its opposite, unemployment. Feelings and views about being in work and feelings and views about being unemployed are two sides of the same coin and we cannot understand why work appealed if we do not understand how unemployment repelled. Andrew (43, currently unemployed and single) said:

> "Work? Very important, just to get out the house and that. There's nowt worse than not working. It's so depressing. It's awful, just awful. Like I say, when I'm working I'm a totally different lad, totally different and when I'm not working I'm just down.... It's hard to explain. It's just it does put you on this totally, like, puts you on a proper depressing mode."

How and why unemployment can be a negative and sometimes debilitating personal condition has long been researched in social psychology. One of the most influential contributions to this literature is from Marie Jahoda (1979, 1982), who drew on research from the 1930s and the 1970s to explain the pattern of social psychological decline typically associated with longer-term unemployment. For Jahoda, work provides 'categories of human experience' that are essential for psychological well-being. In modern capitalist societies work, for most people, is organised as employment (although she acknowledges the potential for some individuals, perhaps such as artists or those with consuming hobbies, to locate the positive benefits of work outside of formal employment). While the material incentive – wages or salaries – is crucial in explaining why people might want to work (and higher levels of welfare benefit can ameliorate to an extent the social psychological harm of unemployment), she suggests that work also has five latent functions. It enforces activity, usually on a daily basis. Work structures time – the working day, week and year. Without the time structures of employment Mondays feel the same as Sundays. It provides goals and purposes for people that can bring some sense of meaning to life. Work brings individuals into contact with others so that there are social dimensions to the value of work. Finally, work gives social identity. 'What do you do?' remains a question strangers wonder about each other when they meet. In short, Jahoda (1982, p 59) sees employment as providing:

> ... the imposition of a time structure, the enlargement of the scope of social experience into areas less emotionally charged than family life, participation in a collective purpose of effort, the assignment by virtue of employment status and identity, and required regular activity.... [They are] a psychological requirement in modern life.

Jahoda's 'latent functions' approach to understanding the apparent psychological value of work has been criticised for 'not taking into account differing and changing social contexts and differing life stages of the individual' (Ritchie et al, 2005, p 8). Much of the research on which her ideas depend, from the 1930s, was undertaken with specific social groups, typically male, manual workers who had been made redundant from jobs. She limited attention to how social factors such as age, gender, alternate social roles available, individual employment commitment and the potential declining stigma of long-term, widespread unemployment may affect the well-being of the unemployed and vary the social psychological consequences of unemployment at individual level. In a context of 'intergenerational unemployment' or widespread local worklessness 'not being in employment is the norm', according to Ritchie et al (2005, p 9), which may ameliorate the psychological impact of unemployment. Warr (1994, cited in Ritchie et al, 2005) has extended Jahoda's research with the 'vitamin model' in order to try to overcome some of these apparent criticisms. It identifies aspects of the environment that are known to be beneficial to well-being (for example, variety, opportunity for personal control, skill use, interpersonal contact) and helps to explain psychological well-being through the relative availability of these 'vitamins' in different contexts (for example, better-quality jobs, underemployment, unemployment).

Drawing on available evidence from the 1980s, Jahoda (1982) responds to some of these criticisms (for instance, in identifying that the damaging experience of unemployment may be nuanced by age or gender). Even more importantly for our study there is an implication that all employment, regardless of its type or quality, will provide positive psychological benefits. Jahoda acknowledges the psychological harm that low quality employment can sometimes bring – and a key thrust of her work was to argue for the humanisation and improvement of conditions of employment – but concludes, in general, that work is better psychologically for people: 'that the intensity of deprivation, financially and psychologically, is greater in unemployment is ... indicated by the fact that the overwhelming majority of the unemployed want a job' (1982, p 48).

In Chapter 7, where we discuss the experience of employment for participants, we comment further on Jahoda's thesis. In Chapter 8 we examine further how ill health may be related to unemployment *and* to poor work. In Chapter 9 we describe further how people described their experience of unemployment – and of being on welfare. For the time being we can state that the categories of experience that Jahoda says work provides were strongly evident in participants' narratives about the appeal of work (to the extent that at times it almost felt that interviewees were reciting Jahoda's latent functions of work back at us!) When Andrew described the importance of work as "just to get out of the house" and John told how he "loved work" because he was "just busy all the time ... always moving, being busy", they stressed how employment *enforced activity* over the lethargy and listlessness often associated with unemployment. Mary, like others, described the *time structure* and rhythms of working life: "... going to work every day and having something to do. I would drop Jack off at school and I would go to work. It was just nice to actually go to work." Those men we interviewed who were in the long-term process of desistance from crime and/or drug dependency often emphasised the necessity of having the *purpose* in life that work gave: "if I got a job I could start picking me life up and getting better" (John). When Tara, 31, said "I like going out to work, because ... you get to meet people, [rather than] just stuck in the house talking baby talk, sat in front of Jeremy Kyle" she emphasised the *social contacts* that come from jobs. Achieving a new *social identity* through employment (other than offender or drug user) was part of the business of 'going straight' for some. Women who were mothers also often stressed the importance of work to identity:

"I can be me instead of just 'Mam'". All felt, and resisted, the stigma that came from the social identity of unemployed welfare claimant (see Chapter 9).

In sum, work motivation was at least in part spurred by the social and psychological benefits it was known, through personal experience, to provide. The positive value of work to people's social and psychological well-being was confirmed by their knowledge of the negative effects of its opposite, unemployment. Depression proved to be a particular consequence of unemployment, as described later in Chapter 9. In general, people felt better in work than when they were unemployed.

Work motivation in the long term

So far we have described examples and aspects of work motivation as expressed by individuals across the sample. An important finding of the research, in addition, was that the commitment that individuals described lasted over time. For the older half of our sample it is not surprising that they described enduring work commitment; after all, this group were purposefully recruited because they were of a particular age (41–60) and engaged in the low-pay, no-pay cycle. By definition, they are likely to have retained a commitment to employment. That said, it is illuminating to understand how and why that commitment maintains in the long term (as we have attempted above) when one might hypothesise that a recurrent experience of low-level jobs and unemployment would serve to diminish the commitment to work. A key part of the 'discouraged worker' thesis argues that a worker, faced with persistent inability to get secure, rewarding employment, facing repeated rejection by employers and spells of unemployment will, eventually, become demotivated and give up the search for work. Evidence for workers either deciding not to enter the labour market, for instance, by continuing in or returning to education, or reducing or halting their efforts to find work in difficult labour markets, is well established and cross-national (see, for example, Raffe and Willms, 1989; Benati, 2001; van Ham et al, 2001). Our older participants, however, are proof that the condition of the 'discouraged worker' does not apply to all who face the circumstances said to generate it. This is what Andrew (43) said: "I'm out of work more than I'm in it. It's just getting harder and harder. Like sometimes I might get two days' work and I will take it. If someone says 'there's one day's work', I'll still take it." Simon (36), who had had nine bouts of worklessness and 12 jobs since leaving school, commented that "I want to work 'til they put me in a box."

As described in Chapter 3, we did not recruit our sample of younger participants (those aged 30–40) *knowing* that they were currently engaged in the low-pay, no-pay cycle. We knew they had been when we last spoke to them, typically at least six years earlier. Finding that they were *still* engaged in churning between jobs and unemployment is again evidence of the durability of work motivation over time. Murad also finds a similar class-based 'work ethic and enthusiasm for work' among excluded groups in continental Europe, describing its 'persistence in current times' as 'remarkable' (2002, p 98). Of course, interviewees talked about how at particular moments in their working lives they had felt demotivated and dispirited, but these were described as *episodic*, not lasting feelings about work. Marge, 31, described to us how her husband had a serious, limiting illness but that this had not sapped his commitment to employment (despite Marge's preference that he worked less or less hard):

> "I think if he just didn't work it's [sic] be easier but he wants to try and work and.... But he gets stressed at work. If he's off sick he has to have a meeting about his sickness so obviously he gets stressed and that makes his illness worse. But for him it is about more than the money. It's just to get out, isn't it? And to socialise, to feel like you are earning some money. Enough to bring into the house – although he would be better off and healthier if he didn't work!"

Conclusions

This chapter has begun the description and explanation of the low-pay, no-pay cycle. Our earlier research on Teesside showed a pattern of churning around low-paid jobs, unemployment and government training programmes to be the *predominant* and *long-term* labour experience for young adults in deprived neighbourhoods. We found that this pattern continued for them as they reached their thirties. This runs counter to a dominant view that low-paid, insecure jobs provide stepping-stones to better employment. Furthermore, this pattern of movement around jobs and unemployment is, for these young, working-class research participants, best not understood as reflection of a new, choice-rich, experimenting life phase of 'emerging adulthood'. While there is debate about the real extent of precarious employment (see Chapter 2), there was no shortage of older people, aged over 40, in this locality who shared in the same low-pay, no-pay cycle, from whom to recruit participants for this study. There were some differences in the detailed shape of the overall pattern, but churning between low-paid jobs and unemployment was the norm and characterised working lives in the long term, for younger and older workers, for men and for women.

As a first step toward understanding the low-pay, no-pay cycle (and its connection to recurrent poverty) this chapter examined the motivations of people towards work – what brings them to want employment in the first place. The personal imperative towards work lasted over time, despite the set-backs and insecurities inherent to the low-pay, no-pay cycle. We have tried to disentangle the multiple motivations that participants described. Financial reasons were, of course, important, given the everyday material hardships people faced when dependent on unemployment benefits (see Chapter 8). The non-monetary attractions of employment were, however, also strongly emphasised by interviewees: having a life outside of the home; the social contacts and social identity that employment brought; the sense of personal pride and dignity offered by working for a living; and the structure and purpose of employment (which was particularly valued by some as an alternative to lives centred on offending and/or dependent drug use). Reflecting the working-class culture history of their town and culture of their families, many stressed how their commitment to employment was an outcome of what they had learned from their parents, in their families, a commitment and outlook they hoped would benefit their own children. Crucially, participants' motivation to being employed was shaped and shadowed by what they knew of the opposite, being unemployed. It was better, generally, to have a job than to be without one and thus, overall, we found a strong resonance between theories about the social psychological benefits of employment and the informants' descriptions of the value of work.

In the next chapter we continue our exploration of the low-pay, no-pay cycle by discussing how these motivations towards work were put into practice, that is, how people went about the business of searching for jobs and the skills and qualifications they brought to that search.

6

Searching for jobs: qualifications, support for the workless and the good and bad of informal social networks

Introduction

We now turn to the processes and practices that underlay participants' experiences of searching for work. The formal services provided through the state, voluntary and private sectors to help the workless into jobs are described, from the point of view of our interviewees. A key finding of the chapter, with implications for social policy and practice in this area, is that the informal methods and practices of job searching tended to prove more successful in locating jobs but, as a corollary, tended to limit people to the poor work done by others in their social networks. We begin, however, by describing the educational backgrounds, skills and qualifications that people brought to the labour market.

Education, skills and qualifications

In Chapter 5 we documented the strength of the sample's motivation to work. This strong commitment to employment was not matched by high levels of education, qualifications and skill. Overall, these were relatively low level. Virtually all had left school at minimum school leaving age and many had had disappointing experiences of school, typically leaving with a few low level passes at GCSE (or their equivalent predecessors). The reasons for working-class educational underachievement are well documented (Evans, 2007) and our interviewees gave depressingly familiar explanations, for instance: of the perceived irrelevance of the curricula (and, for some, of educational qualifications per se); of being bullied and victimised (by pupils or teachers); of problems in their wider lives not being recognised or appropriately cared for by school; of pupil cultures that encouraged educational disengagement and truancy; and of poor-quality teaching and educational provision in schools that failed to provide a successful education comprehensively to all pupils (see MacDonald and Marsh, 2005). This is not to say that *all* were low qualified and low skilled. Some of the older men were skilled tradesmen, having completed apprenticeships early in their working lives. A handful of people also possessed higher level educational credentials: undergraduate diplomas or degrees.

A second point of note is that negative *experiences* of secondary school did not set negative *attitudes* to education in stone and a good number returned later to some sort of post-16 education or training. Most common were qualifications gained through vocational training and education courses for 16- to 18-year-olds (such as the Youth Training Scheme [YTS] and its successors). Similarly, a number of participants had returned later to further education college as 'mature students', often on a part-time basis, to undertake National Vocational Qualifications (NVQs) usually at Level 2 (courses designed to qualify for childcare and teaching assistant jobs were the most often mentioned). Several had also passed shorter training courses offered, for instance, by training providers in local community centres (for example, gaining certificates in basic computer skills, computer repair, literacy, numeracy, and first aid). It is important to stress, therefore, that there was a willingness to re-engage with education and training in order to improve labour market prospects. Other motivations included participating in courses as an alternative to the purposelessness, inactivity and social isolation typical of unemployment (see Chapter 9). Underlining the material hardship that informants like these faced, in our earlier Teesside studies more practical reasons for attendance at these sorts of courses were sometimes given, for example to benefit from the free crèche, cheap cafe and free heating provided in community centres (MacDonald and Marsh, 2005). Nevertheless, informants' main rationale can be summed up by Carol-Anne, 34 (who obtained her classroom assistant job after completing a short training course, delivered locally with 'family-friendly' hours):

> "Yeah, yeah I do [think qualifications and education are important] … just to give yourself the best chance you can to get a job, because at school I didn't try my hardest and I wish I had. I wish I'd gone to college and I didn't."

There was some evidence that gaining further qualifications did help some in the search for jobs in indirect and direct ways. Simon, 30, had

had a typical, churning labour market career (see Chapter 5). After repeatedly losing jobs and being unemployed, he invested his savings of £2,000 to take a course that led to him passing his HGV driving licence. This opened up new job opportunities (which also, as it turned out, tended to be insecure). Debbie, 43, had completed an NVQ Level 2 in Health and Social Care, working with disabled children on her work placement. Not only had the course helped boost her confidence about returning to work after a long period looking after her own children, it had led directly to a part-time job:

> "It was the best thing and I absolutely loved it from the minute I walked in. Loved it. Completed the course and I've still got in there the appraisal the woman give me because I was that proud that she'd said I'd done really well and I did that, finished it and they gave me a [school] lunchtime supervision job after!"

Having noted the positive attitude of interviewees toward gaining further training, skills and qualifications, and that there were clearly instances where this benefited people, we concur with Crisp et al (2009, p 6) that 'skills development is not an automatic passport to better employment opportunities' and with Newton and colleagues (2005, p 3) who concluded that 'overall, the evidence suggests that a focus on qualifications would appear not to contribute to an individual's employment outcomes, due to low emphasis on these in recruitment' (see Chapter 4). Many participants had completed training programmes (for example, under the New Deal for Young People programme or vocational, college-based courses) yet remained on a merry-go-round of insecure jobs and unemployment:

> "I'm thinking about going on another training course but I get a bit fed up going on them ... two or three times a week I do job search and there have been applications I've sent off and I've got a reply but no job offers yet as such.... I did a business enterprise course. I think I got a certificate for doing that.... They are never a waste of time cos I was always learning something but the main thing at the end of it is to get a job, well that's the main idea to me." (Sid, 55)

Don, 40, was another who had had disappointing experiences of training courses. He "didn't really like school" – he was repeatedly bullied because he was very tall – and he "left early, which I shouldn't have done." After returning from working away in London, he enrolled at a local college to take a year-long course in injection moulding:

> "I was roughly about 24, 25. The dole place pestered me to go on that. I went on the course for over a year. You just got your dole and went to college say 32 hours per week, summat like that. It was supposed to be a year. This is the best laugh! After 10 months we were ready to do our exams and we found out that they [the college] are not qualified to do the exams for the injection moulding course what we'd been doing. So what a waste of 10 month that was! And then they sent me on this course placement and if you were alright they kept you on, but they made me sweep up for a week. £10 for sweeping up for a week! Then they decided they had enough people anyway.... Oh it was good at college, because I got like the equivalent of an A level in Maths but no certificate for it because they weren't allowed to give them out so that was just a waste of time really.... No, no jobs came from it, just that sweeping up one."

Notably absent from most participants' work histories was explicit or formalised skills-based training or qualifications *with* the employers they worked for. Typically, the jobs they got did not offer anything more than a basic induction into the necessities of the work role (see Chapter 7).

We know that some forms of training and vocational courses offer much greater labour market value than others. Roberts and Parsell (1992), for instance, showed how youth training programmes in the 1980s were stratified, with those offering most success (that is, chances of employment afterwards, recognised skills qualifications) being those where young people trained *with* large, national-level employers (who had integrated the training programme into their recruitment practices). These training programmes 'creamed off' the best YTS entrants. Courses at the bottom end, often in community-based centres with limited connection to employers, fared much worse in placing participants into jobs (Bates et al, 1984). Furlong (1992) argues that many youth training courses added nothing to, or even detracted from, participants' later success in the labour market. There are echoes now of this same failure of vocational training programmes to consistently help participants towards employment. The think-tank Demos has highlighted the glaring lack of policy (and, we would add, academic) attention to 'the structure of opportunities' available to the 'forgotten half' of school-leavers who do not progress on towards higher education

(MacDonald, 2011). They comment that 'there is a dearth of evidence about what happens to these young people post-school' (Birdwell et al, 2011, p 33), and that 'the rush to expand university places has taken attention away from other educational routes into the labour market' (Birdwell et al, 2011, p 54). *The Wolf report* (Wolf, 2011) has provided some evidence, however, and its conclusions are damning. It paints a picture of post-16 vocational education as confused and muddled and that many vocational courses at NVQ Level 2 (exactly the sorts of courses that the research participants were encouraged towards to improve their skills) have low or zero value in the labour market: 'young people ... are being deceived, and placed on tracks without their full understanding or consent' (Wolf, 2011, p 82). It concludes that:

> The staple offer for between a quarter and a third of the post-16 cohort is a diet of low-level vocational qualifications, most of which have little to no labour market value. Among 16 to 19 year olds ... at least 350,000 get little to no benefit from the post-16 education system. (Wolf, 2011, p 7)

Some such courses are known, however, to increase job prospects, because there is a labour market demand for such skills, and one example is in the field of health and social care. As noted above, interviewees like Debbie experienced a direct connection between completion of a course and getting a related job. Even when completion of job-related training was likely to be beneficial, barriers were often in their way (for example, in Don's case, above, the failure of the programme to provide necessary accreditation). Mark, 36, was keen to take a training course in Aberdeen that would qualify him for working on offshore oil and gas platforms. He needed this in order to comply with the requirements of a job he had been offered via an employment agency:

> "I tried me hardest to get it at the job centre but they said 'We can't help you, you don't qualify'. So I came down here to Pathfinders [a voluntary sector employment support agency] and they said 'The maximum we can give you [sic] £150'. He said 'Try Working Futures' [another such agency]. So I rang them: 'You've got to be referred off the job centre'. I went there: 'I want referring'. They said 'We can't refer you, you don't qualify, you're not in this criteria'. So I did it off my own back. I phoned and phoned and phoned and eventually got the £400 for the course, and the £96 travel and £150 for my digs, from here there and everywhere. So

I did take it and went to Aberdeen, got that course – and no better off. They're all getting laid off."

Overall, a very significant finding of the study is that for the interviewees, levels of educational attainment did *not* straightforwardly predict improved labour market fortunes. The sample included even better qualified people (with degrees and diplomas) who at times in their working lives found themselves caught up in low-pay, no-pay churning labour market careers in the same ways as the least qualified. We return in Chapter 10 to a discussion of processes of supply and demand in the labour market and how employer requirements shape the low-pay, no-pay cycle (see also Chapter 2), but we remind readers here of a key finding from interviews with local employers (see Chapter 4). In listing the things they looked for in new employees, very rarely were particular types or levels of skill, qualification or educational background mentioned.

Searching for jobs

Research shows that job hunters use a variety of methods to search for work and this was also true for the interviewees (Lindsay, 2010). Repeated spells of unemployment defined their churning labour market careers and when out of work interviewees typically maintained an active search for employment, sometimes investing considerable amounts of physical and emotional effort in these searches:

> "Well I go job hunting four days or five days a week, just to get out. I walk down to the Willowdene 2000 offices first [a local community organisation, which offers job search support], then I walk down to that place in the town [another welfare to work agency], and then coming back just, like, I've got the routine. I know where all the scaffolding firms are. I just walk round. Well, they all know me now anyway because I pop in every week, but there's nowt … what narks me is the way you send out all these CVs, all these forms to these employers and you give 'em your phone number and you don't get a response. You're just struggling every day, waiting for the phone to ring or for someone to get in touch. They should have the decency; it's only a phone call to get back in touch with you." (Andrew, 43)

"At the moment my typical day is: get ready, get the bus down town, go to Pathfinders, do a job search, have an interview with me client adviser, apply for jobs, get the print outs, phone them up in the phone booth, apply from there – I also go to Learn Express now to do computer work. A lot of jobs now are on email so I want to be able to go on a computer to be able to do me own emails, rather than relying on other people sending them. So I do keep myself busy." (Sid, 55)

"I'll get up; go over to my mate's. We're both looking for a job at the moment. He's been out of work 12 year! He's got back trouble but they're bringing everyone off [Incapacity Benefit]. He said rather than argue he'll look for a job but he can't sit down for too long and the doctors said he can't really work but they're trying to get everyone off the sick at the moment ... so, we have a cuppa, decided whether we're going to walk over the job centre or if we're just going to look on the computer. Tuesday we went over the hospital; the [advertised] jobs were already gone. But if they're not gone you've got to look on the computer. I'm one of the lucky ones; I've got a laptop so it's one of me only luxuries. At the moment – look [Don pointed to holes in his shoes], I need some new trainers, I haven't got the money for trainers." (Don, 40)

As with Andrew's case, above, responses to the numerous job applications people made were very rare. There is great emphasis in government policy on the responsibilities of the workless to actively seek work and to regularly apply for jobs (and to be able to demonstrate that they have as a condition of eligibility for benefits). There is apparently no perceived responsibility on employers to respond to such efforts, even in the negative. This could 'nark' jobseekers and make them feel 'worthless', but the evidence of this research is that it did not deter them from continuing the search for work:

"I've applied to Iceland, I've applied to Tesco to see if there's any vacancies, you know? Home deliveries and things like that. The only one that bothered to let me know was that Dales Hotel ... I mean I write ... I put an application form in or fill a form in and my CV ... I hand write my CV and ... they don't even respond or send a letter or reply.... I get annoyed sometimes. I don't know why they don't reply. It's just impolite I think." (Ronnie, 57)

"There's quite a few people who don't bother sending you correspondence back. Some do and it's nice to know you've been considered. You're waiting for the postman, aren't you? Thinking 'What's gonna happen this time?' I must have sent a CV to every single [double-glazing] window company round here but they're not taking on. It's horrible, really. Like I said it, makes you think you're worthless ... oh no, it doesn't put me off, definitely not." (Alan, 38)

The participants predominantly searched for work in their immediate locality, that is, within the town of Middlesbrough. Several had worked further afield, within the wider conurbation of Teesside or in surrounding areas, often when an employer laid on transport for workers. For instance, an employer for whom many participants had worked, known locally as 'the turkey factory' and based some 15 miles away, used coaches to pick up workers in Middlesbrough in the early morning, bussing them back in the evening. Mirroring to an extent the old political rhetoric that urges the unemployed 'to get on their bikes to look for work', there has been considerable policy interest in how the workless might be connected to job opportunities in more buoyant labour markets and how, in this and other respects, some deprived neighbourhoods seem to have improved when others have not (IPPR, 2010a). The Institute for Public Policy Research (IPPR) conclude that several factors are important in understanding processes whereby some neighbourhoods might 'get left behind', including the motivation and attitude of those without work and the scope of their job search horizons. They also conclude that good public transport provision was significant and the most successful employment support schemes were ones that were 'linked into opportunities in the surrounding area' (IPPR, 2010a, p 5). A 'crucial' factor also was 'the context of the local labour market, including the availability of accessible entry level jobs ... proximity of jobs matters more for people accessing entry level employment, meaning the location of entry level jobs is important' (IPPR, 2010a, p 5).

Self-evidently, widening the geographic parameters of job search activity increases the likelihood of finding a job. Yet policy or political exhortations to this end tend to overlook some of the realities of life for those who are workless and living in poverty. Interviewees talked about how the time required (especially when added to childcare duties at home and school times), the non-affordability of buying and running a car, the awkwardness of bus timetables and delays in connecting services and, finally, the financial costs of travel (set against low-paid employment) together often ruled out looking for jobs outside of the town they lived in. It is important to recall, as well, that some employers interviewed for this study *preferred* workers to live locally (sometimes very close to the place of employment, because this meant that they were less likely to be absent from or late for work) (see Chapter 4).

An alternative to extending the travel to work area is to relocate to where there may be more jobs. As discussed later, tried and tested methods of job search tended to rely heavily on locally based social networks. This cultural practice tends to restrict the geographic (and social and economic) parameters of job search activity and militates against uprooting from the locality to find employment elsewhere (Kelvin and Jarrett, 1985; MacDonald et al, 2005). Emotional ties to families and friends (see Chapter 8) and the difficulties of locating suitable, affordable housing also tend to keep people in place. Nevertheless, a few in the study had moved away for jobs. These were all older men. Teesside, like other northern industrial cities, has a tradition of skilled, male workers seeking (more lucrative) employment in other parts of the UK or overseas (as in the TV comedy 'Auf Wiedersehn, Pet'), often in the construction or offshore oil industry. Don, 40, was unusual in that he had moved away to work as a teenager without a skilled trade behind him. Here he describes his younger life and his current experience. Don recalled hearing "Margaret Thatcher saying 'you Northerners get on your bike and go to London if you want a job'", and with a friend he travelled to London, gaining employment working in a pub: "we got there at one o'clock and we started work at half past one; got a job straightaway. I went down there for a few month and stopped there for seven year. It was alright. For the first six weeks I lived in a tent under the M25 but that's a different story...." He was paid £300 per week and now commented, "this is like 23 years down the line, you know? When I think about it now I'd be over the moon to come out with £300 here [in Middlesbrough, currently].... There's just nothing here." This dearth of decent local employment opportunities meant that those who felt they had skills to sell sometimes considered moving away for work. Mark was 36 and a trained joiner:

> "I used to be on £20 an hour as a joiner – £15, £20 an hour. Now they're paying joiners like me £6.35 an hour. I had it out with the job centre. I said 'I won't get out of bed for that. I've done 20 year and that's what they pay kids. You

get more than that and you're sat on your backside all day'. I'd never, ever thought I'd have to travel – maybe I have to go Leeds, an hour a day [each way]. I'm willing to work at London for two weeks or whatever and come back. With the rigs you can be away for three weeks and back for a weekend but its still £1,000, £1,200 a week that's getting sent back home. My wife and I have never been apart, we've always been that close, but she said 'If you have to go where there's work, you have to do it, and I'll have to cope'."

Jobcentre Plus and welfare to work agencies

Many participants had regular contact with Jobcentre Plus and other welfare to work agencies in their periods out of a job (although this was not the case for all, as described later in Chapter 9). We turn to voluntary sector welfare agencies shortly showing that, when they were accessible, they tended to be positively evaluated. Jobcentre Plus was much less well regarded.

Interviewees were overwhelmingly negative about their experiences of this service. Our time spent in Jobcentre Plus offices during the fieldwork – and our interviews with Jobcentre Plus staff – alerted us to a difficult relationship between staff and clients, with negative attitudes on each side, and a general 'us and them' feel to encounters (see Chapter 4 for other research evidence on this). At times, some staff appeared unsympathetic to the troubles and distant from the lives of interviewees. Commonly, informants felt belittled simply by being out of work (Chapter 9) and having to attend the job centre, and this discomfort was often exacerbated by how they felt they were treated by its staff. Mary, 30, described her partner Andy's recent, unhelpful encounter:

> "'Look, I want to get back into work'. They said 'What do you want to do that for? Keep claiming'. And he said 'I don't want to do that, there's nothing wrong with me' and they were like 'Go to the doctors and get a sick note'. They were so rude and so unhelpful and that's why a lot of people don't go back to work because they're not getting the help they need. It's quite sad really."

Tara, 31, also talked about the way her recently redundant husband had been treated:

"He's constantly glued to that laptop, looking at jobs ... he's applied for a few so we're just sitting fingers crossed now ... he went down to the job centre last week and he wasn't very impressed. He sort of wasn't very happy with the way it all was. I mean, he's never been in a job centre. He left school and went to work so this is a new thing and he come out and he said they were more interested in giving him Jobseeker's Allowance than they were in finding him a job. He said 'I don't want that [benefit], I want a job'. He said their exact words were 'Well you've paid into the system'....Then they were saying he'd have to be willing to give up his college course – even though it's part time – to actually give him anything anyway. He has to agree that if a job came up and his college course overlapped it, would he give up the college course, because otherwise he's not actively seeking work [laughs]! He only does eight hours a week on a night [at college]! And yet they say 'train, re-train' ... it's just they say one thing but actually want you to do another ... we haven't been impressed, full stop."

Because of these sorts of problems with statutory services, because of resistance to signing on for moral reasons and the stigma associated with unemployment and because they hoped that the period out of work would be too short to justify the hassle of establishing a benefits claim, some interviewees did not claim benefits during periods of unemployment (see Chapter 9). Others were in receipt of Incapacity Benefit that did not require regular contact with agencies. However, government welfare reforms to 'migrate' Incapacity Benefit claimants onto Employment and Support Allowance (ESA) will be complete by 2014, meaning people in this situation will be faced with increased 'conditionality' on their receipt of benefits ('welfare reforms' like this are discussed in Chapter 10). Together these cases meant that a significant proportion of the interviewees felt that they received little support in seeking work from agencies funded to do exactly this. In this sense, echoing the phrase used by one of the welfare to work agency practitioners we interviewed, they were the 'missing workless' (see Chapter 9).

More generally, the very nature of the low-pay, no-pay cycle – and the relatively short periods of unemployment they experienced – meant that the interviewees simply did not fit easily with the support on offer. This was often the case with some of the more specialised, voluntary sector support services discussed by interviewees and which served only the longer-term unemployed, not those with the shorter periods of worklessness typical of the participants:

> "Pathfinders are good, I think, aren't they? I don't know how some people are supposed to find out about them because some people just don't know about things. Andy [Mary's husband] went to the job centre and did say 'I wanna be fast tracked to Pathfinders 'cos you have to be on benefits six months before they refer you. But I think they've changed it. I think it's 18 months now. You'd think they'd want people back into work." (Mary, 30)

> "I'm stuck here trying my best to get a job. I've been down Pathfinders and they say 'you can't come for 18 months, that's how long you have to be out of a job'. That's terrible. You don't want to be on the dole 18 months." (Andrew, 43)

> "No, I think I have to be unemployed longer to qualify for things like that [support from a particular agency]. I haven't had any sort of advice from anywhere. I actually did it all off my own back [that is, exploring options for retraining as a maths teacher]." (Alan, 38)

Yet it seemed that even those with longer spells of unemployment could also fall through the net of support. Shaun, 56, received Incapacity Benefit for a longstanding eyesight problem incurred in his childhood. This did not mean, however, that he was unable to work. He had previously held down jobs and, currently, did voluntary work for local community and youth groups six days a week. When asked whether he had ever had any help or advice about finding another job, he said: "No, no, if you want it you have to go for it. You have to find out yourself basically, you have to go out and look for it that type of thing. You don't get that advice." Linda, 33, also seemed to have been left virtually untouched by services designed to help people back into work. She had "really enjoyed" the YTS she did in a butcher's shop when she left school. The owner selected which of his two YTS trainees would get a job at the end of the work placement by setting 'an adding up test' which Linda failed, because she was not as quick as her colleague. Now 33, since then she had spent a lot of time looking after her children, in receipt of Incapacity Benefit (for depression and other health problems), volunteering as a youth worker and doing unpaid cleaning work at her brother's takeaway business (in exchange for free pizzas). She was keen to get a job and hoped to enrol on an NVQ Level 2 course in childcare. At age 33, she could not recall receiving any advice or support about training or getting a job since she had completed her YTS scheme at the age of 18.

In contrast, those we spoke to who *had* participated in voluntary sector-run welfare to work activities tended to speak highly of the empathetic attitude of staff and the personalised support on offer compared with more generic services offered by Jobcentre Plus (see our discussion of Chris, in Chapter 8). They benefited from help with CVs, interview techniques, confidence building and various short courses (for example, in basic literacy and numeracy). One agency, Pathfinders, was spoken of particularly positively and seemed able to offer substantial support to jobseekers, as Angus (47) describes:

> "I got that job through Pathfinders, not the job centre. Because I'd been on the dole for 18 month I had to go on to them ... got a security officer job, it was on the wall. While I was there they paid for me driving licence, me theory [test], me photos – paid for all my driving lessons. They even paid for me passport, 'cos I never had a passport. They give you a mobile; never met a company like them! I've only used them that once because I was on long-term unemployment. It was about four years ago. As I went in there I thought, 'yes!' At the dole [job centre] it's just 'Have you found 'owt?' With Pathfinders it's 'go and have a look there'. So I thought 'I'll have that', went for it."

Micky, 31, also received positive help via Pathfinders. He said:

> "I applied to go there. They weren't even going to put me on it. They were going to leave me in the job centre.... I said to them: 'Look, you're not really doing nowt for me. Why don't you sign me over to Pathfinders? I might have a chance of, like, getting a job?' 'Cos every time I go job searching it says 'Needs driver's licence, needs this, needs that qualifications, whatever'."

As well as support to buy a provisional driving licence and driving lessons, Micky appreciated the help he got in preparing his CV (in multiple copies), in writing application letters and job interview training: "I've never had a job interview in my life!" Pathfinders offered him funding to buy new clothes should he get an interview and costs for travel to interviews.

Under the Coalition government's Work Programme, private and voluntary sector welfare to work providers have been given greater responsibility to assist people into jobs with an emphasis on 'payment by results', that is, agencies receive funding for those placed into jobs (DWP, 2010). There is a particular emphasis, to be applauded given the findings from this study, on placement into 'sustainable employment'. Government contracts to welfare to work providers are staged according to the length of time the 'client' stays in a job with providers being paid by results (the longer a client remains in a job the more payment the agency receives; see Wintour, 2011). Although this approach is to be welcomed – and is discussed further in Chapter 10 – it potentially clashes with the strong motivation towards securing *any* sort of job, of whatever duration, that was evident among some interviewees (see Chapter 5). A not dissimilar funding regime operated with Pathfinders, as Don, 40, discovered:

> "The dole place says to me 'You've been out of work six month you've got to go with Pathfinders'. So you go over to Pathfinders, you look in the paper there's a job here; 'Eight weeks' work'. Pathfinders are telling you not to take it because they want you to have a job [that lasts at least] 13 weeks so they can get the money off the government for you, so they're telling you not to do it, but that eight weeks' work would sort me out."

Private employment agencies

Private employment agencies are significant in any discussion of precarious work because, in the main, the employment they offer is explicitly temporary. Gray (2002) describes the potential benefit of employment agencies to disadvantaged groups in the labour market in that they can potentially help bypass employer prejudices in recruitment (at least in tight labour markets). Overall, however, private employment agencies are heavily implicated in the growth of more flexible and contingent forms of work by providing a service to employers who seek to reduce standard labour costs (Atkinson, 1984; Abraham, 1988). As well as helping to cover staff leave, agency workers can be used as replacements for full-time, permanent staff in the face of fluctuating or uncertain demand. There is some evidence that employers also now recruit permanent employees from agency staff (Forde, 2001), and that agency workers may be used instead of probationary contracts so that employers can 'try out' potential permanent recruits with little risk (Houseman et al, 2003).

Many research participants registered with private employment agencies in seeking work. These agencies were used increasingly, particularly by men, as they reached their twenties and thirties. There are many such agencies in a constellation of streets in Middlesbrough's town centre (see Chapter 4), and Richard, 30, said, "I think I'm registered with every agency in the town." Furlong and Cartmel (2004) implicate private employment agencies directly in the churning labour market careers of disadvantaged young men in their study in Scotland. In our study, too, they were the subject of plentiful criticism:

> "I had to fill in, like, a 40-page book. Then they say 'We'll let you know'. Well, I waited a week and these jobs they'd had advertised said 'Wanted immediately'. Another week goes by, another week, another week. I keep phoning them. With them, Wright Stuff, it was really bad because they lost my details. Got a phone call off 'em: 'Could I go and fill it in again?' I said 'I give in, mate, if you've lost my details on a job that was immediately'. So I went back with Blue Star who I'd been with in London. It's just a con for you to get on their books so they can rip people like you off. They pay you minimum wage and get two, three times as much for you ... [text removed by authors]... no wonder they're offering to put a minibus on to get you to work." (Don, 40)

In this extract Don alludes to the profits made by employment agencies: "They pay you minimum wage and get two, three times as much for you." Purcell et al (2004) have examined the role of private employment agencies and the relationships they need to establish with employers, and with potential workers, if they are to be commercially successful. Putting it simply, in order to make profits, agencies pay their registered workers less than employers pay the agency for the workers' labour. Beynon et al (2002, p 224) describe how employment agencies need to offer substantial 'offsetting economies' in order to win contracts with employers (to provide them with workers). In many cases they do this by lowering hourly rates of pay (often the National Minimum Wage, as Don notes), reducing or eliminating associated benefits of employment and minimising hiring and training costs. As a consequence, many of the attractions of standard employment (reasonable pay, employment-related benefits, relative job security) typically do not apply to agency workers, especially those least in demand because of their low skills or limited work experience (Purcell et al, 2004). Although Richard, 30, had used agencies extensively, he was now disillusioned with them:

> "They would phone me up and say there is a job in a factory and I would be there for a while and they just kept on bouncing me from job to job for about eight month.... They say they will find me continuous work and then me signing off the dole and they give me a couple of days here and a couple of days there but [because I have signed off benefits] I'm having to pay rent and council tax and electric and gas. When me wages are short they don't want to know. They just want the money, don't they? So I've just come to a decision to just not work for an agency anymore – through the debt I've got into with it with me rent and stuff like that."

A key problem for Richard had been the uncertainty of work from employment agencies. As was common across interviewees, promises of longer-term contracts were often not fulfilled. When Richard started taking contracts via agencies he 'signed off', meaning that he also lost various benefit entitlements that helped him get by, particularly Housing Benefit. He had hoped that the pay from jobs via employment agencies would allow him to cover all of his outgoings. The work he got was, however, intermittent, uncertain and often short term (he was only paid for the days he worked), and therefore it did not make practical sense to sign back on for days or weeks when he was not working. On one occasion he signed off on the promise of several months work via an employment agency only for this work to last a matter of a few weeks. Because of the time it took to re-establish benefit claims (including for Housing Benefit) he was forced to take out a loan from a 'doorstep lender' at a high interest rate (to cover basic living costs and his rent). He ended up seriously in debt (see Chapter 9 for a discussion of the wider experiences of debt). When interviewed he was unemployed and living on an extremely tight budget, with a proportion of these debts taken at source from his weekly JSA. His period of working via employment agencies was directly responsible for the parlous financial situation he was now in.

'For me it's always been not what you know, but who you know': the power of informal social networks in finding work

Regardless of the uneasy or unhelpful encounters they had with Jobcentre Plus, the difficulties they sometimes had in accessing more useful help from voluntary sector organisations and the inherent problems of private employment agencies in establishing them in work, the interviewees repeatedly found employment via informal social networks, confirming findings from our previous studies (for example, MacDonald et al, 2005) and other research (Watt, 2003). We quote first from an interview with Angus, age 47:

> Interviewer: "You say 'lucky break', would that be jobs through someone you knew?"
>
> Angus: "Oh yeah, always someone you knew ... it is always was word of mouth. One of my friends he used to work on the vans there and my work was factory work but he put a word in for us and I was there ever since."
>
> Interviewer: "So you didn't have to have an interview or anything?"
>
> Angus: "It was only until recently, believe it or not, that I had my first interview after all these years!"

As Lindsay (2010, p 25) points out, 'a particular area of policy interest has been access to social networks among disadvantaged job seekers in inner-city areas characterised by high levels of unemployment and deprivation'. The social capital embedded in such social networks can aid access to employment (Strathdee, 2001; MacDonald et al, 2005). As can be seen from the extract from Angus' interview, the informality of participants' job search methods ranged from the methods by which they heard of job openings (typically via extended social networks of family, friends and acquaintances) through to the means by which they were offered posts (for example, on the recommendation of one of these contacts, often in the absence of any formal written application, CV or job interview).

Let us consider first the issue of job information and recommendations. Newton et al (2005) argue that the unemployed can be disadvantaged by employers' recruitment methods, which are often based on word-of-mouth and informal methods of advertising, that is, the unemployed may become detached from networks of people in jobs and therefore be excluded from tip-offs and recommendations. Hasluck (1999) also argues that there is a potential mismatch between the informal, word-of-mouth methods that smaller employers in particular use to recruit for jobs and the job search practices of residents of deprived neighbourhoods, where networks and contacts for jobs are poor. Dickens (1999) describes this as 'network failure', arguing it to be an important part of the process whereby people in deprived neighbourhoods remain detached from employment. This problem of 'network failure' was not apparent in our study, with most interviewees seeming to remain connected to social networks that included people who were in jobs, arguably because of their continued, repeated engagement with the labour market. Informal network contacts accounted for most of the jobs they entered and, as Mary (30) suggests, reciprocal favours were expected in this exploitation of social capital:

> "Every job I have had I've got through somebody I know, like family or a friend and his [her husband's] Mam. I got her a job in my old nursing home and then obviously she might be doing the same for me.... I have been looking on the internet on the job centre website to see if there's anything too but a lot of them, they're [private employment] agencies and you phone up and they're trying to ship you all over the place."

Mark, 36, described how he had applied for a job as a joiner he had seen advertised in the job centre (a formal job search approach). He thinks he was successful in his application, however, because of informal connections: "maybe because I knew the foreman on there. My dad used to work with him at Wimpey's [construction firm]." Watt's (2003) study of social housing tenants in Camden, London, also confirmed that recommendations via social networks were crucial in the circulation of 'reputations', by word of mouth, about potential employees. Having the right reputation and social contacts were very important in the process whereby Watt's respondents got jobs (even as important as the possession of formal qualifications). The following extracts confirm the value of having well-placed family connections in gaining work through informal methods – and hint at the potential for exclusion from informal job distribution processes for those who lack locally embedded networks of family and friends:

"The main thing people will tell you is 'It's who you know, not what you know'. I don't care if you've got all the skills in the world, you'll get a good job off someone you know. Everyone around here is in the same boat at the moment but it is all to do with who you know, not what you know. I know people who've got good jobs, £1,000 a week. It's because one of their dad's mates is the boss." (Don, 40)

"For me it's always been not what you know, it's who you know. Like I say, I've been lucky with my dad, him being a site agent, and he's got me on his jobs as well as other lads." (Mark, 36)

Lindsay (2010) concludes that for longer-term unemployed people, the job search networks they might have built up through employment will diminish over time. While this sounds plausible, the interviewees' *recurrent* engagement with jobs – and relatively short-term periods of unemployment – seems to have kept job search networks alive over periods in and out of the labour market. Crucially, their financially and economically impoverished neighbourhoods were rich in locally embedded forms of bonding social capital, typical of many other residentially stable, (largely) mono-cultural white working-class locales (Kearns and Parkinson, 2001; MacDonald et al, 2005; Chapter 8, this volume). People knew each other and had friends and family here. The experience of unemployment – and of insecure jobs – was common. Tips and help about job possibilities were shared within these networks, even when someone faced longer periods out of work. Of more significance to the interviewees – rather than becoming detached from informal job networks – was the recent and general decline in job opportunities in the latter part of the 2000s. Several – including Andrew, 43, and Alan, 38, below – commented that one impact of the economic recession was to make these networks less effective, simply because there were fewer jobs to report informally:

"There's just not the jobs there. Any jobs I've had I've got meself or word of mouth. I've never had a job out the job centre. Say I'm not working, like, I'll phone my mates and say 'Where you working?' and they'll say 'Yeah get down here' then I'll phone up and you just get took on, no interview – nah, it's a long time since I've had an interview! But like at the moment, every one I've spoke to not one of 'em is working, you know what I mean?"

"People who used to tell you through word of mouth, I think they're more concerned about their own job safety now, if you know what I mean? So they're not exactly going to brag about vacancies at their place in case ... well, that's what I think, in case it pushes them out."

The informal job search activities of the participants is evidence of a level of vibrancy of at least a facet of a working-class community sometimes regarded as on the wane by social commentators and theorists. Reliance 'on *who* you know, not what you know' and word-of-mouth recommendation is a long-standing feature of working-class job search practices (Jackson, 1968; Marsden and Duff, 1975; Morris, 1995) that, according to our study, persists in contemporary contexts where formalised methods via the statutory, voluntary and private sectors are encouraged and abundant.

The quotes from Andrew and Alan (above) remind us, however, that no matter how effective – compared, for instance, with the activities of Jobcentre Plus – or long-standing such informal methods might be, they are reliant on the availability of employment. While we can regard this job search activity positively, especially given the weakness of more formal assistance from support and employment agencies, it also served to tie individuals into low-level work. Their networks did not range to better-paid, better quality employment. Kearns and Parkinson sum it up neatly: 'the neighbourhood for poorer people has more often served as an arena for "bonding" social capital that enables people to "get by", rather than as a platform for "bridging" social capital that enables people to "get on"' (2001, p 2105). In the postwar boom decades of Teesside's economic history such informal methods rooted in working-class social capital *did* allow access to more stable, regular, better-paid working-class employment (Beynon et al, 1994). Now, for the interviewees, the opportunities they led to were not only normally of low quality but also drying up. In a tighter labour market, stripped of better-quality working-class employment, 'who you know' not 'what you know' now confined interviewees to the sort of low-level, low-paid work these days done, in the main, by the sort of people they knew. In other words, because of the massive deindustrialisation of Teesside coupled with a relative abundance of lower quality jobs, old, durable, class-based, job search practices that once provided accepted, informal pathways into decent working-class employment now provide routes to 'poor work'.

While these informal methods of job search are characteristic of industrial working-class communities, informal strategies for recruitment can *now* be understood as characteristic of lower segments of the labour market *and* as reflective of employers' flexible, casualised practices (see Chapter 2). Some research has pointed to how employers and the unemployed can use different 'search channels' and how this can be an obstacle to the latter getting jobs (Campbell and Meadows, 2001). This did not seem to be the case in our study. Rather, the casualised systems that employers in the lower rungs of the labour market use to recruit workers fitted nicely with the informal ways in which these now economically marginal working-class people looked for jobs. When Simon, 30, says that he has "never actually got a job where I've had to apply for a job, wait and go for an interview ... it's more or less people who've wanted someone. I've been in the right place at the right time, I suppose", what he is describing is not good luck but a facet of the casualisation of employment. As described in Chapter 4, what these employers required primarily was a willing worker physically capable of doing the job who possessed 'the right attitude'. Polished CVs and interview performances were usually not required. The interviewees accessed employment that did not appear to discriminate against them on the basis of educational qualifications, skill levels or work history (even if we heard discriminatory attitudes linked to age and gender in our interviews with employers; see Chapter 4). The relative openness of this segment of the labour market is amply demonstrated by the fact that a number of interviewees who possessed records of earlier criminal offending and/or problematic drug use were now displaying low-pay, no-pay careers similar to the rest of the sample (see Chapter 8). Casualised, poor work was on offer in spite of criminal records, previous drug dependency or chequered work histories.

Conclusions

Interviewees' strong work motivations, as described in Chapter 5, were not matched by strong educational or qualification profiles. The value and role of qualifications and skills was complicated. Earlier disappointing experiences of or negative attitudes towards formal education (from school days) did not lead to a lasting rejection of education and training. The effects of undertaking post-16 training courses on labour market prospects were mixed, however, as was their apparent quality. Some programmes (for example, those providing vocational training that qualified individuals directly for specific jobs) clearly benefited participants, whereas others had not. Even some better-qualified people (with university degrees) struggled in the low-pay, no-pay cycle.

Despite recurrent churning between jobs and unemployment, and the potentially demotivating effect of repeated failures to secure jobs and the common lack of response to their applications, people continued to search for jobs. They did this in a variety of ways. Unsurprisingly a locality with high, long-term worklessness has relatively plentiful provision to help people from 'welfare to work' (Chapter 4). Difficult relationships and what was regarded as unhelpful advice tended to mar interviewees' perspectives concerning Jobcentre Plus (see also Chapter 9). When they could access them, the more tailored and fuller services of voluntary sector agencies were more positively reported, but these tended to be targeted towards the longer-term unemployed. Private employment agencies were widely used, especially by men, and were a significant driver of the low-pay, no-pay cycle and employment insecurity and casualisation. Most widely used were informal, word-of-mouth job search practices. Most jobs held by participants had been got in this way, reflecting findings of our previous Teesside studies and long-standing, cultural practices associated with working-class communities. This finding is a double-edged one; informal methods clearly worked 'better' than, for instance, the statutory service of Jobcentre Plus in terms of placement into jobs, but the bonding social capital that underpinned networks of family, friends and acquaintances now limited individuals to the sort of poor-quality work that was done by the people they knew and, in the depressed labour market conditions of the time of the study, was beginning to fail to do even this. Rather than explaining informants' experience of labour market churning as some sort of mismatch between what employers require (for example, in terms of skills or qualifications) and how they might prefer to recruit workers, we argue that there is, in fact, a strong fit between the informal methods of job search practised by the interviewees (and their durable motivations toward work) and the forms of casualised, insecure employment available in the lower reaches of the labour market. Casualised, insecure employment *requires* the sort of resilient work motivation and informal, persistent job search practices displayed by the informants (this is a theme developed further in Chapter 10).

In reviewing the sorts of job search practices used by the informants in this chapter, and their general, strong motivations to work in the previous one, we can begin to see that many of the interviewees might be described as 'the missing workless'. This is a discussion we return to in Chapter 9, where we explore people's experiences of welfare benefits and unemployment. Some people chose not to register for welfare benefits (because of the stigma and/or hassle of doing so, especially if they perceived their likely spell of unemployment to be relatively short). This is one sense in which they might be regarded as 'the missing workless': they are not counted in figures of the unemployed and do not claim welfare benefits while unemployed. We have also seen in this chapter that many seemed to be missing from systems of support geared to move people into employment. This is despite the strong emphasis of government policy on getting those that can work into employment and the profusion of support agencies available locally. We argue later in Chapter 10 that those engaged in the low-pay, no-pay cycle, and who tend to face shorter episodes of unemployment, appear to occupy a particular blind spot in policy and practice provision for the workless. That this failure of practical support be communicated to policy makers was one reason why several interviewees agreed to participate in the study.

7

Poor work: insecurity and churning in deindustrialised labour markets

Introduction

In this and the following chapter we seek to understand the interviewees' work histories in more depth. In Chapter 8 we examine the 'supply side' of the labour market – how personal issues and family circumstances, often rooted in wider social disadvantages, had an impact on people's engagement with work. In this chapter we are concerned with the 'demand side' of the 'employability' equation (Lindsay and McQuaid, 2005), or more precisely, how research participants experienced the sorts of employment that they did and what we can learn about the low-pay, no-pay cycle from their descriptions. We begin by noting the deindustrialisation of Teesside's labour market and how this has created a context where the jobs available to the research participants were now defined by their low pay, low skill and insecurity. The following section, introduced by three cases, examines in depth the experience of doing poor work. Reasons for leaving and losing jobs are then discussed. Despite the predominant experience being one of poor work, interviewees still found work to hold positive social and psychological benefits, the focus of the penultimate section. Finally, we briefly note the exceptional cases of individuals who had managed to locate better quality employment and escape the low-pay, no-pay cycle.

Teesside's deindustrialised labour market

> "Everything's just gone. The clothing industry went, the steel industry went, the shops are going ... my friend's daughter, she's been to college, but she can't even get a job in a shop. They're not taking people on. She put her name down for Argos, all places that do well at Christmas, but just

nothing. There's that many people got their name down for these jobs, there's nothing for this area." (Janice, 56)

"I think it's absolutely terrible. When I was 18 my dad got me a job at Corus [local steelworks] and that's all changed now. Your parents can't just get you in. It's all changed now." (Chris, 32)

"It's even worse at the minute. Everybody's looking for the same thing. Even my dad who's been in a job since he left school [as a bricklayer] it's the first time he had to sign on." (Richard, 30)

Younger and older interviewees were aware of the dramatic changes that have affected Teesside's economy (see Chapter 3). Some, like Richard above, reflected on their family's working history and how older relatives were now struggling to find steady work – and how tried and tested methods of accessing jobs via personal recommendations were faltering (see Chapter 6). As Beynon et al (1994) describe, one outcome of the economic crisis to hit Teesside in the latter third of the 20th century was not only an overall decline in skilled manual employment but also the casualisation and degradation of some of that which remained. Employers sought greater 'functional flexibility' through sub-contracting that typically resulted in the provision of employment under worsened terms and conditions (for example, temporary contracts and lower rates of pay) (see Chapter 3). Some of the interviewees had experienced this decline in opportunities for reasonably paid, skilled or semi-skilled manual work first hand. Don (40) told us "When you used to go on a shut down [a standard phase of production at the steel works] years ago it used to be good money. Now the shut downs are just above minimum wage." Mark (36) recalled how 15 years ago he used to earn "£15, £20 an hour for joiners like me and you go on jobs now – £6.35 an hour." Lash and Urry (1994) describe how places that once thrived on a robust manufacturing base now mainly offer 'junk jobs'. While there are still remnants of better quality working-class, manual employment in Teesside, the impact of long-term economic change in the structure of the local economy combined with the national recession (at the time of fieldwork) to create very difficult conditions for the unemployed.

Working in a deindustrialised local economy: low pay, low skill and insecurity

Even though the older participants now accessed low-skilled, short-term, National Minimum Wage jobs in the lower levels of Teesside's economy, several had earlier in their working lives been employed in better-paid, more secure jobs. To repeat, while 100,000 jobs were stripped from Teesside's manufacturing base between 1971 and 2008, 92,000 jobs were created during the same period in the service sector (see Chapter 3). Typically, these were part-time and lower-skilled positions. Reflecting these changes – and typical of national economic trends – service sector employment was widespread among the sample, but it was not the only sort. Interviewees got jobs in care homes for the elderly, in nurseries as carers for infants or in schools as classroom assistants. Several had worked as cleaners. Many had worked on production lines in food processing and textile factories. Some were able to get jobs at the steel works, but only temporarily and in unskilled roles. They served in bars and fast food restaurants and call centres. They worked as shop assistants and delivery drivers. Some had been security guards; others had driven forklift trucks or heavy goods vehicles. Some did construction work, in particular labouring and scaffolding. Importantly for our critique of the 'entry-level jobs as stepping-stones' thesis (see Chapter 5), there was little age differentiation in the types of work done.

There was, however, some predictable variation by gender. For example, it was only men who did construction work and it was usually women who did caring jobs. We would not, however, be in complete agreement with some analysis of changing employment opportunities that posit the gendered exclusion (or self-exclusion) of men from more abundant service sector work. For instance, Crisp and Nixon (2010) argue that forms of working-class masculine habitus and culture (that emphasise 'real' work as work involving manual skill and mastery) are not suited to the types of service sector, customer-focused employment now said to dominate local labour markets (McDowell, 2003). From their studies, they describe how older working-class men in particular can be excluded from new forms of interactive service work that demand emotional labour. Lower-skilled, young and older working-class men alike struggle to adapt to the new employment conditions of contemporary society and the requirements of 'the service encounter' (see also McDowell, 2001). On the basis of our research, this is a perspective we would wish to moderate rather than deny. First, while service sector work has proliferated, it is not the only sort. In one of our previous studies of young adults in Teesside in the late 1990s and early 2000s (MacDonald and Marsh, 2005), the modal average type of employment ever undertaken by informants, and equally balanced by gender, was factory work (working in textile, electronic assembly or food processing firms). It was also a significant form of work in this study. Second, the inability of working-class young men to adapt to the demands of service sector employment can be overstated (see McDowell, 2001). Roberts' (2011) study of working-class men's employment in the retail industry provides a nice corrective to wilder claims about the 'crisis of masculinity' vis-à-vis job opportunities. In our study several forms of service sector work were not gender-segregated. Working in fast food restaurants, bars, shops, call centres and as cleaners were examples of forms of employment that recruited both men and women.

Three things united the jobs that these working-class men and women did: they were typically *low skilled*, *low paid* and *insecure*, with only a few caveats and exceptions. In sum, then, this was 'poor work' (see Chapter 2).

By low skilled we mean the jobs that they did did not require much in the way of previous experience, training or qualifications. Employees were expected to be able to perform them without training or experience. These were mainly routine jobs that offered little scope for autonomy, decision making, creativity or the expression of skill. As confirmed in interviews with employers and welfare to work agency staff (see Chapter 4), physical ability to do the job and possession of the 'right attitude' (that is, be willing, reliable, hardworking and 'flexible') were the key qualifying criteria. Describing these jobs as low skilled should not be read as any derogation of their value. They are the sorts of jobs that are essential to the functioning of economy and society and some of them (those in the caring field stand out) demanded uncommonly high levels of personal commitment and social skills.

By low paid we mean that most were National Minimum Wage jobs. Interestingly, interviewees (employers, welfare to work agency staff and workers) would often describe this pay as 'fair' or 'good'. This is a small but intriguing finding, given that it is the lowest pay legally possible. This, we think, can be explained by three related factors. Some employers in the most casualised, deregulated sectors still pay below the National Minimum Wage (Citizens' Advice Scotland, 2011). We had an indication of this in interviews, including with one employer. Thus, in comparison, the National Minimum Wage is 'good pay'. Second, the introduction of the National Minimum Wage has lifted pay levels at the bottom of the labour market, so compared with wages received prior to the National Minimum Wage, these were regarded as 'good'. Finally, most interviewees had little experience of better-paid jobs; they were deprived of vantage points that would look down on these as low-paid jobs.

Defining insecurity is more complicated. There is considerable debate about how best to define 'insecure work' and the nature of trends in respect of it (see Chapter 2; Auer and Cazes, 2003; Fevre, 2007; Vosko, 2006; MacDonald, 2009). In respect of the participants, the most straightforward case was that some jobs were offered on temporary contracts. This was most evident in those accessed via private employment agencies, where jobs of sometimes just a few days were assigned (see Chapter 6). Some interviewees had accessed grant-funded posts in the social welfare fields (for example, in youth or community work roles) that were time-limited and their extension dependent on the winning of further funding. Some had accessed jobs that were formally permanent but had been made redundant by their struggling employers. Others' contractual situations were less clear, more informal and unwritten. Regardless of the legal status of employment contracts, very often informants were unable to say precisely whether the job was 'permanent' or 'temporary', only that it had ceased, and sometimes they were unclear as to exactly why it had (discussed later).

Doing 'poor work'

In order to give a flavour of some of the 'poor work' done by interviewees, we begin this section with a brief description of the experiences of Debbie (43, as a sales assistant), Don (40, making tents) and Pamela (54, a care worker).

A few years previously – and deep in debt at the time – Debbie, 43, had been "desperate" to find a job. She had "applied for any job going" but had had repeated rejections (or, more precisely, non-replies). Eventually she managed to land a three-month sales assistant position in a department store, for the Christmas period:

> "I hated it, hated every single day of it ... because my legs used to hurt I was on my feet all day. The staff room was on the fourth floor and staff aren't allowed to get in the lifts because obviously you could be nicking 'owt so I used to cry going to work. I used to cry coming home from work *I hated it so much* [her emphasis] ... it was minimum wage, £5.60. I'll never forget it the way people [customers] used to talk to you: 'I don't deserve this for £5.60 for you to

talk to me like this, it's not my fault it's company policy'. I hated it but I stuck it out and did it from the day I started to the day I finished and I still carried on applying for every job going."

Don, 40, had had a classic churning employment career. Over the years he had increasingly used private employment agencies, on one occasion getting temporary employment putting together tents for the Army:

"They [the agency] said: 'Do you fancy making tents?' Well for someone like me – six foot eight – on me knees all day, it was no good, building tents. There was seven weeks work. I done the seven weeks but I was in agony, wasn't I? I used to walk about like Quasimodo cos you'd been on your knees all day. I used to come in like all hunched up and all. That was alright but you've still got the wrong people in charge, snotty people who's there on a bonus and they're pushing you, pushing you harder and harder 'cos they're on the bonus. *You're* not on a bonus, making big tents for the Army. You're like 'why do I bother doing this?' I think it was £4.50 an hour ... then we got laid off, summat happened and it was out of their control, summat to do with the Army, and six weeks later we went back for another five weeks and it was like that, on and off."

After some time out of work, Pamela had got a job as a carer (employed by a private social care agency). One of her friends from her estate who also worked for the company told her of the vacancy. She was hired despite lacking relevant qualifications and much experience: "I phone 'em up, got an interview, no qualifications. I had none – apart from I'd looked after my gran." She went on:

"I got this job. No training. I was thrust out there into the big world doing jobs, you know? Giving morphine to somebody, washing naked men – which I loved by the way! I'm really good at that, putting men at ease. Things like hoists, changing catheters. *No training!* They're really the worst firm I have ever worked for – but the job in itself was so rewarding."

She described some of the problems of the job such as: "low pay ... it was £5.30 an hour"; being contracted and paid to work for 16 hours but sometimes working 40-hour weeks; having to walk lengthy distances in bad weather between appointments (and not being paid for this travel time); and being booked to provide half-hour care sessions in people's homes but being encouraged to "literally run in and run out so I could get to the next appointment on time: just cutting corners all the time and they did that to every single carer." Pamela also criticised the "training" she had eventually been given: "after two years they said 'everybody has to do their NVQ 1 and 2' because the government has said you can't work in care unless you have this qualification." The training was done 'in house' with care workers completing worksheets in between calls (when they were not paid). Pamela said that she was told she had passed her NVQ 1 and 2 after two weeks' study ("it should have taken a year at least. I thought 'we've done bugger all'"). Pamela said: "I've got my folder here. It says I've got health and safety, food handling, hoist lifting and I never did one of them!" She had previously passed a course in infection control:

> "… when we looked through all our folders everybody had the infection control certificate with my serial number on it! They'd just photocopied them all! All those carers are out there with qualifications that they've never even done! Don't ever get old!"

Pamela left this employment after suffering an accident at work when she was trying to lift a wheelchair user onto a bus ("never pushed a wheelchair in me life, had no training"). She suffered major damage to her back ("I was crippled with agony"). After some private osteopathic treatment ("£30 a time – how could I afford that?") she returned to work but she still "wasn't right, I was in agony." Pamela then took sick leave for two weeks:

> "… when you go back they [the employers] make it bad for you. They were sending me on calls miles away and I said 'I can't do it'. I had difficulty walking and I carried on for a few weeks but I just couldn't. They were getting increasingly nasty to me so I just wrote a letter to them one day. I handed my notice in."

She claimed for damages against the care company (who denied she had been working on the day of the accident) but the case collapsed after a year when Pamela was unable to ensure that she could pay legal costs. She now regarded herself as unable to work because of the injury to her back (she was receiving extensive medication for it) and acted as the full-time carer for her disabled daughter.

The general story

Although only three cases, Debbie, Don and Pamela give a flavour of the general experience of poor work done by the interviewees. Despite repeated attempts to get jobs and unwanted spells of unemployment, when they did access jobs they often did so on the basis of less than stringent recruitment practices. Previous experience, training or relevant qualifications were often not necessary (see Chapters 4 and 5). Jobs were typically hard graft, mentally and physically demanding (Debbie, Don and Pamela all talked of the *physical pain* their jobs caused them). It was often dull and repetitive work that lacked space for individual autonomy or skill. Interviewees talked of feeling like "robots" and "machines". Where there was potential for more creative or interesting work – as with Pamela's caring role – the intense pressure of work sometimes overrode this. Investment in workers, via employee training, rarely featured and, if it did, it was often perfunctory, of poor quality and of little wider labour market value (and, in Pamela's case, workers were – allegedly – fraudulently awarded qualifications).

Pollert and Charlwood (2009) describe how many 'vulnerable workers' face problems at work yet lack union representation, and how 'low paid and unrepresented workers face a significant risk of being denied their employment rights' (2009, p 354). In our study, workers described being required to undertake tasks that seemed unreasonable, outside of their normal role or job description or for which they were untrained. An unsympathetic attitude from employers to periods of ill health was commonly reported. Sick pay was often not forthcoming and several reported being sacked for taking (certificated) sick leave (in one case, a day's leave) (see Chapter 8). Some talked of missing out on other statutory rights (such as maternity allowances) because of employers' bureaucratic errors. Jobs often entailed unsocial (evenings, nights, early mornings and weekends) and sometimes 'flexible' and unpredictable hours. So-called 'zero hours' or 'on call' contracts meant that some employees did not know from one week to the next how many hours they would work and be paid for (with serious repercussions for very tight household budgets and benefit claims). Additionally, many times interviewees reported not being paid properly for the hours they did work (see Don, below). Several people talked of being required to do extra hours at very short notice (with the threat of the sack if they did not). According to the interviewees, 'compassionate leave' or requests to leave work early (for example, to look after a sick child) were often denied by employers.

While poor work was widespread across many forms of employment and the industrial sector, we heard most complaints about what is locally known as 'the turkey factory' (see MacDonald and Marsh, 2005). Food processing factories like this were reported as offering easy to get but hard and demeaning work. A report by the Equality and Human Rights Commission (2010, p 2) provides a graphic insight into the 'widespread poor treatment of agency workers' in the meat processing industry, including verbal and physical abuse and lack of attention to health and safety practices. Don (40) described how he had got work at 'the turkey factory' via an employment agency, and the casual approach the firm took to payment of wages:

> "It was me that caused the strike! I don't like to admit to this but ... I go to the turkey factory. I get a good job. I'm over the moon! 'Do you wanna do some overtime Don? You're reliable. You're here every day. You're working on your day off. Do you want any overtime?' So I got overtime. The coach was picking us up like an hour-and-a-half before you start.... I'm getting there I'm earning some money for Christmas. I'm over the moon ... the first week's wage come in. I'm supposed to be picking up £280 and I get me wage and I'm £110 short! They said 'It'll be there for you next week, Don'. But the next week I'm £60 short so that's £170 and £60 short! I was sat in the canteen with some of my mates from the estate and they had the same thing [underpayment of wages] and we say 'We're not moving until they sort out it'. By this time word had got around and three of us are not moving, within half an hour 70 of us were not moving! *The Chronicle* [the local newspaper] comes down and 'cos it's an embarrassment for them, they sorted everyone out. I said 'I'm willing to stop [the strike] as long as I get paid'."

While Don described being "over the moon" at his "good job" at the turkey factory, others were less positive. Richard (30) and Alfie (46) talked about their time there:

> "It was just minimum wage I think it was about £5.12 an hour ... pretty rubbish really for the hours you put in – but it was just a job at the end of the day ... you're like a

machine [laughs quietly]. It's just the same thing, day in day
out. It used to do your head in after a bit."

"The management, they just don't care about the staff. They
treat you like robots…. If you went over and said 'I've cut
my finger off', they'd just say 'Make sure you don't get any
blood on the food'. That's what they were like."

Eventually Alfie's resentment at what he saw as unacceptable working
conditions boiled over and he confronted his boss about pay and
working conditions, only to be told, "If you don't like it, don't do it".
By this time, Alfie had simply had enough: "I threw me card at him
and walked out."

Losing and leaving jobs: 'it all tends to dry up'

Resigning was a relatively rare explanation for how employment
ended in these low-pay, no-pay work histories. Based on research with
low-income mothers in the US, Brooke-Kelly (2005, p 83) argues
that 'quitting may be one of the only forms of resistance available to
workers' in low-paid, flexible jobs. Challenging a dominant discourse
that sees workers who quit as lazy or feckless, she suggests that where
employment is low paid and constraining, quitting becomes an
expression of resistance on the part of the worker. Active resistance of
this sort was uncommon in our study, with Don's 'strike action' and
Alfie's resignation at the turkey factory being rare examples. Typically,
interviewees described the negative aspects of poor work in 'taken
for granted' tones rather than in ones that stressed the unfairness and
injustices of poor work. This was something we also found in our earlier
studies with young adults in Teesside (MacDonald and Marsh, 2005).
Caution is required in considering the reasons people left jobs because
– again, echoing earlier findings (MacDonald and Marsh, 2005) – the
exact, formal reason for the cessation of a period of employment was
sometimes fuzzy to interviewees. Nevertheless, it was clear that the
pressures of work, coupled with their limited wages and nil prospects,
would occasionally cause interviewees to quit. Care also needs to be
taken here in interpreting the choice to resign. Often these seemed
like 'forced choices'. Interviewees felt pressure to quit, often related
to physical and mental health problems (discussed in more detail in
Chapter 8). Earlier we saw how Pamela had resigned from her care
assistant post following a work-related injury and what she felt was
the unfair treatment she received after taking sick leave. In such cases,

resignation seemed more like self-preservation than either active worker resistance or lack of employment commitment.

Other reasons given for why informants decided to leave jobs included the rising costs of or increasing difficulties of travelling to work (for example, a friend no longer able to give a lift to a workplace some distance away). Perhaps the major factors that caused people to resign from jobs related to personal health problems (sometimes caused by the job) and responsibilities and pressures in their wider lives, particularly caring for others (these are factors that we discuss in more detail in Chapter 8).

Some reported being dismissed from jobs, but this was relatively rare. When it did happen, interviewees reported that their employers had, for instance, felt that their work performance had not been satisfactory (for example, not meeting sales targets) or had sacked them for taking (certificated) sick leave or because the employer wished a relative to have the post instead. Thus, several losses of jobs seemed to result from unfair and perhaps illegal dismissals.

Much more frequent than quitting or being dismissed was the wholly *involuntary* cessation of the posts that people worked in. Those who worked for private employment agencies were, obviously, employed on temporary contracts (even though they sometimes found that contracts lasted less than they had been told; see Chapter 6). Others, too, knew that their posts were only temporary (for example, some people had worked as teaching assistants or youth workers in posts that relied on winning recurrent grants to keep staff in post). More generally, however, interviewees talked loosely of being "made redundant", work "coming to an end", the job "just not being there any more", being "laid off", the employer "not having enough work", important "contracts not coming off" and so on. Richard (30) had had nine relatively short-term jobs since he was 16, never having quit or been dismissed from a post. As he put it:

> "I've never finished a job through me own misconduct just laid off due to lack of work and stuff like that … it's just it all tends to dry up. It makes you wonder if you'll ever find a job that you can actually stick to, you know? It's just a carry on all the time."

Talking of one of the longer-lasting jobs – as a forklift truck driver – he said:

"I just ended up getting laid off after seven months. It was just due to the way everything went, like. He was putting in for grants to expand his business and he was getting knocked back so he had to make cutbacks himself. It was a case of last in, first out. I loved it as well. It was a good job. I was always working weekends, like, it was a choice to. I used to like going to work. I used to enjoy getting up on a morning to go to work. It was a proper company as well so I felt safe and secure in it. I knew everybody in there and they were good lads so it was just gutting when I got laid off."

The attractions of work: 'I absolutely loved it'

We have described above the negative experiences of poor work and how people lost and left jobs. If we look back to where we began our description of poor work, we read about Pamela's dismal experience of working for a social care agency. Her comment that "they're really the worst firm I have ever worked for" was followed in the next breath with "but the job in itself was so rewarding". Richard, above, similarly talks of how he "loved" the jobs he had had, even though they were insecure and low paid. We found that the same interviewees who could describe the unpleasantness and hardships of particular jobs could talk very positively about the attractions of work in general (and sometimes in respect of the actual work they did in jobs or for employers they regarded negatively). In Chapter 5 we described people's motivations to work, and here we provide just a brief description of the attractions of poor work by returning to the case of Debbie, whose dismal experience of shop assistant work was presented earlier in the chapter.

Through her twenties and thirties Debbie, now 43, had spent most of her time having and raising her children. She had had few jobs until relatively recently (including a stint over Christmas as a sales assistant in a department store). She had also been involved in two violent and abusive relationships that had affected her mental health and her confidence about getting jobs (indeed, one ex-partner had been convicted of grievous bodily harm against Debbie, the original charge being attempted murder). She also suffered from chronic physical ill health that required extensive, daily medication. In her thirties, she completed a course in Health and Social Care and managed to get a job as a school-based carer for a child with disabilities:

"… and that was me working in a school! I used to get her from place to place. She was physically disabled. In break times I used to have to do all her physio and I used to get quarter of an hour for my lunch then take her for hers and then we'd have some fresh air and stuff and I absolutely loved it! The teacher had said to me I'd make a really good classroom assistant or go for teaching 'cos I was a natural with the kids and then after three months unfortunately she [the child] moved to France so the job finished, right back at square one. There was nothing out there."

After a further period of unemployment, interspersed with a short spell as a 'dinner lady' (from which she resigned because her violent partner was coming to the school and threatening her in the playground), Debbie found a post working as a part-time youth worker in a local community organisation on her estate (for whom she had been doing some voluntary work). She earned £16,000 pa pro rata for a 22.5-hour week. When she was told she had the job:

"… absolute panic set in because I thought I was gonna fail. The first thing I thought was 'I can't do it, I dunno how to do it I dunno why they've given me it I can't do it'. Him upstairs [her husband] bless him said 'You can do it, you're good at it, you've been doing it so shut up' basically. You have to work with kids age 0–19 and engage them in activities and keep them from going into anti-social behaviour and I thought well over the three-year period I dunno what happened, just a completely changed person, I put all these ideas forward, I was able to go and talk to people I'd never met before, go into meetings … it was just that it made me feel like a better person inside."

She said of her current job:

"I love it, absolutely love it. I enjoy going to work. I enjoy having summat [something]. You have your days where you're drained and you're tired and you're cold but you have days when you come in and think 'I've just achieved something; that wouldn't have happened if I hadn't gone in and done it'. You know, to go in and help a family out, I love it. I can tell [young] people from my own experience – 'I was you years ago but I ended up going back to college and you've got the chance now, your only chance now'. Every day's different … just like the way that it's different, you meet different people.... To me, I class work as my therapy with my illness."

Debbie's effusive description of the attractions and appeal of her job stressed the social and psychological rather than financial aspects – the sense of achievement she got from helping others, the variety of experiences and social contacts it brought, the boost to her self-confidence and self-esteem after years out of work (and suffering in violent partnerships and long-standing ill health). Work, for women like Debbie, signified important, positive, biographical change. In Chapter 5 we noted how some classic social psychological theory originating from the 1930s helped explain people's opposition to being unemployed and their negative experience of unemployment. The same theory, despite being subject to criticism (see Chapter 5) for its potential lesser applicability in the contemporary period, or to women as well as men, or to the frequently unemployed, is argued to fit well with the descriptions given by the interviewees. Remarkably similar findings have come from Batty et al's (2011) investigation of the working and wider lives of residents living in a variety of UK neighbourhoods undergoing social and economic change and regeneration. They acknowledge that, as with our study, the employment people got could involve 'low pay, long or unsocial hours and pervasive insecurity', but they also conclude that such jobs:

> ... could bring a number of valued benefits. These include financial independence, social contact, a sense of purpose, a feeling of 'making a difference' and social status. This suggests that individuals can invest meaning and significance in employment, in spite of otherwise onerous terms and conditions. (Batty et al, 2011, p 23)

Batty and colleagues also note that this sort of work could sometimes have a negative effect on the well-being of their interviewees. We return to questions about health and precarious, poor work in Chapter 8 and, for the time being, only reiterate how the social and psychological benefits of employment helped explain how even poor work was attractive to people – and how this is a crucial motor that drives the low-pay, no-pay cycle.

Better-quality employment

As a counterpoint to the general experience of poor work described by informants, here we note the significance of better-quality employment to the three people in the sample who had managed to secure it, focusing on the case of one of these, Marge, 31. For those who appeared to have escaped the poverty and churning of the low-pay, no-pay cycle, work of this sort had been critical.

Marge had trained as a hairdresser when she left school, eventually getting a job in a local salon, part of her work involving training young people. She said, "That was the worst job. It wasn't actually the job it was more the management. The manager ... actually picked on people and that was awful. I ended up looking for another job because of her." Becoming unemployed she began to regret her decision to leave but, on a whim, applied for a job working with a local voluntary sector agency that helped disadvantaged young people: "Thank God I didn't stay there [at the salon], it's changed so much for me." Since her early twenties she had worked for this same youth support agency. Her youth worker job was temporary because it was based on recurrent grant applications. Comparing this with earlier jobs as a hairdresser, she said:

> "This has been my best job because, you know, it's satisfying other people's needs and you're there supporting people ... and the company as well that I work for is absolutely fantastic. They're supportive in all ways, with home, childcare; in your job as well they listen to you. You can self-manage, really."

Over her time with this organisation, Marge had had a child and her husband had experienced chronic ill health. She described her employer as very "sympathetic", providing support she needed in terms of time off to care for her child and husband. The employer had also provided time to allow Marge to complete a part-time undergraduate degree in Youth Work (and paid her course tuition fees for this).

In this and other cases it is worth noting that better-quality employment was found with voluntary sector, 'not for profit' organisations that operated with social as well as commercial goals (as we note in Chapter 10, these are, however, exactly the sorts of organisations that have come under increasing threats to their survival with current government cutbacks in public spending). Smaller commercial businesses were more likely to offer poorer-quality work and have unsympathetic, unaccommodating attitudes to workers. Even here, however, there was the occasional example that showed that this need not always be the case. Sharleen, 33, was a single mother with six children and worked part time in a local butcher's shop. She was full of praise for her employer:

> "They're fair. I mean, ours is only a small shop. There are only three of us and I basically go in on their days off. It's really good. They're dead flexible so if I need, say, if the kids need a doctor's appointment there's no questions asked. They'll just swap the day off so I can go in on a Monday or a Tuesday or whatever.... The other week I was really poorly. I had a chest infection and the doctor told me I had to stay off work for a week but I don't get sick pay because I'm only part time, so she was really good to me and she said come in on Saturday and then all day Friday to make my hours up."

Conclusions

At the heart of the discussion in this chapter – indeed at the core of this study – is a paradox. Contemporary political discourse about the unemployed and the poor in the UK is increasingly governed by a view that the poor are so because of their own failures and that the workless do not want jobs, but prefer a life on benefits. This discourse is not only popular with many politicians but increasingly so with the UK public. The British Social Attitudes Survey (NatCen, 2011) found, for instance, that 54 per cent of respondents thought that 'unemployment benefits were too high' (a figure that has climbed from 35 per cent in 1983) and that this 'discourages the unemployed from finding jobs.' It also found that 63 per cent believed that parents who 'don't want to work' are a reason why some children live in poverty. Yet our findings, as developed in this and previous chapters, stand in direct contradiction to these ideas.

In Chapter 5 we discussed what people 'brought to' the search for work – their skills, qualifications and motivations. There we described a strong commitment to employment, or more specifically, to the value of working over being workless. We explained this in terms of a range of 'functions' that work, in the shape of employment, provided and which benefited people (and how people through experience knew these to be lost or absent in unemployment). In this chapter we have described the experience of work in practice. For the interviewees, labouring in the shadows of Teesside's prodigious industrial past, the deindustrialised labour market is now comprised of low-quality poor work, typified by its low pay, low skills and insecurity. Certainly the jobs people did can be described as degraded, casualised and poor quality (and interviewees like Pamela, Debbie and Don were able to point to the hardships they faced in them, albeit in often muted tones).Yet – a second paradox – workers *retained* a strong commitment to employment even when this commitment was recurrently repaid only with poor work. These were not 'discouraged workers' (see Chapter 6). The commitment to work that people expressed as an attitude was replayed as a practice, over decades. The 'good' of work could (even) be found in jobs, or with employers, that were 'bad'. For a small handful in the study we have seen how better-quality employment can harness this commitment, allowing workers to escape the churning of the low-pay, no-pay cycle. Most, however, were trapped in jobs that led them nowhere – apart from a usual speedy return to unemployment. Exits from jobs were predominantly involuntary and reflective of the insecurity of the lower echelons of the UK labour market.

This was also a main finding of the Joseph Rowntree Foundation recurrent poverty programme, of which our study was one element (see Chapter 2). It identified a range of factors that influence an individual's and a household's chance of experiencing recurrent poverty (Goulden, 2010). It confirmed, however, that better-quality employment provided the best defence against poverty and that 'structural labour market factors remain the strongest influence' (Goulden, 2010, p 11) on the risk of recurrent poverty. It argued that policy effort should be geared toward improving the pay, conditions and security of employment as well as increasing its availability (we return to this discussion in Chapter 10). In conclusion, then, at this point in our book we identify two prime drivers of the low-pay, no-pay cycle: the relative availability of insecure poor work for individuals in places like those we studied and those same individuals' resilient commitment to work, whatever the job.

'The ties that bind': ill health and caring and their impact on the low-pay, no-pay cycle

Introduction

As stressed at the end of Chapter 7, the prime driver of the low-pay, no-pay cycle was the insecurity of employment on offer coupled with a strong motivation to work and to avoid being 'welfare dependent'. In other words, the 'demand side' of the local economy – the spread and type of jobs that were available – was unable to properly accommodate people's need and appetite for jobs. Yet this was not the complete story that was told to us in interviews. 'Supply-side factors' also served to shape the low-pay, no-pay cycle. By this we mean that, in some situations and at some times, the circumstances and conditions of people's lives meant that they were unable to fully engage with employment, despite their enduring motivation to do so. In this chapter we focus on those issues that were most prominent in interviews in this respect: ill health that affected individuals or their families and the caring responsibilities that people had for others. As we will see, these were often closely related.

We will also argue, however, that it is difficult to separate out 'demand-side' and 'supply-side' factors in any simple way. Biographically focused interviews that explored individuals' lives holistically and over the long term revealed the complexity of the relationships, for instance, between ill health, unemployment, poor work and an experience of extended precariousness and insecurity. At the simplest level, ill health could limit labour market engagement: people were not well enough to work. Engagement with the labour market, however, could also generate ill health which served to then limit people's availability for jobs: poor work made people ill. Being unemployed, however, also had negative health effects: unemployment also made people ill! The first part of the chapter describes and illustrates these relationships, in an attempt to unravel this complexity.

The second part of the chapter focuses on how caring commitments interacted with the low-pay, no-pay cycle. The availability of suitable childcare was a problem for many interviewees in their efforts to establish themselves in employment. Caring responsibilities were wider than this, however, and were often tied to problems of family ill health. Growing up and living in recurrent poverty and in neighbourhoods of multiple deprivation meant that the participants experienced the concentrated problems of social exclusion as they bear down on poor neighbourhoods. Just one example of this is the destructive impact of problematic drug use and, in our case, a thriving local heroin market.

In the final section we draw the first two strands of the discussion together and show, through one unpredicted finding from our research, the way that problematic heroin use, and its negative impact on health and wider well-being, affected some of the individuals and families in our study, particularly in respect of new and demanding caring responsibilities that in turn limited engagement with jobs.

How ill health can stop people getting and keeping jobs

Given the socioeconomic situation of interviewees and the deprived neighbourhoods they came from it is not surprising that ill health featured regularly in interviews, both in respect of interviewees themselves and their families. The fact and social determinants of class-based inequalities in health are well established (Graham, 2000; Marmot, 2010), as is how these may be compounded by area-based effects of disadvantage (see, for example, Joshi et al, 2000; Exeter et al, 2011). As Smith notes, in general terms, health inequalities 'are ubiquitous: the less affluent have always had worse health, they have worse health wherever they live, and they suffer more from all forms of ill health' (2005, p xii). In 2004 Middlesbrough was ranked 11th out of 354 local authorities for the proportion of the population living in the most deprived 10 per cent of wards in the country (Index of Multiple Deprivation, 2004). In relation to health deprivation specifically, 14 out of its 23 wards were ranked in the 10 per cent poorest nationally in respect of health and disability. Common diseases were significantly more prevalent among the Middlesbrough population than the national average: deaths from lung cancer were 50 per cent greater, from circulatory diseases 16 per cent greater and from suicide and undetermined deaths 42 per cent greater (Middlesbrough PCT and Middlesbrough Council, 2006). Within Middlesbrough, rates of ill health were even higher in the most deprived wards like those we studied.

In respect of physical ill health, chronic problems such as arthritis and respiratory and cardiac disease, visual impairment and musculoskeletal problems (particularly 'bad backs') were most common among the older interviewees. Predictably given their age, chronic physical ill health was less common among young interviewees (but some had experienced acute incidents – for example, injuries resulting from car crashes or other accidents – that had had consequences for their employment). For younger interviewees ill health was mostly psychological in nature (depression and anxiety and stress-related problems). Psychiatric conditions, particularly depression, were also apparently common among the older participants as well as the younger ones. Hammen (1997, p 56), reviewing numerous studies, concludes that 'poverty is associated with increased risks of virtually all forms of psychological disorder ... also unemployment or employment in lower status occupations are typically more associated with depression.' Interviewees' stoical attitude to their ill health meant that they only sometimes sought medical help and/or applied clear definitions to their conditions. This was particularly the case with some of the younger men who described clear depressive symptoms but who had not been formally diagnosed with depression, nor sought medical help for these difficulties, reflecting findings of other research that shows how 'hegemonic forms of masculinity' can inhibit men from seeking medical help (Frosh et al, 2002; Emslie et al, 2006).

John, 40, had lived a troubled life. He told us how "a family friend" had sexually abused him as a child and he had, a few years after this, then been accused of raping his sister (a charge that was later dropped but which lay at the root of long-term estrangement from his family). Addiction to heroin fuelled acquisitive offending during his teens and twenties, which led to spells in prison. (Interestingly, Allen's 2007 ethnographic study of young heroin users also found that childhood abuse, as well as bereavement, shaped later patterns of problematic drug use.) John had managed to get occasional, short-term jobs – and fiddly jobs 'on the side' now and again – but at the age of 40 was living alone, persisting with his drug treatment programme and hoping to get a proper, steadier job. He described how he had been to a number of employment support agencies and one staff member had raised the prospect of undiagnosed depression with him. He reported that he had not been to the doctors, despite the Jobcentre Plus staff also advising him to, because he was "worried I make myself look like an idiot". In John's case we can see how long-standing and successive difficulties had had a negative impact on his well-being. Mental health problems, particularly undiagnosed depression, were for him a key but not the only barrier to him accessing jobs. More generally in the sample, mental and physical health problems had the same effect – limiting access to jobs and making it difficult to last in them even when jobs were gained.

Bereavements were sometimes tied up with interviewees' ill health and poor sense of well-being. Ronnie (57), for instance, said that he had suffered two "nervous breakdowns", plus some other more minor health problems. His wife died when she was in her forties and he attributed his long-term depression to this and the "pressures of life". As with our earlier research (Webster et al, 2004), bereavement was a common experience for research participants, many of whom had suffered multiple bereavements in quick succession. Ribbens McCarthy (2005, pp 64-5) has argued that 'experiences of multiple bereavements or compound disadvantages are likely to be unevenly distributed across localities, given the known link between premature death and inequalities related to social class and geography.' We interviewed Janice, 56, and her husband Lennie, 57. Both had suffered from depression for several years. They attributed this to several, successive family bereavements including the deaths of two of their grandchildren. Song et al (2010, p 269) describe how 'the death of a child disrupts parents' health and well-being both during the acute phase of bereavement and for extended periods over the course of their lives.' Such consequences can also be felt by grandparents, as Janice describes:

> "We were really bad with the first one. We had never been through that before. She [her granddaughter] died in the March and I lost my brother in the August to cancer. Then me mother got diagnosed with a brain tumour that year, so I had her stopping here and I had to watch me mam die ... it all built up, you know? Then, like I say, two years ago me other granddaughter died. So, it has been hard ... when you lose a grandchild. It's just something that you never get over. Plus, you know, you have other members of the family dying and it all builds up."

For Janice her ensuing, long-term depression was a key barrier to her getting a job. It sapped confidence and energy and now Janice rarely went out. With her husband, she seemed very socially isolated:

> "... you just don't feel like socialising because if I did go out I know I wouldn't be good company for people. So I might as well not go. It'd just spoil the night. And then that

depresses you because you don't go anywhere ... it's just a vicious circle, really."

Lennie described his wife's situation and his own dawning realisation that he, too, was clinically depressed:

"Janice got it before me because of the amount of deaths we had in the family. She suffered badly at the time. I had me work, but she lost her mother and her brother, and the grandkids, just everything, everything piled up and just made her very ill. I thought one day she would end up hurting herself ... then one day it just hit me. You just think, there is something wrong here. You know there is something wrong, but you can't put your finger on it and then you go to the doctors and they tell you, 'You've got depression'."

One of Janice and Lennie's daughters herself became ill and had to give up her job; in Janice's words she suffered a "nervous breakdown" after the death of her child (Janice and Lennie's grandchild). Both Janice and Lennie had worked in a series of jobs earlier in their lives. Neither had been able to get a job during the last few years. While we should not conclude that ill health was a straightforward cause of their distancing from the labour market (after all, there are many older workers in Teesside who do not suffer ill health but who are also unable to get jobs), both Lennie and Janice would admit that at least part of the explanation for their worklessness rested on their long-term depression (itself largely the outcome of multiple family bereavements). In Chapter 9 we note how Lennie had been deemed 'fit for work' and removed from sickness benefits. He was still without work and now not receiving any benefits.

How jobs (and unemployment) can make people ill

In Chapter 5 we described participants' strong motivation towards work and delineated a variety of reasons for this. A key motivation was that interviewees knew, from direct personal and family experience, that being out of work was not good for a person's well-being – unemployment made people ill. In Chapter 5 we also saw how the social psychological decline associated with unemployment has been well described in extensive research literature over decades and associated with feelings of boredom, listlessness, social isolation, apathy, depression and in some cases, despair. The informants described all these feelings in interviews, when they recounted what it was like, or had been like, to be unemployed. The depression that was common in the sample was said by several interviewees to be directly related to their unemployment.

We know that unemployment can cause ill health. It is less commonly reported that employment can, too. Waddell and Burton (2006, p ix) argue that 'work is generally good for health and well-being' but add that 'job insecurity can have an adverse effect on health' (p 10). They conclude from their review of the literature that work is generally good for your health and well-being, provided you have 'a good job': 'good jobs are obviously better than bad jobs, but bad jobs might be either less beneficial or even harmful' (p 34). Australian research by Butterworth and colleagues (2011, p 807) makes a similar argument, concluding that 'overall, unemployed respondents had poorer mental health than those who were employed. However the mental health of those who were unemployed was comparable or superior to those in jobs of the poorest psychosocial quality.' Ritchie et al (2005) review research about underemployment and well-being. They note that, in contrast to the extensive research showing the relationship between unemployment and negative mental and physical ill health, 'the amount of research into the relationship between well-being and economically inadequate employment is extremely limited' (2005, p 30). The evidence is scant and in some cases contradictory, but Dooley (2003, p 16, cited in Ritchie et al, 2005, p 32) concludes that studies do provide 'evidence that economically inadequate employment is associated with adverse mental health effects similar to those of job loss'. That precarious, poor work might be a source of depressive illness is beginning to be recognised in public policy research in the UK (Baumberg, 2011).

There was certainly evidence in our study that undertaking poor work could have negative consequences for people's physical and mental health (see Chapter 7, where we discussed the physical pain sometimes caused by the jobs people did). Simon, 30, provides a good example. In Chapter 5 we described the pattern of his work history as being an archetype of the low-pay, no-pay cycle. The reasons for him losing or leaving work were *not*, however, characteristic in that for him ill health was a regular explanation (see Chapter 7, where we discuss reasons for the cessation of jobs). He had struggled with long-term depression since his teenage years (which he linked to serious bullying while at school). Work sometimes got on top of him, worsening his mental health. He had moved between unemployment, training schemes and over a dozen jobs of different types since he left school. One of these was working in a local call centre. He described how it affected him: "I had a tough time there. I was having panic attacks all the time so I wasn't there as much as I'd have liked to have been. I think it was just due to the job, really." He had resigned from a job as an assembly line worker in an electronics components factory because working night shifts over months in a stressful job was making him ill. He had also quit a job he had had as a heavy goods vehicle driver, saying:

> "I mean it's not so much about confidence it's more about ... I get depressed and down ... especially in the heavy goods, starting at eight o'clock and I wasn't getting back home again till six or seven on a night so sometimes it's 14-hour days ... it's no good really ... you'll get in, have a couple of hours at home then going to bed and doing it all over again. So it's just ... it's hard."

Interviewees also talked about physical injuries that they incurred at work. Often these arose from poor training or just generally hard working conditions (see the case of Pamela, in Chapter 7, who suffered a serious injury while working as a carer, which eventually led to the loss of her job). In Chapter 7 we also mentioned how the local 'turkey factory' gave an example of some of the poorest terms and conditions of employment that the interviewees reported. Yet in previous studies (MacDonald and Marsh, 2005), and this one, it was a regular provider of employment to interviewees. The Equality and Human Rights Commission conducted an enquiry into the meat processing industry, and while they found examples of good practice, they also reported some shocking treatment of workers, some of which they argued could breach human rights legislation. For example, they reported that:

> ... some workers had been prevented from visiting the toilet by their line manager. This included pregnant women, women with heavy periods, and people with bladder problems. Interviewees described the lasting humiliation of workers urinating and bleeding on themselves while working on the production line. (EHRC, 2010, p 11)

Thus, the poor-quality work that people did often caused or exacerbated the ill health that interviewees reported. A number of the interviewees had experienced accidents at work that were often downplayed or ignored by employers, in ways that also appeared to contravene their legal duties. Interviewees typically felt compelled to try to keep working when they were ill, fearing they would be sacked or lose their jobs (a fear which was not without foundation, as several cases showed).

Importantly, the sorts of jobs that interviewees did were frequently not ones that could accommodate even short periods of illness. Employers were often not tolerant of interviewees' ill health. Lloyd and Warhurst (2011) suggest that after low pay, 'bad jobs' tend to be also characterised by limited benefits, such as sick pay, leave and pensions. Salaried, professional employees have the benefit of statutory sick leave cover that is usually adhered to by their employers, and often, too, the support of occupational health professionals should work-related illness arise. This was not the case for people in our study. Not only did they do jobs that were more likely than most to generate ill health, they worked for employers that were as quick to fire as they were to hire. Here we might argue, then, that the people in our study directly confronted inequalities in health because of their class position (Scambler, 2002). They were more likely to encounter work that generated ill health *and* face a stronger likelihood of speedy expulsion back to unemployment when they suffered it. Consequently it was not unusual for the interviewees to report that they lost jobs because of even very short periods of illness. Carol-Anne (34) had worked as a junior administrator in an office, a job that she initially "loved". Mistreatment by her employer meant that she had soon begun to "hate" the work: "It was a small family business with a very high staff turnover and I was off with a tummy bug for a week so they sacked me." Although she had a doctor's note to prove her illness:

> "… I didn't feel at the time that I could do anything about it. I just didn't have the confidence. And I just felt it was all my fault … that was sort of when my depression started really. Felt really bad about myself."

As we saw in Chapter 7, when we discussed Pamela's decision to quit her care worker job (after her injury at work she received apparently malicious treatment from her employer because she took time off), it was sometimes an employer's response to periods of illness that prompted people to leave jobs. We noted in Chapter 4 how some employers preferred to recruit workers who lived close by, sometimes very close by, the place of employment. We quoted Kevin, a care home manager, who liked to employ workers "who lived within half a mile". The reason given for this was that he perceived that his workers might be more reliable and punctual if they lived nearby. It also, of course, allows managers to enforce more immediate control over, and apply pressures to, workers as the needs of the business demanded. Elizabeth, 30, like Pamela, had also had a job as a care assistant, working in a residential care home. She took a week's sick leave from her care home job after she had had her wisdom teeth removed:

> "All week I had them [her employers] knocking on the door for me to go in. Every day. and I thought, 'No I've had enough'. I went back the following week and just went to see the manager and said, 'Look, I'm leaving'."

Caring for others

Despite objective indicators that label the sort of neighbourhoods we researched as displaying multiple deprivation, they are also places in which high degrees of informal social support among residents can be found (Kearns and Parkinson, 2001). We have noted elsewhere how the sort of 'bonding social capital' present in close family and social networks can help to ameliorate the adversity of living in conditions of deprivation (for example, via emotional support and friendship, informal loans of money, informal sharing of childcare and other forms of care, recommendations and tip-offs about jobs, protection from and redress after criminal victimisation) (MacDonald and Marsh, 2005). We have also argued, however, that while crucial supports to 'getting by', this form of bonding social capital can serve to keep people in place, geographically and socially, and limit an individual's chances of escaping deprived situations (MacDonald et al, 2005). One example is in respect of people's reliance on informal social networks for searching for jobs. These were vital for helping people get work but tended to limit people to the sorts of poor work done by people they knew (a key argument of Chapter 6).

We have described how ill health limits people's engagement with the labour market. Caring for people who were ill (family members or friends) could have the same effect. We interviewed Alice, 30, three times over 10 years. Over the years she had had a range of part-time jobs, including most recently as a dinner lady in a school. Her husband, Danny, worked for the council as a gardener. In the most recent interview she told us how her son, Ross, had been diagnosed with cancer, when he was three years old. She and Danny now spent regular and lengthy periods staying with Ross as he received treatment at a hospital in Newcastle, over 40 miles away from Middlesbrough. Because of his regular absences from work, Danny had to leave his job: the council "could not keep the job open" for him, given his persistent absence. The couple struggled to access benefits because Danny was deemed to have 'voluntarily left his job'. Even when they were eventually successful in making a claim for benefits, they suffered serious financial difficulties as a consequence of their son's life-threatening illness:

> "Danny was a gardener and he had to pack it all in. So he had to go on benefits, but then because we were up there [at the hospital] he couldn't get back down here to sign on so he had to go to the doctor's and get a sick note to cover him while he was up at Newcastle so the doctors put it down to stress and he got a sick note for six months. Because he missed signing on one week they were like dead funny with him so he explained about Ross and they said 'You need to go to the doctor's and get a sick note'." (Alice, 30)

Losing employment at times of family illness and the inevitable stresses this brought also often resulted in additional financial strain. Responsibilities could weigh heavily, not just limiting people's ability to engage in work, but also having an impact on their own well-being (see the case of Janice, earlier who, despite her own ill health, gave up work to look after her daughter when her daughter, Janice's grandchild, died). Interviewees often talked about having to put their family caring responsibilities before their commitment to work. Diane, 40, had had a string of mainly part-time jobs during her twenties and thirties (for example, as a bar maid, party organiser, payroll clerk and cleaner). This low-pay, no-pay career had stalled, however, as a combined result of illness in her family (her own, her husband's and her son's). She had not worked for several years and now acted as a carer for her husband and son:

> "I had a nervous breakdown and I have 'type two bipolar' which is manic depression and I have severe asthma attacks. My husband's ex-Army and he was hurt during the Falklands [War] so he can't really work ... he has post-traumatic stress disorder as a result of his injury, not quite what I expected [from life]! And my son has cerebral palsy, ADHD [attention deficit hyperactivity disorder], learning difficulties and he's partially sighted and that's due to him being born 15 weeks early. Everything stresses me ... if there was a gold medal in getting stressed, I'd have it. I'd get a golden medal in worrying as well."

Even faced with multiple hardships (numerous family illnesses, bereavements and so on) interviewees often displayed remarkable stoicism and resilience (MacDonald and Shildrick, 2012). Diane went on to talk about how her son's disabilities had inspired her: "I'm just acutely aware of how lucky I am ... he [her disabled son] keeps on going and going and going ... I mean if he wasn't the way he was, I wouldn't have learnt to drive." Similarly, Mary, 30, reflected on how the death of her partner (who was the father of her first child) in a car accident had affected her:

> "It shocks me sometimes actually when I think actually did get through it. Sometimes it seems like a different person it happened to. You think you're never going to get through things, don't you? It's the end of the world ... I think it's made me a lot stronger, though. I think if I can cope with that, I can cope with pretty much anything that's thrown at me."

Mary certainly had experienced further troubles. Her new partner, Andy, had also suffered a serious car accident, resulting in a long period out of work. He had eventually returned to a job but had recently been made redundant. At the time of interview, Mary was hoping to return to employment herself, having spent recent years looking after her young child (and then Andy, as he recovered from his accident). So while the interviewees sometimes faced a barrage of personal troubles in their lives, particularly in respect of family bereavements and personal and family ill health, their effects typically were not to permanently dislodge a motivation to engage in employment. Caring responsibilities that resulted did, however, serve to make it even harder – sometimes impossible – for people to take up job opportunities when they arose or to hold down jobs, and were responsible for some of the longer stretches of 'no pay' in our overall mapping of the low-pay, no-pay cycle.

Unsurprisingly it was women who tended to bear the brunt of caring responsibilities. Cunningham-Burley and colleagues (2006, p 389) have examined the difficulties women face in balancing motherhood and paid employment, particularly during periods of family ill health. Their respondents described the 'complex juggling of work, domestic and childcare responsibilities' and expressed concern about 'unpredictable events, especially sickness, which would upset the precarious balance between home and work.' The women in their study were largely unaware of any family-friendly policies in their workplace in relation to sick leave or more generally, confirming other research on this topic

(Bond et al, 2002, cited in Cunningham-Burley et al, 2006). It is the impact of childcare more broadly on the lives of the interviewees that the next section explores.

Childcare

In our study of the low-pay, no-pay cycle the impact of gender played out most obviously in relation to the effects of childbearing and childcare on men and women's work histories (in Chapter 5 we described how this affected the typical pattern of the low-pay, no-pay cycle with women sometimes having longer periods out of the labour market). Over recent years a number of measures have been put in place to try to make working arrangements more flexible and 'family friendly' (such as flexible working conditions for parents and extended maternity and paternity leave). Dex and Smith (1992, p 7) report that:

> ... in the context of growing business and family pressures, this interest in more flexible working arrangements has developed as a potential way of helping families and employers to cope with the real life problems of being carers and employees in a competitive business environment.

Yet the reality was that for many of the interviewees the sorts of jobs that they undertook rarely offered these packages of support and assistance (echoing Cunningham-Burley et al's 2006 findings). It has been well established by research over decades that it is women rather than men who take most responsibility for domestic labour, and particularly so in respect of childcare. More recently, Warren and colleagues (2009, p 2) found that 'it is mothers, rather than fathers, who bend their jobs to meet family needs', suggesting that this relegates some women to marginalised sectors of employment, experiencing indirect discrimination, poor conditions and discontinuous work histories built around part-time jobs. Saraceno (2011, p 59) concurs, saying it is most often mothers who will 'rearrange their modes of participation in the labour market' to allow them to take care of their children. Grant (2009) has shown that women living in areas of disadvantage face even greater problems in achieving this juggling act of accessing local, flexible employment at the same time as finding manageable and acceptable childcare.

Our study confirms these findings. For instance, mothers in the study were more likely than men to search for work in their immediate neighbourhoods. Mary, 30, who we discussed above, commented that:

"A lot of them, they're agencies [private employment agencies that she had enrolled with] and you phone up and they're trying to ship you all over the place. I'd rather go for something that's a bit more secure. I like to know what my hours are and what I'm doing so I can sort the kids out."

Mary felt that she needed to be present for her son, Dylan, at key times in the day, which limited the sort of hours she might be able to work (and the distance she was able to travel to work). This, however, had to be balanced against the extent to which she would actually be better off financially in part-time employment (rather than on benefits), which in turn was balanced against the advantages of a full-time wage versus higher childcare costs:

"If I do 16 hours [per week] we'll only be £10 a week better off which just covers your bus fare so you'd be going to work [for little extra income] ... so I said really ideally I need to be doing 30 hours a week. I didn't really wanna do that with because Dylan's at an age where he doesn't get in from school till half four ... don't want him to be falling behind because I'm at work day in, day out."

Others were also concerned about the difficulty of offsetting the costs of childcare with the low wages that might be on offer in the sorts of jobs that they would be accessing. Balancing up whether one would be financially better off was often unclear to many of the mothers. For instance, going to work, after the costs of paying childcare, would have left Carol, 44, '£20 a week better off', but from this she would have to pay bus fares to get to work. The Daycare Trust and Save the Children (2011) has found that a quarter of parents in severe poverty had given up work and a third had turned down a job mainly because of high childcare costs, and a quarter had not been able to take up education or training, all because of difficulties in accessing childcare (and they were more than twice as likely as better-off parents to have done this).

This issue of the potential insecurity of working hours, their inconvenience in relation to the demands of childcare and the costs of the latter in respect of the low wages they might get in jobs were common themes among mothers who were looking for jobs. Sinead, 36, had had a string of jobs with short-term periods of unemployment in between when she did not claim benefits (see Chapter 9). She was made redundant when a high street chain store closed down, and since then had been searching for work. The family were surviving on her husband's wage and were experiencing severe financial hardship:

> "The employment that I need is to work around my children. I can't do nights and I can't do weekends, so it's quite hard. [In respect of a particular job she was considering, she said] you started really early on a morning and you're finishing at 6 o'clock so it's no good because I'd have to pay out childcare as well so it's not going to be worth it, like ... I don't really want to put him into full-time childcare but then I'd have to see if I got a job working full time. How much would it take out of my wages for childcare? So it's a catch-22 situation, isn't it?"

Fitting childcare responsibilities in with the demands of college and training courses, undertaken to improve job prospects (see Chapter 6), was also reported as a problem. Thwarted attempts at betterment could have debilitating impacts in themselves. After a long spell of unemployment, Amanda (48, currently unemployed) had decided to return to a further education college to take a vocational course that she hoped would give her more chance of a job:

> "... it [the course] was supposed to be over two years but they crammed it into one which eventually got the better of half of us. We just couldn't do all the reports and presentations and with the kids – travelling from college to the childminder's – I was literally going to bed about 3am, because I had to do me washing, homework, shopping, ironing, out the house at 6am, one [child] to the childminder's, then nursery, run round to the college for 9am ... because they didn't take into consideration, your family. They were cramming it. I got depressed because I thought 'This is ridiculous, I can't be a mother and a career woman'."

Laura, 31, had had several jobs in the past but since becoming a mother she had not had a job. Her situation was complicated by the fact that she had previously suffered with severe postnatal depression, which was treated with medication she found to be 'highly addictive'. She says, "it took me years to get off them." She had been keen to return to work but the costs of childcare for four children made this difficult. The family relied on her husband's intermittent employment as a scaffolder (which paid relatively well when he was in work but work had been very sporadic, so the couple tried to save money to tide them over periods when he was not employed). Laura expressed the same frustration as Amanda, above, and a sense of being trapped by the constant demands of motherhood. She hoped (and planned) to go to university but knew this was going to be a struggle for her to manage:

> "Well I'm hoping to apply next year and.... It's been really, really difficult and plus my age and the fact I've got four children now. Yeah I'm finding it quite difficult [baby crying in background]. Ah, she's tired she's been up since half past five this morning! Childcare's alright at the minute, but it's going to be a problem when I start university next year because ... and I mean, what are you supposed to do? Leave them at home on their own? I don't think so. Either that or lose your benefits, it's stupid."

The government-sponsored Sure Start initiative was not widely accessed by our sample, although those who had used its childcare and other services tended to talk positively about it. For example, Sharleen (30) found that the programme gave her the motivation to get back into work:

> "Before we went to Sure Start I used to get up, clean up, go to my friends or our Leanne's and we used to just sit and drink tea and smoke fags all day, that's it, and, like, maybe nip up into town and that'd be [it]. We all said one day, 'Is this our lives?' and we all got up and got jobs and we did!"

When Sure Start was accessed it could be a great support to parents, yet supporting other research which suggests that working-class women are sometimes wary of formal childcare (Griggs, 2010), the interviewees tended to express a preference for self or family childcare over that which might be provided by agencies or outsiders. This was the case with Winnie, 44. When her daughter was very young, Winnie had not been employed, preferring to stay at home to look after her. Currently Winnie was undertaking two part-time cleaning jobs in order that she could also care for her grandson (in Chapter 9 we describe the severe financial hardships that resulted for Winnie as a consequence). Her daughter preferred not to use – and did not regard it as feasible to pay for – formal childcare, so relied on Winnie for this:

"Yeah, it has definitely had an effect on my work. I mean, I actually give up a full-time job so I could look after my grandson. To make it easier for my daughter so that.... Well, I mean I didn't work when my daughter was young because I didn't want to put her in childcare. Without my grandson [to look after] I could either go into full-time work and be bringing in more money or without him I could take on another job so I'd be doing three [part-time] jobs for more money, but I don't want my daughter ... my daughter doesn't wanna be trapped in that cycle of being on benefits and stuff. So I'm trying to help her – but I'm not really helping myself."

Ill health, caring and the low-pay, no-pay cycle: the long-term and intergenerational impact of heroin dependency

Problematic drug use – specifically, dependence on heroin and the social, medical and legal problems this brought – was a dominating feature of the life histories of some of the young people who participated in our earlier research (Johnston et al, 2000; Webster et al, 2004; MacDonald and Marsh, 2005). Teesside provides a classic example of a place that suffered a 'second wave heroin outbreak' in the mid-1990s (Parker et al, 1998; MacDonald and Marsh, 2005). A vibrant heroin market and an associated criminal economy quickly became established, concentrated on the most deprived neighbourhoods. Studies show that neighbourhood deprivation and problematic drug use are strongly linked. Indeed, drug problems are indicative of localities in the UK that have undergone processes of rapid economic dispossession and social exclusion. For some, drug use offers criminal opportunity; for others, respite from the stress and boredom of living in poor areas (Shaw et al, 2007). MacDonald and Marsh (2002) argue that in these contexts, heroin can be described as a 'poverty drug' and its appeal understood in respect of the psychological pressures and social hardships that users face (see the discussion of John, earlier in the chapter).

Our previous research charted how young adults growing up in these places at this time, both users and non-users, were greatly affected by the problems generated by the drug economy. Some of those we re-interviewed for this study, all men, had made transitions to adulthood overshadowed by long-term, intertwined 'careers' of heroin use and crime. As all of the interviewees were over 30 – and given what we know from criminological research literature about age-related desistance from careers of crime and drug use (Maruna, 2001; MacDonald et al, 2011) – it is not surprising that most of those who earlier had problematic engagement with heroin had either desisted from drug use or were in the process of doing so (and receiving drug treatment, usually in the form of a methadone maintenance programme). Most were now struggling to access the labour market (more purposively than had been the case earlier in their lives). Their difficulties in doing this included physical and mental health problems accrued over years of risky drug-using behaviour. Relative lack of work experience (and for some, recurrent periods in prison) meant that they sometimes did not have the knowledge, skills or confidence to be able to easily get jobs. Their potential CVs were not impressive. Chris, 32, was a recovering heroin addict, starting his use of this drug in his late teens (as had both his brother and sister). He had had occasional short-term jobs after leaving school but then lost a more promising job at the steel works, achieved via a recommendation from his father, because of his poor record of attendance (associated with his heroin dependency). His struggles to get off heroin and the health problems it had caused (for example, he had suffered from deep vein thrombosis, leaving him unable to walk for six months) meant that he had not been employed for over 10 years. At the time of interview, he wanted to get back into work and was seeking help in this process:

> "Because I hadn't had a job since, like, back then, I was petrified, proper scared thinking 'Is it going to be...? Can I handle this?' Well they [Jobcentre Plus] got us in and we had a talk. They sent me to Pathfinders [a voluntary-sector based welfare to work agency] to build my confidence and all that up and done us a CV and all that. I'd never been to an interview because my dad got me that job at the steel works. Honestly, I was just like proper scared and like I was thinking it [a job interview] was going to be like going in front of the headmaster and I thought 'Ooh, I dread that'."

We quote Chris at length again to demonstrate the emotional, psychological and physical health problems that can affect those with long-term careers of problematic drug use, how for some such individuals these provide a substantial barrier to re-engagement with the labour market and how the intervention of voluntary sector-based agencies can sometimes make a strong contribution to this process (see Chapter 6):

"Well, at Pathfinders they said as soon as I'm properly sorted, because I am on the methadone now still, as soon as I'm sorted I go there and she'll get me, like, my provisional [driving licence] and get me some driving lessons. When I was on the heroin my teeth were just proper bad, rotten, and I was frightened of the dentist and at Pathfinders they got my confidence up. I just … I'd bottled it for too long. Anyway I just went and they sent me to hospital and they took 16 [teeth] out on the same day! It was the best thing that I've ever done. It's helped me because I didn't ever smile, now look [shows interviewer his teeth]. It's brilliant! Sandra [his adviser at Pathfinders] has, like, brought me from here to here [motions widely across the table] where I was just doing that before [motions to indicate slow, small steps forward]. It was taking ages and ages and she was just, it was summat about her she made me believe in myself. When I was on the drugs I always felt worthless and she hasn't half helped me. I'm waiting to go back there because she said she can get me in touch with places that give ex-criminals a second chance."

Problems recovering (or recovered) heroin users faced went beyond problems of lack of confidence, limited work experience and health issues. Others pointed out that they felt discriminated against when applying for jobs (see Chapter 4 for research evidence on this point), although they reported this with no sense of complaint, and more than one person said that they would do the same if the positions were reversed. Richard, aged 30, was now engaged in the low-pay, no-pay cycle in similar ways to the rest of the sample (see Chapter 7). This is despite the fact that over the course of our last interviews with him (until the age of 24) he had been heavily involved in problematic heroin use, acquisitive offending to support his habit, repeated imprisonment and failed attempts at rehabilitation. Over the last six years he had been 'clean', and repeatedly engaged in short-term jobs. One explanation for the difference between Chris's and Richard's work history is the fact that, fortuitously, Richard did not suffer any serious or lasting health consequences from his drug use; another relates to the duration of their 'drug careers' (Chris was still struggling to get clear of drugs whereas Richard's exit from drug use, and treatment, had been several years earlier), and the fact that Richard had managed to sustain fuller engagement in the labour market in his teenage years and twenties (and thus had more work experience and contacts). Additionally, Richard admitted that he tended not to disclose his drug and criminal history to employers. In any case, our general finding has been that even those with such histories are able to access low-paid, insecure work (MacDonald, 2011). A key explanation for this is that the sorts of employers they worked for tended not to be so interested in people's past (and rarely asked for full CVs anyway): physical ability to do the job and 'the right attitude' were more important (see Chapters 4 and 6).

The importance of employment as an aid to processes of desistance from crime and drug use is well-established in the research literature – as is the difficulty, especially in times of high unemployment, of people with these sorts of biography getting jobs that might help them desist (see, for example, Webster et al, 2004; Farrell et al, 2011). Less commonly reported, and of direct relevance to the subject of this chapter, is how *caring for* working-age children who are troubled by problematic drug use can seriously inhibit engagement with employment. This was an unexpected finding. We did not expect issues about heroin use to be significant for study (given our main research questions) and our sample (given knowledge about age-related desistance). Yet many of the older research participants described, unprompted, the impact that having a heroin-dependent son or daughter had had on their lives in general and their labour market participation in particular.

Even though Brian, 54, was one of the better-qualified interviewees (he had completed a university degree in Human Resource Management in his thirties), he still had a chequered employment career including working in food processing factories. In recent years he had been unemployed. He attributed this partly to ongoing problems the family faced with their son, Jamie, who was addicted to heroin. Jamie had repeatedly stolen from them and they had had to take formal custody of one of Jamie's children, their grandchild (the other was taken by a grandparent on the mother's side). Consequently, Brian's wife reduced her hours at work and was currently off sick with stress:

> "My son, he's a heroin addict to put it bluntly ... it's 10 year now, he's coming up to 26. It's been difficult to try to cope with what he does. He's been away to prison and they try to get him back on track.... It is quite sad, so at the moment, we've actually had to become foster, kinship carers ... so it's a bit of a mess at the minute.... It's a huge financial drain having someone like him [Jamie] about, not just in terms of what gets nicked but it's also in terms of the things you need to do to keep them together.... It's

an investment in time and other things cost, like food and electric. Even just running around – they're not good with appointments and things like that. We've got a calendar up on the wall; it's the only way to cope with it. And children [the grandchild they were caring for] as well now, that's an additional thing remembering to get their jabs and stuff. So it's a huge investment in time, a huge investment in money and what that tends to do, it depresses your ability to actually do anything else, you become emotionally drained."

Barnard (2005, p 1) suggests that the 'tendency for policy and practice to focus on the individual with the drug problem has eclipsed consideration of the severe and enduring impacts of problem drug use on many families'. She points to the effects on siblings in the family and their own greater risk of drug use, but also reports how many parents of drug-dependent children 'linked deterioration in their [own] physical and psychological health to the stresses of living with their child's drug problem' (p 1). Brian, above, seems to be exactly caught up 'in the maelstrom that drug problems almost inevitably create' (Barnard, 2005, p 1).

Butler and Bauld (2005) argue that parents of drug users face a multitude of problems, ranging from guilt about what has happened to their child, to feelings of shame, isolation and embarrassment. Although suffering from health problems herself (a long-term depressive illness, partly connected to the situation of her own daughter, Faye), Carol, 44, cared full time for her grandson, Thomas, on account of Faye's long-term problematic use of heroin. Aside from the physical demands on her time and the limits this placed on her ability to take paid work (Carol was unemployed), she also referred to the emotional dimensions associated with caring for a grandchild when one's own child is a heroin dependent:

"You see, Thomas is proper attached to me because his mam comes and goes. She's a drug addict so he thinks I'm going to disappear, half the time. He thinks I sit and wait for him outside of school all day. That's what he thinks [laughs]."

Research shows that there are 200,000 grandparents and other family members raising children because they can no longer live with their parents (Grandparents Plus website, 2010, http://grandparentsplus.org.uk). The role of grandparents in supporting families is relatively little discussed, yet one in three families rely on grandparents for childcare (ONS, 2009), with the value of this care estimated at £3.9 billion (ONS, 2009). Recent research by Griggs (2010, p 9) has shown that grandparents from low-income families are more likely to play crucial roles in respect of caring for grandchildren: 'when a grandparent becomes their grandchild's parent they often experience considerable emotional trauma and stress, retirement savings may be depleted and grandparents' work arrangements disrupted.' This research also points to the added financial strain inflicted on those who may already be experiencing economic hardship. In the US, Engstrom (2009, p 2) highlights the plight of grandmothers who undertake care of grandchildren while their daughters are in prison or addicted to drugs. We found a number of similar cases in our study – as with Brian and Carol, above – of grandparents bearing the strain of family heroin problems, with clear implications for their capacity to engage in paid employment as well as wider financial and emotional ramifications for their own lives. These financial costs not only included a much reduced ability to earn income through employment but also the purchase of care and treatment for the drug user as well the costs of thefts of family property (to fund drug purchases). Some parents repeatedly purchased basic clothing and furniture for their drug-dependent sons and daughters, only to find it quickly sold on to fund their drug habit.

Conclusions

Living and growing up in neighbourhoods of multiple and concentrated deprivation meant that the interviewees faced wider disadvantages beyond their difficulties in accessing decent, lasting employment. This chapter has drawn attention to particular examples. Reflecting the spatial concentration of social class inequalities in health, illness and the experience of bereavement was common among the research participants and their families. The chapter has sought to demonstrate, however, that the relationship between ill health and the low-pay, no-pay cycle is complex, multidimensional and, critically, recursive in that ill health could be a cause of, and caused by, difficulties in the labour market. Speaking of mental health problems, for instance, the Department of Health (1999, p 7; emphasis added) notes that these 'can *result* from a range of adverse factors associated with social exclusion and can also be a *cause* of social exclusion.'

Undoubtedly chronic and sometimes acute mental and physical illnesses (of the sort typically associated with disadvantaged, working-class people) inhibited individuals in their search for work or in their ability to hold down jobs. Depression was a particularly widespread problem. But both poles of the low-pay, no-pay cycle – poor-quality work and unemployment– could each also cause, or add to, ill health. The negative health implications of worklessness are well-known. Recurrent experience and threat of unemployment was one cause of depression for people in our study. The detrimental health impacts of employment are less well known, or accepted. The orthodox position, established by research over several decades, is that unemployment is bad for personal health and employment is good for it (see Chapter 5). Coates and Lekhi (2008, p 6) report, however, that:

> … the quality of employment has an impact on health, life expectancy and life chances. While it is clear that unemployment has a corrosive effect on physical and mental health there is equally strong evidence to show that a good job is better than a bad job. If we care about the capabilities of individuals to choose a life that they value then we should care about job quality.

Clearly, a good job is better for personal well-being than a bad one and this question, of how to improve the quality of poor work, is one we confront in Chapter 10. On a similar theme, and in reviewing research literature on this issue, Ritchie et al (2005, p 32) speculate that 'it is certainly conceivable that it is equally or more stressful to be in inadequate employment than remain workless.' This is, of course, possible, but our research method does not allow us to closely estimate whether low-quality jobs are 'worse' than unemployment for health. Nevertheless, as we document in Chapter 5, even poor work was, in the main, positively appreciated and preferred by the informants (to worklessness and claiming welfare benefits) because of its comparative social psychological and moral value. As this chapter has shown, however, these sorts of jobs could nonetheless also exacerbate or cause ill health among those who did them.

While research on the ill effects of worklessness is extensive and of poor quality jobs still relatively limited, Ritchie et al (2005, p 32; emphasis added) go further and highlight the need to 'understand the impact on mental well-being of work histories that are characterised by *cycles* of unemployment, inactivity and low-paid insecure jobs'. We feel we have gone some way towards meeting this research aim. To summarise: first, ill health could limit labour market engagement; second, poor-quality jobs could generate or add to ill health (which in turn limited labour market engagement); third, unemployment could also lead to ill health; and fourth, if we understand these impacts processually, as they were lived by the individuals in our study, we can surmise that *cycling between* unemployment and poor-quality jobs over time is likely to have a *cumulative*, negative impact on well-being.

Caring for others was the second theme of the chapter. The weight of caring responsibilities, whether for family members who were ill or for children or grandchildren, usually fell on women, particularly mothers. Childcare difficulties were often a barrier to sustained employment. Obviously our first theme, ill health, is related to our second one. The extent and sometimes unpredictability of ill health as it affected individuals and families caused difficulties for those simultaneously trying to care for others and to get or hold down jobs.

The third theme of the chapter, which brought together a discussion of ill health and of caring responsibilities, was about the destructive effects of problematic drug use on the communities, families and individuals in our study. This is an example of how one of the wider set of disadvantages and problems that can affect deprived neighbourhoods can have an impact in different ways on different generations. For some younger participants, who were or who had been users, problematic heroin use limited labour market engagement (for several different reasons, including negative impacts on health). For older participants an unpredicted finding of the study was that they sometimes found themselves in the position of limiting their own employment to care for heroin-dependent children (or for their grandchildren).

We conclude this chapter by returning to its introduction, where we noted the different emphasis of this chapter (on 'supply-side' issues) to the previous one (which focused on the 'demand side' of the labour market and the poor work available to people). We have shown the complex interrelationships between these sides of the 'employability equation' with the focus on ill health. Supply-side factors (the ill health of workers) limited people's ability to work, but demand-side factors (poor-quality jobs) also generated ill health – which limited people's ability to work. But in trying to consider the way that the supply of labour meets the demand for it from local employers – and doing this from the *point of view of workers* caught up in the low-pay, no-pay cycle – this clear separation is less easy to make in practice.

Ill health becomes amplified as a 'supply-side' barrier to work *when* the sort of employment available to people, 'on the demand side', is so uncaring of, and unforgiving to, workers when they are ill (as noted, dismissals for certified sick leave were not uncommon). The same applies to issues of caring responsibilities, specifically childcare. The work that was available to people was often low paid, irregular, insecure and sometimes carried out in unsocial, non-family-friendly hours. *This made* suitable childcare difficult to afford (on low wages) and obtain (for example, childcare that was flexible enough to fit with changing employer demands, that could potentially be terminated at short notice if a job concluded, and that was available in the early mornings, evenings and at nights, and at weekends). In other words, in each case – of ill health and caring – the difficulties and 'barriers' people 'brought to' the labour market have to be understood, at least in part, as a product of what the labour market offers them.

9

Poverty and social insecurity

In this chapter we turn to the interviewees' experiences of poverty. A primary aim is to show how these experiences related to encounters with employment, with the welfare system and with debt. In other words, the chapter aims to examine the relationship between cycling between low-paid jobs, unemployment and poverty. While inadequate benefits and low pay were each important factors in explaining poverty, it was also the case that moving between these different states – between employment and unemployment – was in and of itself a key contributory factor to the informants' financial hardship.

The first part of the chapter examines the way that research participants talked about poverty, focusing on the intriguing disjuncture between people's objective situations and their renouncement of 'poverty' as a description of these situations. Second, we describe the everyday hardship that was common across the sample. Third, we discuss the fact and experience of 'in-work poverty', how poverty continued even when people got jobs. Fourth, we explore encounters with the benefit system paying particular attention to the ways in which these fed into and exacerbated poverty. Here we report informants' widespread antipathy to making benefit claims and the complexities and difficulties of doing so. Finally, the chapter examines the experiences of debt and how these were cumulative, difficult to escape and long lasting, overshadowing the lives of research participants, when they were in jobs and when they were out of them. In summary the chapter highlights how people lived in lasting, everyday hardship, because of their experiences of welfare and of low-paid jobs, and also because of their repeated movement between the two.

Talking about poverty: moral discourses of 'the poor'

Our methodological approach was well placed to allow us to investigate subjective understandings of poverty from the perspective of those experiencing it. There is a lack of research evidence of this sort in the extant literature. As Lister notes, the voices and views of those experiencing poverty are rarely heard: 'the poor' are 'frequently talked and theorised about but are rarely themselves in a position to have their thoughts published' (2004, p 2). In discussing these issues in interviews we found that interviewees overwhelmingly rejected 'poverty' as a label that captured the condition of their own lives (people were much more willing to admit to 'struggling to get by', 'to feeling the pinch' or to 'things being tight'). Linda, aged 33, who had two children and was currently living on benefits, with her husband, was typical: "Not really [poor], no, not really, no." Alan, 38, was also currently unemployed and living on JSA. He stressed he was: "No, not poor, no."

Poverty was often imagined to be a situation that only people in developing countries might face. Where it was believed to exist in the UK, interviewees held strong views about its causes. Poverty was typically interpreted to be a result of personal failure and to be associated with destitute, homeless people or problematic drug users. In other words, the interviewees thought that 'poor people' were very much different to them: "Living on the streets, most of them are on drugs anyway" (Linda, 33). Alcock notes that the public tend to think of 'the *deserving* poor' as those 'not felt to be able to do much to help themselves, generally the elderly, children or the sick and disabled' (2006, p 9). In our research interviews there was little reference to 'the deserving poor'. In contrast, interviewees had clear views on 'the undeserving poor', and felt free to castigate and blame them. These were those thought to be workshy, to be claiming benefits illegitimately or to be engaging in inappropriate consumption habits (for example, spending money on alcohol, cigarettes or drugs rather than on food for their children). According to Spicker (2007, p 93), poverty 'is a moral concept as well as a descriptive one' and this was clearly evident in our study where poverty in the lives of others was viewed as a personal failure of morality or character. Mary and Dawn, both 30, said similar things:

> "Over the other side of the estate, yeah, very poor. Some of the places that are over there are awful. There is crime constantly and they are very poor and the kids haven't got much, but that's because the parents are spending it all on drugs or getting drunk every night."

> "Some people struggle because they are too busy drinking. They don't manage it. They either go out drinking or drinking in the house every day and there's drugs and stuff. That's what makes people so poor."

These 'others' – 'the undeserving poor' – are difficult to locate, empirically. MacDonald and Marsh (2005) heard similar comments about how "*we* are not like *them*" in their research with young adults in these same neighbourhoods, and interpret them as distancing narratives whereby individuals and families sought to maintain respectability and distance themselves from the shame and stigma of living in poverty by denying their *own* poverty, casting the label onto others and then denigrating and blaming those who were, they said, in this position. This sort of perspective was evident in our interviews where hardship in the lives of others was often viewed as a consequence of individual culpability or of personal moral failure.

British 'attitudes to those in need have hardened', with explanations citing social injustice declining and those blaming individual failings rising significantly over the past 25 years (Rowlingson et al, 2010). Castell and Thompson (2007, p 7) rightly assert that there is 'still a mountain to climb even just to get people to "base camp" in terms of [their understanding of] the causes and consequences of poverty in the UK.' We argue that these responses are part of a wider dismissal of poverty – of denying its existence or seeing it as self-inflicted. It is a viewpoint that is perpetuated by policy makers and the media. As Dorling (2010, p 256) argues, 'that people end up at the bottom' because they are undeserving has become the 'homogenising myth of our time'. These ideas draw on a powerful and important discourse that is clearly not just the preserve of the powerful. Informants felt very strongly that poverty was something to be ashamed of, a self-inflicted condition and failure on the part of them, 'the poor', to 'manage' in conditions of hardship. In contrast, the interviewees stressed how they personally *did* 'manage' and 'cope' and, in doing so, distanced themselves from the shame of poverty. In emphasising *their* ability 'to get by' – and in their renouncement of 'poverty' – they were buttressing a sense of self-respect and family respectability in social conditions that are increasingly hostile to 'the poor' (Skeggs, 1997; Jones, 2011).

Everyday hardship

The interviews were full of examples of the struggles and financial hardships people faced. Some interviewees lived in 'deep poverty'. By this we mean that they were unable to clothe or feed themselves properly or furnish and heat their homes adequately. For all, day-to-day life was frequently a juggling act which demanded strict routines, such as getting to the shops to catch the daily price reductions, careful decision making about purchases, and long-term planning for special events (that brought extra pressure) such as children's birthdays and Christmas. Leisure lives were limited by lack of money (and further constrained by family responsibility) and often focused on home-based activities. Holidays were rare and several people reminisced fondly about holidays they had been on in their childhood. Their absence – and the aspiration to have a family holiday – was repeatedly mentioned and emphasised in interviews, which we interpret as symbolic of what it meant to live in financial hardship. Lennie, 57, described how he would love to be able to afford this sort of 'luxury'. He 'dreamt' of a job which might pay "maybe £9 or £10 an hour – just enough to live on and put a bit aside and have a holiday. I don't know when we had our last holiday. I cannot remember our last holiday." In Chapter 5, we quoted Linda, 33. For her, one of the attractions of employment was that she could give her children a better life and show them the value of working. It would also allow her to take her family away on holiday: "… my ideal situation would be to be able to say [to the children] 'we're going to Disneyland Paris in six weeks!' That'd be absolutely brilliant, instead of just sat here thinking 'I'll never go on holiday with the kids'."

The pressures of poverty described in this study were the same as we have heard in previous research with young adults, particularly those who were parents. MacDonald and Marsh (2005) quote an interview with Kelly, a single parent, who described her attempts to budget carefully and to shop around, remarking: "You've got to be a millionaire to go in Morrisons! [a mid- to low-budget supermarket chain]." The same pressures are well illustrated by Chris, 32, who described not only the constraints of living on a low income (his JSA benefit), but also the strategies and sacrifices that 'managing' and 'getting by' demanded of him:

> "I put a tenner on each ['pay as you use' gas and electric meters] but sometimes that doesn't do. I mean I've sussed out turning off all your plugs and that helps you: just daft things just to save a couple of pennies [laughs]. Baccy [tobacco] – I don't get it from the shop. Fag houses [residential houses whose occupants deal in cheap, illegally imported cigarettes]. Because in a shop it's £13, odd. I get it for £6 so that saves me a bit.…Yeah, I go to all the cheap places like Heron [a discount frozen food shop] because there is bargains there, but I'm a fussy eater I can only eat like fish fingers, chips, burgers, sausage, pies – just plain things. I've just found in Sainsbury's they do four meals for £3 and they're big meals, like shepherd's pies, toad in the holes, things like that. I spend between £15 and £20 a week [on food, that is, around £2.50 per day]."

Like many interviewees, Chris paid for his utilities via pre-paid meters, but as the children's charity Barnardo's (2012, p 6) have found, such customers 'are most likely to be [from] low income households', 'paying a premium when compared to those on other standard or direct debit tariffs' and 'are more likely to be in fuel poverty than those using other payment methods.' This report goes on to state that at least 'four million households in England are living in fuel poverty' (Barnardo's, 2012, p 4), emphasising in particular the problem of this for families with young children and for disadvantaged young adults. In our study, older people, too, were also sometimes badly affected by 'fuel poverty'. This problem was not just one associated with the difficulty of meeting the costs of gas and electricity, but could also be caused by an inability to pay for expensive repairs. Janice, 56, and her husband Lennie, 57, had been unable to fund repairs to their broken boiler. They, like some of the other interviewees, had bought their council house under the Right to Buy scheme in the 1990s. As owner-occupiers they were unable to receive complete Housing Benefit towards mortgage payments when they were unemployed (as they were currently) and, of course, were responsible for household repairs. People in this situation sometimes seemed to face extreme hardship. Our interviews with Janice and Lennie were held during the winter months:

> Janice: "I mean we can't afford to get the heating done and that's not ideal, especially with me getting chest infections – but we can't do anything about it. You just have to get on with it, keep going sort of thing. Heating broke five weeks ago and we can't afford to have it fixed."

> Interviewer: "So how's it been for you? How have you managed?"

> Janice: "Cold! [laughs] There's no heating, there's no hot water...."

> Lennie: "We've been sleeping down here [in the living room, in front of a heater].... We listen to the weather forecast and because the past couple of nights it was due to plummet, so we stayed down here because up there [in the bedroom] it's freezing cold...."

> Janice: "It's bitter cold ... you can't even go in the bath to get warmed up because there's no hot water. There's

the shower but you're that bloody cold when you get out. So I go to me daughter's next door but one for a bath ... my bones ache, don't they? Really ache. I just cannot get warm. He puts that on full [points to electric heater] but I still cannot get warm, so it's pointless wasting the electric."

The Barnardo's report on fuel poverty (2012, p 5) found that people in financial poverty are 'increasingly having to decide between keeping themselves and their families warm or having sufficient food to keep them healthy', pointing to the impacts that this can have on 'all other areas of their life from relationships to mental health and other general health issues'. This resonates with our findings. In Chapter 8 we noted that it was women who took most of the responsibility for caring for others, including children. We also found that it was women who primarily had responsibility for managing household budgets (see, for instance, our later discussion of debt). Unsurprisingly, then, it was women who talked most explicitly about financial strain:

> "I walk to my eldest daughter's house and I'll ask her to give me a meal. I go to Sainsbury's about nine o'clock and look for all the reduced items. You'll buy a loaf of bread and it'll last you for four days. Reduced eggs they'll last you a week. I got half a dozen free-range woodland eggs for 20p the other day! So you've got six eggs. A loaf of bread, reduced vegetables, whatever it is, and I'll have vegetables with rice, bread and egg." (Amanda, 48)

> "If I want clothes or the kids want anything, it's always like getting the loan book out [from a doorstep loans agency], you know? I would, like, have to miss something to get something, if you know what I mean? It's awful. There's never anything in my purse. It's always empty. If someone said 'Do you want to go somewhere?' I couldn't just get up and go out and do it." (Sophie, 30)

Support from relatives helped interviewees to cope with these difficulties (see Chapter 8).

Being unable to provide essential items for children was often a source of great stress for the interviewees – particularly mothers – who frequently described going without things so that they could better afford things for their children. As we heard in Chapter 8, these stresses and strains could have implications for the interviewees' health and well-being. Mary, 30, was typical in her depiction of the effects of managing on a low income and how these stresses could filter out into daily family life:

> "We argued a lot [Mary and her partner Andy]. Not because of anything other than we had no money, just frustration at not being able to do the things we needed to do because we had no money coming in. Dylan's at the age he is where he's asking for pocket money and if he can go and do things with his friends and we couldn't do it and that was very difficult … it's just when the kids are wanting something and you can't do it, that's the worst. I think if it was just me and Andy we'd think 'It's fine we can manage on that' … [but] Dylan's just come home and said 'They're changing our uniforms at school', that we spent £200 on last August! So we have to fork out again and things like that. It's going to hit you and they have set up a thing where you can pay weekly but you don't want to be the kid at school who pays weekly. You want just to be able to go buy it so, stuff like that."

This picture of compromise, hardship and struggle that comes with poverty is a story that is rarely heard (Toynbee, 2003). Instead the public, once again, hear a clamour of tabloid media portrayals that shout that those living in poverty and relying on welfare benefits for survival are 'scroungers', 'the workshy' and 'benefit cheats' (Golding and Middleton, 1982). Yet our findings chime *exactly* with other more truthful, qualitative investigations of the lives of people living in poverty. Hooper et al (2006, p 4) also argue that in their study with families experiencing poverty:

> … poverty meant going without what the vast majority of people in the UK take for granted. Their lives were significantly restricted by poverty. Many could not afford basics such as a cooked meal each day for adults or toys for children. Constant prioritising and juggling were required – "robbing Peter to pay Paul" as some put it. In this context, the smallest things, such as deodorant or moisturiser, could become luxuries that had to be saved up for. Poverty was often self-perpetuating – for example, where poorly insulated housing meant increased heating bills. Many went

into debt to get essential items such as clothes or to pay utility bills.

Despite this financial strain, the participants were also keen to stress that they budgeted properly and managed well. They took pride in coping in adversity. Interviewees described their experiences with little sense of complaint which, as noted earlier, was part of their own moral narrative about themselves (positioned against others who failed to 'manage'). An angry sense of social injustice was notably absent from interviews, as was the case in our earlier studies with young adults (see MacDonald and Shildrick, 2010).

'In-work poverty'

In our investigation of the low-pay, no-pay cycle a key question was about the extent to which moving into jobs enabled people to get away from poverty. An important finding was that it did not, in any substantial or lasting way. 'In-work poverty' was a common experience for many informants. Welshman points out that 'poverty, work and wages have been the focus of much of the work of social investigators over the past hundred years' (2011, p 39), even if this has only come to the fore in UK government policy in the last few years (see Chapter 2, this volume). Holmes and Mayhew (2012, p 1) argue that the idea that 'the UK labour market has become more polarised into high wage "lovely" occupations and low wage "lousy" occupations' has gained currency and, like other commentators, they point to an 'increase in low wage work in the UK' (2012, p 1) (see Chapters 2 and 10). That employment provides the best route out of poverty was the mantra of the New Labour government and continues to be an axiom of the present Coalition government. The movement from 'welfare to work', rather than retention in work or tackling poverty that might remain even when people are in jobs, has been the predominant policy imperative. Of course, as this book shows, 'a job does not guarantee that work alone will raise enough income to escape poverty' (McKnight, 2002, p 97).

In 2011 the National Minimum Wage rose from £5.93 to £6.08 and, on the face of it, an adult working full time (on the National Minimum Wage) should receive an income that takes them (marginally) above the formal poverty rate. The reality is, however, more complex. As Ray et al (2010) conclude – from research within the Joseph Rowntree Foundation Recurrent Poverty programme (see Chapter 2) – issues to do with the nature of the job, household composition and costs and personal debt can all work to keep people in financial hardship even when they are in work. The Child Poverty Action Group (CPAG) (nd) have also noted that people who are unable to work *full* time – or who have other household members who are reliant on benefits – are also at risk of 'in-work poverty':

> Paid work is not, on its own, a guarantee of being free of poverty. In 2009/10, 58 per cent of income-poor children were in households where one or more adult in the house was in work. Low wages, part-time work and not having two adults in work in a couple household all increase the risk of poverty.

Each of these factors affected people and households in our study, undermining financial gains which could be accrued from being in work and diminishing the prospect of a job being a route away from poverty. For instance, Winnie, 44, had worked throughout her life (apart from when she took a break to care for her daughter when she was young), moving between jobs in caring, cleaning and shop work (see Chapter 8 where we discuss the impact of caring responsibilities on her and others). She was currently working in two part-time cleaning jobs so as to give her sufficient time to look after her grandson, thus leaving the opportunity for her daughter, a single parent, to work full time and not be "trapped on benefits". Because Winnie was working part time and fewer than 16 hours a week, she told us she did not qualify for Working Tax Credits, a benefit designed to 'make work pay' for low-paid workers. Thus, Winnie was someone we defined as 'persistently poor' (see Chapter 3). Indeed, she seemed to be in deep poverty. The income from her jobs gave her £576 a month. After her outgoings she was "left with barely anything":

> "I struggle, really struggle because by the time I pay my bills, gas, electric and water rates, TV, all that I'm left with a couple of pound that's it ... I wanted to work. If I didn't work I think I'd go crazy ... I mean, to be honest, somebody in my situation, I would probably be better off on benefits."

For others, the wages they earned were not enough to lift their households out of poverty when other family members were unemployed or reliant on benefits. As noted in Chapter 2, while the previous New Labour administration made some strides in tackling poverty for some sections of the population, 'the delivery of

Labour's anti-poverty ambitions was hampered by an unwillingness to countenance a wider range of labour-market interventions to reduce employers' reliance on low pay' (Coates et al, 2012, p 9). In other words, interventions such as Working Tax Credit – introduced in 2003 for certain low wage earners – have been criticised for subsidising and therefore entrenching low pay (see Chapters 2 and 10). Working Tax Credit payments are also limited to those working over 16 hours a week (set to rise to 24 hours with incoming, government 'welfare reforms'; see Chapter 10). Hence, many low-paid, part-time workers (like Winnie) simply did not qualify for support. Additionally widespread administrative problems have been reported with the administration of Working Tax Credits (Smithies, 2007), with some recipients reporting 'disastrous' experiences in claiming, resulting in payments that were unreliable and subject to frequent change (Dean and Mitchell, 2011, p 17). Furthermore, reliable sources predict that the introduction of the Coalition government's much heralded Universal Credit in 2013 will erode some of these gains (a discussion we return to in Chapter 10). The Institute for Fiscal Studies (2012) has argued that the changes to taxes and benefits will leave some households on average £160 worse off in 2012–13, rising to £370 a year thereafter. Furthermore, 'households with children and those in the lower part of the income distribution will feel the biggest impacts as a proportion of income' (IFS, 2012, p 1). Low-paid working families are going to be particularly hard hit. As Joyce (2012, p 2) points out:

> Projections of income poverty suggest that, on average, those on lower incomes are set to fare even worse in terms of changes in real income than those on middle incomes; in particular, the government's child poverty targets continue to be utterly unrealistic under current policies.

The changes to Working Tax Credit that came into effect in April 2012, which altered the number of hours needed to be worked in order to qualify from 16 to 24, have been argued to have a negative impact on working families, especially those on low wages. The Chief Executive of CPAG, Alison Garnham, said at the time:

> This will pull the rug from under the feet of hundreds of thousands of families desperately trying to make ends meet. It's shocking how many children in some places are going to be hit by this change and it is inevitable that many will be thrown into poverty. Just imagine how hard

it will be on low pay, with low hours and with kids to take care of when suddenly up to £70 a week gets taken away. (Garnham, 2012)

The problem of low pay was one of the most important issues that faced the interviewees. It was a crucial factor in understanding their experiences of poverty. Most interviewees accessed jobs on the National Minimum Wage (see Chapters 5 and 7 for a discussion of the exceptions). To repeat, this was a wage that those paying and those being paid it tended to refer to as a 'good' or a 'fair' wage (Chapter 5). Yet the reality is, of course, that the National Minimum Wage is the *lowest* legally payable. It falls substantially short of what others have defined as an acceptable 'Minimum Income' (Hirsch, 2011), or what has now become more widely known as the 'Living Wage'. As Savage notes, 'there are still 5 million workers – 20% of all employees – earning less than the living wage which is designed to provide a "minimum acceptable quality of life"' (2011, p 1). In short, moving into jobs that paid the Minimum Wage did little to relieve the interviewees and their households of poverty. Even when these wages managed to shift interviewees marginally above the poverty line, these 'poverty exits' were short in range (and often duration) and they rarely took workers to income levels that would allow for a reasonable or acceptable standard of living. The participants sailed perilously close to the poverty line, sometime rising slightly above it when in jobs, but they only ever found short-term relief in a status or group which, in the US, Newman and Tan Chen (2007, p 5) have called 'the missing class' or 'the near poor', a large group of people who 'no one pays attention to' and who work in low-paid jobs. They argue that 'the near poor' live 'close to the margins' (2007, p 5) and have a 'bleak existence' lived out 'cheek by jowl with the real poor' (p 8). For some of the interviewees, moving from being poor and sometimes deeply poor, to being temporarily 'near poor' did little to alleviate their predominant experience, which was one of everyday, lasting hardship.

Engaging with the benefits system

By definition, all the participants had experienced periods of unemployment. At these times, people were usually reliant on state welfare payments to survive. Benefits are not generous and purposefully set low under rules of 'less eligibility' (see Chapter 2). They provide meagre resources for people who typically have little, if anything, in reserve. Benefit payments fall short of official poverty levels and are even further from the MIS (proposed by the Joseph Rowntree Foundation) that the general public believe to be acceptable levels of income. Hirsch (2011, p 14) argues that 'basic out-of-work benefits provide well under half of the minimum income (net of rent and council tax) required for an adult with no children and somewhat less than two-thirds for families with children'. To give an example using the government's '60 per cent of median income poverty definition': the UK median income (before housing costs) for a couple with two children is £623 a week. Sixty per cent of that figure is £374 a week. If a family with two children have an income of less than this they are deemed to be living in poverty. A workless household with a couple and two children in it would receive £270 per week in benefits and would therefore clearly be living in poverty (Crossley, 2011). In respect of the MIS definition of poverty, Hirsch (2011, p 14) goes on to point out that 'over the past three years, small reductions in the adequacy of benefit rates have accumulated, so that the percentage of MIS provided by benefits has fallen'. More recently, proposed welfare reforms by the Coalition government stand to further reduce benefit payments, especially for those with large families or with high housing costs (Joyce, 2012). Quite simply, the inadequacy of the levels of benefits which interviewees received meant that when they were reliant on benefits they were also experiencing poverty.

There were, however, other issues relating to the benefits system, beyond levels of benefit, which impacted on the interviewees' lives and their experiences of poverty. As pointed out in Chapter 5, interviewees shared a strong dislike of claiming welfare. In part, this was a reflection of their commitment to working (Chapter 5), but it was also driven by a moral objection to being reliant on welfare and a desire to avoid the stigma of being in that situation. Across the sample, informants described feeling demeaned and depressed when they had to make claims:

> "Well I'm normally full of life, jolly and like … just the thought of going in and signing on…. Like I said, I just can't stand the place. If I didn't have to sign on – yeah, I'm not bothered about money myself, it's only the council tax and my rent. If I didn't have to pay them I just wouldn't go down there. It's just embarrassing. They make you feel like you're dumb, do you know what I mean?" (Andrew, 43)

> "I don't like it at all [claiming benefits]. I feel, like, suffocated; that they are waiting for me to do something. *I just hate it.*

I'm an independent person. I don't like relying on benefits. I just hate it. They turn into the FBI, questioning your every movement. It's like 'I just don't want to be here'. Just going to the job centre makes me depressed. I just detest it, I really do." (Chrissie, 31; original emphasis)

Making claims was rarely reported to be a simple or unproblematic process. Encounters were reported to be difficult and fraught with confusion and mistakes that often cost interviewees financially. Finn et al (2008, p 1) argue that despite significant changes to the delivery of frontline benefits, tax credits and employment services, there remains a 'failure to meet agreed service standards that agencies set themselves (including lengthy waits for payments, appointments and telephone responses)'. They suggest that:

> Some service users reported difficulties obtaining benefit claim forms. Forms often arrived late and some respondents were given incorrect advice about which forms to complete. The majority of respondents felt there were too many forms and that they were unclear, repetitive, unnecessarily long and time-consuming. Several respondents found completing forms stressful and felt they were too complicated. Some claimants complained of having to repeatedly fill in the same forms and provide identical information to that given previously. (Finn et al, 2008, p 1)

All of these problems were reported in our research. Claims were often described as being slow to be processed and the experience of making them was often mired in confusion. We quote Sinead (36) at some length, who had recently been made redundant from a high street chain store. Her experience was hardly unusual and her account captures the repeated misunderstanding that participants reported, as well as the consequences for their lives:

> "It's awful and because I'd never, ever done it before I didn't know what to expect. I went in [to Jobcentre Plus] and she said 'You're not entitled to any benefits' and I said 'Sorry?' and she said 'You're not entitled to anything'. I mean, I'd worked just about all my life: 'You're not entitled to anything because you haven't paid enough National Insurance over the last three years'. So I said, 'Well what does that mean?' She said, 'Well it means you can't get Jobseeker's Allowance

because you haven't paid enough contributions'. Well, then I got a letter last week to say that 'because I'd reapplied' – and I hadn't reapplied – 'because you've reapplied, you're entitled to £60 a week on Jobseeker's Allowance'. So I phoned 'em up and said, 'What's this about, I've been told I'm not entitled to anything?' and she said, 'Oh yes, you're entitled to Jobseeker's Allowance, £60 a week. It'll go into your bank account on Monday the 16th'. So yesterday I checked my bank account – no money in, so I phoned them up and she said, 'You're not entitled to it because you've got a partner', so I said, 'No, the lady told me I was entitled to benefits' and she said, 'No you're not entitled to anything because you've got a partner, he has to pay for you, phone family credit'. So we phoned family credit up [Working Tax Credit]. They won't give us any extra money till April because the new tax year starts in April. So I can't get no money from anywhere."

When we interviewed her, Sinead and her family were desperately hoping that 'the new tax year', in some months' time, would bring some sort of benefit payment to relieve the hardship the family were facing. As with Sinead's case, it was not unusual for interviewees to be on the receiving end of decisions that they failed to understand and yet felt completely powerless to challenge: "They don't believe you when you say you haven't received the forms but we have to believe them when they say they've sent them out ... in the end it took us nine weeks to get a penny" (Janice, 56).

Occasionally, for some interviewees, their hope that the spell of employment would be short, coupled with some other sort of financial backing (usually gained from a short period of better-paid work coupled with family support), allowed them to refrain from making a claim for any benefits. Aaron, 46, was a qualified French polisher and had occasionally managed to get better-paid jobs. He lived off previous earnings when he lost jobs rather than signing on: "For the first six months I lived on what I had and then I was dipping into my savings, so I went on the dole." Similarly, Laura, 31, and her partner – who had got short-term but well-paid contracts as a scaffolder – had been in and out of employment for years. For her, the process of having to claim benefits was a "right rigmarole ... basically he is out [of work] a lot more times than we claim. So we pay for ourselves basically, but it annoys you. It really annoys you." Avoidance of claiming benefits was not confined to those who occasionally managed to get better-paid jobs that could tide them over during periods of unemployment. André, 33, had worked in several different care homes over a 10-year period with short periods out of work in between. He earned just over the National Minimum Wage: "The whole thing repulsed me, signing on. I just couldn't be doing with it; sponging off the state. It's the hassle as well. You've got to sign on and then sign off and I just couldn't be bothered."

In Chapter 2 we reported how one welfare to work practitioner described the sort of informants to our study as 'the missing workless', because agencies like his rarely came into contact with them because of the relatively short-term nature of their unemployment. In other words, they were missed from many of the services on offer locally to help unemployed people into work. As described in Chapter 6, some actively strove to access voluntary sector organisations like Pathfinders although they had not yet been unemployed 'long enough'. This idea of 'the missing workless' is compounded by the fact that, as we discuss here, a proportion of the interviewees did not formally register as unemployed (or claim benefits) during some of their periods of unemployment. They were not only missing from support services for the unemployed but also from benefits eligible to them and official counts of unemployment. We return to this as a policy and practice problem in Chapter 10.

At the time of writing the Coalition government was rapidly reforming the welfare system and in the process of introducing the new Universal Credit, which, it was claimed, would simplify the benefits system (see Chapter 10). Yet the 'transitional impact' of the changes seems to have produced further problems. Early in 2012, Employment Minister Chris Grayling had to admit that a huge backlog of claims for sickness benefits had built up – 'We are probably about four months behind where we would wish to be and we're in the process of clearing the backlog' (quoted in Fagg, 2012) – resulting in claims being delayed for longer than 13 weeks. Dry ministerial statements give little sense of the personal pains and household hardships that delays and errors in processing claims often produce for those on the receiving end of the mistakes. Those in our research were already living in difficult and precarious financial circumstances and dealing with multiple hardships. They were ill equipped to weather these periods with no incoming money. Jennie, 47, had suffered a long period of illness but her benefits had recently been stopped as she was declared fit to return to work. She had been forced to move in with her mother just so that she could eat:

"And within a week they stopped my benefit. I had to fight it and it was five weeks before I was given a payment. I had to stay at my mam's. She had to keep me and she's a pensioner … I felt guilty because I couldn't contribute so I'd say, 'I'm not hungry, I'll get something later'. She'd say 'Well you haven't had anything today'. I felt like a little girl sometimes because she used to make me sit at the table and she'd say, 'You will eat', but I felt really bad that I couldn't contribute. It took five weeks before I got it back [her rightful benefits payment]."

Our subsequent research (see Shildrick et al, 2012) found much clearer evidence of the harsh effects of Coalition government welfare reforms as they were felt at the sharp end, particularly in respect of people being moved from sickness benefits to JSA. The Trades Union Congress has expressed concerns about the process, arguing that the new Incapacity Benefit tests were failing disabled people because the process has declared 'terminally ill patients and people with severe disabilities fit to work' (Barber, 2012, p 1). In our study, some interviewees, like Lennie, 57, reported that they had lost their sickness benefits and had been (wrongly in their view) told that they had to go back to work. Earlier in the chapter we described the impoverished and cold conditions Lennie and his wife were living in:

"I think it was before last Christmas, something happened with my benefit and I went down [to the job centre]. It had stopped for some reason. I think I had to go for an assessment which I failed and … I honestly can't remember what it was, but you go on a points system … I failed. That says 'You should be going to work, you should be working you should not be claiming'. I was saying 'I should not be going to work, I'm still ill. I know I'm ill. You don't know how I feel'. … I went off the benefit. It just suddenly stopped. So I went down to the Benefits Office with me wife and just said 'Look, all we're living on is just one income which is the wife's benefit, not mine'. They said the same thing back to me, they said 'There's nothing you can do', and we said, 'Surely there must be something you can do? We can't go on living like this. We're going to end up losing the house. We're going to end up on the street'."

From what we could gather from our interviews with Lennie, 57, and with his wife Janice, 56, Lennie appeared to have been recently declared fit to work and had had his Incapacity Benefits withdrawn (and he had not apparently made a claim for JSA – or at least was not receiving it). Janice was the only person to be receiving any benefits in their household, leaving them deeply poor. Given their age, their lack of recent work experience, the ill health that both suffered from (see Chapter 8) and, most obviously, the lack of job opportunities locally at the time, it seemed highly unlikely to us that, despite the official designation 'fit to work', Lennie would get a job. In respect of the welfare reform process of moving large numbers of claimants off Incapacity Benefits, Beatty and Fothergill (2011, p 1) argue that:

> Although some incapacity claimants will re-engage with the labour market, there is little reason to suppose that the big fall in claimant numbers will lead to significant increases in employment. Incapacity claimants often face multiple obstacles to working again and their concentration in the weakest local economies and most disadvantaged communities means they usually have little chance of finding work.

A finding from our interviews with welfare to work agency staff was that, from their point of view, the security provided by benefits was one of the key barriers facing them in trying to assist the unemployed into work (see Chapter 4). We found little, if any, evidence of this in our research and – while we sought out in this study those who were low-pay, no-pay 'churners' (and this might be an expected finding in this group) – we have found similar across all our other research with people living in deprived neighbourhoods (see, for example, MacDonald and Marsh, 2005). Rather than a picture of stability and security on benefits the interviewees' experiences of the welfare system were better characterised by instability, unreliability and insecurity. Indeed, the inability of welfare to protect the interviewees from poverty was one of the key reasons they got into debt.

Living with debt

Welfare benefit payments do not take into account the debts that people may have to pay. The majority of the participants carried substantial debts, many of which had built up over years. Ben-Galim and Lanning (2010, p 4) suggest that poverty and job insecurity increase vulnerability to debt problems. We found that poverty drove people into debt and debts helped keep people poor.

Given their pride in 'getting by' in difficult circumstances there was great reluctance to get into debt: "Desperate, sometimes you get desperate. I mean some weeks if you have to borrow off somebody, the next week you're in an even bigger hole" (Amy, 30). Debt was an added stressor and it was frequently implicated in informants' experiences of depression (see Chapter 8). Credit was often a lifeline for them. At times when they were left with no immediate income it quite simply allowed them to eat and to remain in their homes. Key factors or moments in people's lives that caused them to go into debt were of several types. First, necessity sometimes demanded the purchase of larger, more expensive items (such as furniture or kitchen 'white goods'), here purchasing on credit, particularly through 'rent to own' schemes, was usually the only option. Second, particular moments in the year – family birthdays and Christmas – brought extra expenses beyond the usual weekly budgeting. This was especially the case for those with children who wanted and often felt pressure to provide popular items (such as computers and iPods) as gifts (see Hamilton, 2012). The strain on mothers, in particular, to provide even more 'basic' things for their children was noticeable (Mary, earlier in the chapter, expressed her guilt and anxiety at not being able to provide adequate pocket money – and a new school uniform – for her son Dylan). Goode found in her research that women 'would "do without" basic necessities to privilege their children's needs' (2010, p 101). A third key reason for taking loans was the difficulties interviewees encountered when they were negotiating benefit claims – usually in the transitions from jobs to unemployment. Loans from some source were a necessity, for instance, when 'social security' claims failed, or when payments were slow or delayed, leaving people with no money to live off.

As Perry (2010, p 3) reports from research with low-income families:

> The 'poverty premium' [that is, the higher prices which the poorest families often pay for basic necessities like gas, electricity and banking] is a fact of life for most people on low incomes. Nearly everyone we spoke to was paying more than they might need to through: high-cost credit – using doorstep loans or rent-to-own agreements to pay for basic household items, cookers, fridge freezers or washing machines; prepayment meters/cards for gas and electricity and/or mobile phones; not being able to afford home contents insurance. In most cases, families felt that the more

expensive options were their only option because they were not able to save to pay for items in cash, could not get access to affordable credit, or were not able or willing to pay by direct debit.

Perry's findings were exactly mirrored in our study. Several of the participants did not have a bank account and their sporadic and limited incomes meant that none were able to access credit at normal interest rates. Occasionally people resorted to unregulated 'loan sharks', but most often it was from national chains of legal 'doorstep lenders' or catalogues that they obtained credit. These sorts of company specialise in loaning money to people on low incomes who have poor credit ratings and they also charge very high rates of interest. Expensive doorstep lenders were the predominant form of lending in our study. Such loans were taken for daily living costs as well as for larger goods, but interviewees expressed a strong view that loans should not be used to purchase 'luxuries' (things that others might regard as essential, such as holidays). We quoted Linda earlier and her dream of her going to Disneyland with her family:

> "I'd love to go abroad but in the end, the way I look at it, my house and my bills come before and I won't get in debt to go on a holiday because then you've got the debt to come back to. It's not right, it's not right! I'm not going to get in debt to do something like going on holiday." (Linda, 33)

Fluctuating income levels meant that interviewees often struggled to keep up payments for loans. These difficulties were usually resolved (often at the instigation of credit companies) by taking out further credit (that is, debt). Debts tended to be cumulative and doorstep lenders seemed routinely to offer clients further loans when they struggled to make payments: "Loans, well I've had to reduce everything. It's the worst way to do it, to bail yourself out. Because then you are putting yourself in deeper and deeper anyway, but sometimes you can't help doing that" (Winnie, 44). Pamela, 54, who was now a full-time carer for her disabled son, also told us of her problems with debts:

> "Oh I don't even know the balance! I pay £15 to the first two. The very last one I've told her I can't maintain that. I only told her [the debt collector] last Friday I said 'I'm going to get in a worse state having to borrow to pay you. I don't want to borrow again and get in that situation so

> I've been to the Citizens' Advice Bureau and he's told me to give you £1 a week but I'm not going to do that I'm going to give you £3 a week until my situation gets better. I will pay it off' and I said to her 'You go to doors where people sit and refuse to answer the door and I'm not going to do that to you'."

Sometimes interviewees obtained loans from Jobcentre Plus via the Social Fund, for example, and in these cases payments were deducted directly from benefit payments. This often served as a deterrent for many from taking them out, but additionally many people applied and were refused this sort of assistance, leaving them little option but to go elsewhere. Beyond doorstep lenders and the Social Fund, informants commonly borrowed from friends and family. This was a regular and necessary practice for many in the sample (see Chapter 8) but they could rarely afford to offer more than small amounts. We referred to Sinead earlier, and the confusing, changing and apparently incorrect messages she received in respect of her benefit claim. Because she had been told that she *would* be paid JSA on a given date (her claim was then denied), she borrowed money from her mother to tide her over until that point:

> Interviewer: "So it seems their mistakes and stuff have really affected you?"
>
> Sinead: "Yeah, definitely, because I'd borrowed the money. I said to my mam, 'I'm getting this money on this day and I'll be able to give you it back'. Now I'm panicking but my mam said it's alright. But I don't like to borrow money because I've never had to do it in the past and I don't like to."
>
> Interviewer: "So are your parents comfortable financially?"
>
> Sinead: "No, no my mam's on benefits so it's really hard for her as well. That's why I'm panicking because it's, like, her bill money that she has to pay next week. So if I don't get any money before then, it's making my mam worse off but she said 'Don't worry about it, something will come up'."

One of the key reasons that interviewees took out debts was problems in accessing benefits. Mary, 30, describes how she was forced to take out a loan via the benefits system when her partner, Andy, came out of work:

> "Just to keep us going because we were living off my family allowance [Child Benefit], which doesn't even cover the gas and electric. So we were borrowing money off family and getting loans off people coming to the door, just to keep us. We couldn't afford it so in the end we went to them and said, 'We need some help'. We should really have been entitled to a 'crisis loan' but they said we weren't entitled so we had to claim a 'budgeting loan' where you have to pay it back. They took so long! They are just not bothered there's a family there with no money or any type of income."

Benefit run-on payments that are meant to help people cope with the transition between benefits and employment had limited impact for the interviewees because these run-ons only lasted for a short amount of time, because people did not then access well-paid jobs and because their main difficulties related, in fact, to the period between losing jobs and accessing welfare. Benefit claims take time to establish, as do first payments. Sometimes these were severely delayed. Sometimes informants were not aware of the workings of the benefits system and what they might be able to claim. Liam, 33, said that he had been "lucky with work" and only unemployed occasionally and for relatively short periods. He took out a Social Fund 'crisis loan' in one such period, while waiting for his benefits to be sorted out: "Forty odd pound I got, something like that ... I don't know the ins and outs of the [benefit] system."

We finish this section with a vignette of debt from the study. Although having a work history that contained lengthy periods out of the labour market, as well as several shorter-term jobs, Debbie, 43, was currently employed. Her husband, Sean, was self-employed. The couple had bought their own home, previously a council-owned house, with the aid of a mortgage, even though neither at the time had steady employment with regular income (a classic case of a 'sub-prime mortgage'). She had been hoping to get a job that had then fallen through:

> "... with my money coming in we would have been fine but then that job didn't happen so we all went to pot and to find the money, just to pay the mortgage, never mind anything else, it is such a struggle."

Their fluctuating, unpredictable and sometimes non-existent earnings meant that Debbie and Sean could not keep up regular mortgage payments. The couple had looked into selling their house and moving back into rented accommodation but they faced substantial negative equity, and:

> "… with renting properties you had to have references and clear credit history so no one would take you on. All the waiting lists were so high because people were getting in the same situation. We are stuck between a rock and a hard place."

So, to cover mortgage repayments, they had taken out further loans, which they had then been unable to repay. In her words, Debbie "robbed Peter to pay Paul", selecting each month which debt repayment to default on. On the morning we interviewed her, Debbie had been "hiding from the bailiff" and she had worried that she might mistake our call for his or not be able to let us in case he was nearby: "He's given us 24 hours to pay, they want at the last count nearly £700 and we haven't got that, so…." Debbie was frightened of the bailiff arriving at any time and potentially forcing entry, taking furniture and other household goods – particularly when her children were in the house. She described how her family was "just making it day by day, really". Working at the same time as living in poverty (a description she denied) – and burdened by these debts and threats – felt "just pointless". When asked about the future she said she looked forward to being in a position "in five or six years' time" where she would:

> "…be happy if I could say 'I'm able to pay my bills and I don't owe the bailiffs'; that would be nice to be able to say that. I don't care about extra money and stuff. It would be nice to be able to say 'I can pay my bills'."

Conclusions

A key conclusion of the study is that neither work nor welfare protected the interviewees from poverty. Most struggled to get by when they were in jobs as well as when they were unemployed. Low wages and inadequate benefits combined to leave interviewees in positions of poverty, or near poverty, at all times. These findings tally with those of Ray and colleagues (2010, p 1) in their study of poverty, work sustainability and progression among low-skilled workers: 'many people experienced financial strain and "struggled to get by" while in work.' Importantly, they found that 'those in short-term intermittent work were *especially* prone to feeling financial strain' (2010, p 1; emphasis added). In this chapter we have identified several reasons or processes that might explain this and which worked together to mean that the low-pay, no-pay cycle was one that tied people to recurrent poverty.

First and most simply, when individuals were unemployed they claimed benefits set at levels *designed* to pay below the government's most used poverty line – and substantially below what others argue is necessary for a standard of minimum income (see Chapter 2). The informants in our study were working-class people with few capital resources; their reliance on benefits set them as poor (even if this was a label they rejected because of the social stigma that attaches to it and because of the moral pressure to distance themselves from others they regarded as undeserving and unable to 'manage' common, everyday hardship). This stigma, and the hassles and failures of the benefit system, sometimes allowed by savings from better-paid jobs, meant that some people even avoided claiming benefits during periods of unemployment. This is one of the reasons we characterise them as 'the missing workless'.

Second, while it is difficult to disagree that employment might be 'the best route out of poverty' (see Chapter 2), we have seen that for the people in our study this is not an easy contention to maintain. The National Minimum Wage was intended to reduce 'in-work poverty' but if people only access *part-time* jobs (and the hours worked mean they are ineligible for Working Tax Credits), then the pay from employment can still leave individuals below the official poverty line (Winnie, quoted earlier, was a good example of this predicament). In any case, failures in the payment of benefits, including of Tax Credits, meant that, in effect, households were sometimes left with very little to live on.

Third, poverty is usually assessed at the household level. An *individual* accessing part-time or even full-time work paying at the minimum rate does not mean that the household overall is lifted out of poverty. While packages of benefit support including Working Tax Credits are designed to tackle this problem and 'make work pay', the fact that, by official measures, most children living in poverty live in households where at least one adult is working, signifies the extent of this problem beyond our own study.

Fourth, the jobs people got were characteristically low-paid and the fact of entering employment brought with it costs that, to an extent, offset gains from wages (over benefits). Most significant here were the costs of childcare (see Chapter 8) but travel costs were also, if not a barrier to going into jobs (see Chapter 4), a barrier to jobs bringing a substantial financial bonus to households. Better Off Calculations (BOC) are tools used to encourage the unemployed from 'welfare to work' (see Chapter 4 again). When the costs of going to work are factored in, *in practice*, the outcomes of such calculations did not always show that people would be clearly better off in work. As this chapter, and its predecessors, have shown, however, the limited *financial* advantages of employment (over benefits) were not a deterrent to people continually seeking to make this move from 'welfare to work'. The appeal of work was much more than this (Chapter 5).

Fifth, transitions between employment and unemployment (and vice versa) brought costs to individuals and their families that they usually had to meet themselves, from limited resources. Moving from a job to unemployment was most fraught with difficulty because establishing or re-establishing benefit claims took time and, as we have seen, apparent failures in the process could sometimes leave individuals and their families with no income whatsoever. At these times, borrowing from others – family and friends or doorstep lenders – was a necessity. In Chapter 6, we referred to Richard's experience of private employment agencies. His case provides a perfect example of our point here. The failure of a private employment agency to deliver the extensive work contract it promised meant that Richard had had to take out a doorstep loan at a high interest rate to tide him over (to pay his rent and to buy food) until his benefit claim was re-established. He was now carrying a debt of £500 over his time in jobs and on benefits, and was currently struggling to pay this off from his weekly JSA payment. His was a clear case of how going back to work had a deleterious impact on his financial situation.

Sixth, debts are not included in technical, poverty assessments (or in the allocation of benefits). Even though on the face of it some participants might have 'officially' sat above the poverty line when they moved into jobs, the effect of these debts meant that they were in practice below it (because repayments eat into earnings and disposable incomes). As we have seen, debts were a widespread fact of life for people cycling between unemployment and low-paid jobs and coping with the everyday hardship of life in poverty. Some got caught in a spiral of expensive and cumulative loans that they struggled to manage and pay off. Other recent research has also demonstrated how 'the poverty premium' affects low-income households, meaning that already disadvantaged and impoverished people were further disadvantaged and impoverished by the types of debt and repayment regimes that were open to them.

Finally, and most importantly for our discussion in this book, work did not provide a route or ladder out of poverty, not only for the reasons listed above – and because of the low-paid nature of work available – but because of the inherent insecurity of that work. Income gains that could potentially be made through moves into jobs were not only insubstantial in their amount but, crucially, were not long lasting. For most of the informants, the low-pay, no-pay cycle meant that they might make small, regular steps to just above the official poverty line when they moved into jobs but they also made regular steps back down when jobs were lost. Better than metaphors of 'routes', 'stepping-stones' or 'ladders' away from poverty, the participants seemed more to be caught on a 'waterwheel' that dipped them under the official poverty line before lifting them above it, before the wheel turned again, forever churning between low-paid jobs and even lower benefit payments.

10

Conclusions

Introduction

So what have we learned about the low-pay, no-pay cycle and poverty? The first part of this chapter very briefly reviews the key findings that arose from the research reported in earlier chapters of the book. Following this we discuss how best we might explain and understand these experiences of labour market churning and poverty, situating our case study of Teesside's working poor within a broader, more global discussion of economic change, poverty and place. Following this we discuss the key policy conclusions that arose from the project. Insecurity of work and income (from employment and from welfare benefits) and the poverty that resulted were perhaps the dominant motifs that described the lives of the informants. In the next part of the chapter we enquire into what *could* be done in respect of tackling this insecurity and poverty. There is an emerging body of research that argues and practice that demonstrates that 'bad' jobs can be made 'better', and we discuss some of the strategies that could be employed to this end. In the third part of the chapter, we briefly discuss what *is* happening in respect of current welfare to work policy and poor work in the UK, demonstrating the disconnection between what, on the basis of our evidence, should be done and what is actually being done. The final part of the chapter – 'the great myth and the great illogic' – reflects critically on current policy and politics about the poor and the workless.

Key findings from the research

This book has been about how and why people become trapped in a long-term cycle of low-paid jobs and unemployment (the 'low-pay, no-pay' cycle). This is one of the first concerted studies in the area; relatively little is known about people's repeated movements into and out of poverty over the course of their lives and, in particular, how this recurrent poverty links to the low-pay, no-pay cycle and broader experiences of disadvantage. A key aim was to understand the dynamics of poverty and marginal work across the life course and, drawing on in-depth life history interviewees, to illustrate the consequences of this for the lives of individuals and their families. Our research in Teesside provides a case study example of the wider processes of labour market polarisation that relegate some to a life of hard work in low-paid temporary jobs that neither relieve poverty nor provide pathways up and away from it. As noted in Chapter 2, the problem of people moving repeatedly between work and unemployment is endemic in the UK, rising by 60 per cent since 2006. Importantly the study has shown that this pattern of working is not simply the preserve of young adults but that these patterns continue for most well into adulthood. The inclusion of older interviewees in the sample who also shared this pattern of working life adds to the limited knowledge we have about this sort of work pattern and questions policy assumptions that regard these as 'entry-level', 'stepping-stone' type jobs reserved for younger workers or new economic migrants.

The research points to the resilience and lasting work commitment shown by the interviewees, despite the Sisyphean frustrations and setbacks associated with their repeated periods of unemployment and low-paid jobs. This strong work attachment was learned across generations, where parents and grandparents had also worked and passed on the importance of 'working for a living' to younger interviewees. Related to this, it would not be an overstatement to say that the interviewees deplored claiming welfare benefits, with some, where it was possible, refusing to claim all together. The strong work ethic and loathing of claiming welfare was not just inherited from older generations but was also reinforced by the participants' direct experiences. Being in employment taught interviewees the social and psychological benefits of working, even if jobs did not readily provide financial benefits. On the other hand, being unemployed dealt interviewees detrimental consequences for their health and well-being. These personal experiences all served to bolster their commitment to work.

In the main, the participants were relatively low qualified but had positive attitudes towards gaining further training and skills, and this helped some into 'better' quality jobs. A significant finding of the study was, however, that *overall*, for these interviewees, levels of educational attainment did *not* predict improved labour market fortunes. Even the best qualified – those with degrees and diplomas – participated, at least at times, in 'low-pay, no-pay' churning labour market careers in the same ways as the least qualified. Jobs were most often lost because of deficiencies in the jobs themselves, although as the research has shown, other facets of disadvantage, in particular the sheer preponderance of ill health both across the sample and in their wider family, meant that interviewees sometimes had to leave jobs voluntarily or were sacked for necessary short periods of absence. Ill health and depression were in part influenced by insecure employment and unemployment, and could then in turn inhibit further employment. Mothers often found they had to choose between fulfilling family caring duties and remaining in employment. Similarly, attempts to improve job prospects through education and training were often thwarted by caring responsibilities. These sorts of contingencies and critical events that interrupted work commitment are likely to be more common in deprived neighbourhoods than more generally. People simply did not have the resources to cope easily when things went wrong. The capacity to do and sustain work cannot be separated from household economies or situations, but could be better supported by better-quality jobs (as discussed later).

Contrary to the widely held view that 'employment is the best route out of poverty', the sorts of work available to the interviewees kept them in poverty rather than lifting them out of it. The study found that individuals and households would repeatedly experience poverty both when in work and when out of it. The poorly supported transition period between work and benefits, and vice versa, would often bring additional hardship. Despite the clear hardships that people faced, many were resistant to claiming welfare benefits, and the welfare system was experienced as slow, inefficient and demeaning. It did not provide social security for these interviewees. Interviewees did not describe themselves as poor and they were keen to stress that they budgeted properly, managed well on what they had and that they coped. A sense of pride at getting by and coping in adversity was clung to in opposition to the stigma and shame that still attach to the words 'poverty' and 'the poor'. With only a few exceptions, the defining features of the lives of the interviewees were poverty and economic marginality. Their economic marginality was demonstrated in their relegation to churning low-pay, no-pay careers at the bottom of the labour market. The effect of this marginality was widespread and lasting experience of poverty, over working lives. For us, the most disturbing aspect of our findings is that this occurred among people who possessed strong, resilient work motivation and who had repeatedly engaged with work. An inescapable conclusion is that necessity, along with people's willingness to work – their acceptance of poor work – drives its offer and continuation, trapping individuals in vulnerability and insecurity.

This is what we found in our study, put in the simplest of terms. In the next section, we ask how we might best explain the stories that people told to us. How and why were their lives like this? How typical were their experiences? What sat 'behind' their life stories that caused them to be how they were? What were the broader processes that created the sort of poverty and insecurity that characterise life in low-pay, no-pay Britain?

The myth of the high skills economy, underemployment and poor work: a new precariat?

There is certainly no shortage of evidence that the UK labour market is one that has changed drastically in what many describe as a general shift from Fordism to post-Fordism, during the latter decades of the 20th century. Chapter 2 described some of these trends in general and Chapter 3 did so in respect of Teesside. Sissons (2011) reports that, more recently, over the last decade or so the UK has witnessed a growth in the proportion of jobs at the top and bottom of the labour market leading to even further polarisation of poor and better-quality jobs (see also Holmes and Mayhew, 2012). At the bottom end of the wage distribution, there continues to be an abundance of low-wage work in the UK (Lloyd et al, 2008), the work done by the informants. This is the sort of work that does not require high level or indeed any qualifications (see Chapter 4), and which was predicted to wither if not disappear completely under visions of a 'high-skills, information economy'.

MacDonald (2011) argues that while the supply of better-skilled workers is proportionately set to increase markedly by 2020, this does not necessarily mean that there will be proportionally increasing demand from employers for those skills. In fact, important research by IPPR (Lawton, 2009) argues that although the number of people with no qualifications seeking work in the UK is likely to drop from 2.5 million in 2006 to around 600,000 in 2020, without concerted policy action the number of jobs requiring no qualifications is likely to remain at around 7.4 million. In the same vein, Keep and Mayhew (2010, p 569) argue that emphasising up-skilling as the solution to unemployment or low-paid working ignores 'the scale and persistence of low-paid employment within the UK economy ... the numbers of jobs requiring little or no qualification appears to be growing rather than shrinking'. They report that employers at the lower end of the labour market find 'little difficulty in filling vacancies' and show 'little demand for a more skilled workforce ... low-paid work in the domestic [UK] economy remains and someone has to undertake it if the economy and society are not to collapse' (2010, p 570).

The implications of this predicted mismatch between the supply of workers with higher level skills and qualifications and the demand for such workers from employers are numerous and profound (MacDonald, 2011). Just one of these is that we are likely to see increasing underemployment among better-qualified people, that is, in the sense of individuals working in jobs below their level of qualifications. Already Sissons' analysis of data from the BHPS shows that '5% of immobile low wage earners had qualifications at degree level' (2011, p 26). Even more strikingly, recently released data from the Office for National Statistics (2012) showed that the proportion of recent university graduates employed in lower-skilled jobs has increased from just over a quarter (26.7 per cent) in 2001 to over a third (35.9 per cent) by the final quarter of 2011. It is important to note that 'recent graduate' here means graduated within the last six years; we are clearly not just talking about the normal process of graduates taking time to 'settle into' higher-level jobs. It is also important to dwell on the definition of 'low-skilled work'. This refers to the sort of work that people may be qualified for on the completion of compulsory education (at age 16).

There has clearly been more than a little hype about the economic demand for high skills in the UK economy (see Brown et al, 2011, for an extended discussion). While there is no doubt that particular forms of further and higher education (at particular colleges and universities) are the high road to the better jobs at the top of the labour market described by Sissons (2011), for many others these extended educational transitions are now the low road to lower-quality, lower-paid jobs nearer the bottom of the labour market. One obvious implication for un- or under-qualified people, like those in our study, is that opportunities even for the sort of work they normally got will become more rare, as those with higher skills and qualifications 'bump down' the labour market (even into the lower skilled jobs reported by ONS, 2012). In reflecting on changes in the employment rate that accrue to people with different levels of qualifications as they have changed during and since the recent recession, Sissons (2011, p 19) points out that 'the much greater fall among those with no qualifications' compared to those with degrees is likely to reflect in part 'the nature of increasing competition in the labour market for lower wage occupations'. Recent journalism shows this happening 'on the ground'. Gentleman (2012) quotes a manager from a major welfare to work provider, currently employed under the government's Work Programme (discussed later) to help place workless people into jobs:

> It is a hard labour market and our job is made harder by
> the state of the economy and there not being the jobs out
> there. There are [ex] public sector workers fighting for
> the jobs that our clients are fighting for [jobs such as care
> assistants, security guards and shelf-stackers]. The long-term
> unemployed are pushed further down the list.

Over-qualification for the job is one aspect of underemployment.
There are competing definitions (see, for example, ILO, nd; Scurry
and Blenkinsopp, 2011), but Roberts (2009, p 10) is useful, even
though he focuses on young people, because he includes 'high rates of
unemployment' as well as 'high proportions of employment in part-
time, temporary and otherwise marginal jobs; and over-qualification
relative to the jobs that young people obtain.' Even working with a
narrower definition (that is, those working on a part-time basis who
would prefer longer hours), the IPPR (2010b) report that there are
2.8 million 'underemployed' people in the UK, and that the number
of underemployed men has increased by over a half during the UK
recession. Underemployment is not a UK-specific problem. For
instance, on the basis of his extensive research and analysis in East and
West Europe, Roberts (2009, p 4) has argued that 'underemployment
is the 21st century global normality for youth in the labour market'.
Underemployment is likely to be greater among young people because
they are making transitions into the labour market (and, generationally,
have been beneficiaries of the opening up of extended educational
pathways which, paradoxically, over-qualify them for the work on
offer). It is not, however, a phenomenon restricted to the young, as the
evidence from the IPPR, above, shows.

Following Roberts' definition, clearly what we have been describing
in this book are facets of underemployment (albeit that over-
qualification for the job was not common in our sample): that is, high
rates of unemployment and employment in part-time, temporary and
otherwise marginal work. The most important sense in which the
informants were underemployed was that there was not sufficient,
lasting employment for them.

This discussion and critique of the 'high skills economy thesis' and
depiction of underemployment as characteristic of the informants'
working lives may be steps towards but are not explanations in
themselves of the low-pay, no-pay cycle reported in this book. So,
how might we explain this widespread underemployment – of the
informants and more widely?

There is a tendency – for instance, in theories that posit the emergence of 'an underclass' – to see the sorts of people we engaged with in our research as 'surplus to requirements', sloughed off by rapid economic change and advancement in late capitalism, left behind because of their low skills, lack of qualifications and other personal deficits. This sort of reading positions underemployed and marginal workers as clinging on but soon to be jettisoned by an economy that no longer needs them. This requires belief in the myth of 'the high skills economy', a thesis we have argued to be fundamentally flawed. Low-paid, low-skilled work remains abundant, and even workers with high skills (for example, graduates) are now finding themselves having to do such work. A much better explanation can be found in the analysis by David Byrne (1999) in his extended discussion of 'social exclusion'. This, we think, provides an extraordinarily useful theoretical and political frame for our findings and argument, not least because his empirical examples and arguments so closely match our own. For these reasons, we quote it at some length here. Counter to contemporary theses (see, for example, Bauman, 1998) that position the sort of 'poor people' we talked to in our study as now completely redundant as either consumers or producers, Byrne argues that, in fact, their role as performers of poor work – and this is the term favoured by him as well (see Chapter 2) – is 'absolutely intrinsic' to post-industrial capitalism (Byrne, 1999, p 56). Underclass theory is flawed for many reasons (see MacDonald, 1997), but one of these is its misunderstanding of the common experience of work and welfare for working-class people in post-industrial capitalism. Rather than being a wholly abandoned underclass relegated to permanent worklessness, the informants to this book, Byrne would suggest, are better understood as being members, in the Marxist terminology, of a 'stagnant reserve army of labour' who are 'absolutely crucial' to the contemporary economy (Byrne, 1999, p 56). In criticising underclass theses that posit the complete exclusion from work for those at the bottom, Byrne makes a point that loudly echoes our own findings and argument:

> ... what is missing from that story is the significance of the combination of low wages, insecure employment and dependence on means tested supplements to low incomes. In other words, the [flawed] account is one of separation from work, not obligation to engage in poor work. *Poor work is the big story.* (Byrne, 1999, p 69; emphasis added)

Byrne's analysis of social exclusion is one that emphasises its processual, dynamic qualities. Mirroring our biographical interest in recurrent poverty and long-term work histories, this leads him to try to understand lives dynamically, as biographies through time, rather than in terms of snap-shots of individuals at any one moment. In doing this in respect of working-class people in post-industrial capitalism, Byrne argues that one obvious 'set of experiences' that will be seen is:

> ... long-term unemployment with dependency on low level benefit. However, we might well find, and indeed will find, that a set of individual/household trajectories which involve low paid work as the normal experience with considerable experience of unemployment punctuating such low paid work, is much more significant and represents *the most significant kind of excluded life in our sort of society*. (Byrne, 1999, p 74; emphasis added)

We have found what Byrne predicted would be found. Thus, for Byrne, *the most important form of social exclusion currently is what we call in this book the low-pay, no-pay cycle*. Byrne is attracted to the concept of social exclusion in part because it draws attention to processes of power and asks who or what is doing the excluding. His answer implicates social exclusion as 'a necessary and inherent characteristic of unequal post-industrial capitalism' (Byrne, 1999, p 128), supported by political elites in the UK, almost of all whom argue for the 'necessity for a "flexible" labour market in a competitive globalised world' (1999, p 9) and who have conspired in the 'systematic constraining of the organisational powers of workers as collective actors' (1999, p 128). Thus, if neoliberal, post-industrial capitalism requires a reserve army of labour to be drawn into and out of the flexible labour market that has been created since the 1970s, then governments need social policies that will facilitate that project of flexibility that defines post-industrial capitalism. Workers are required for and required to do the poor work that flexible labour markets create. Prime among these are 'welfare to work' policies. Strongly reminiscent of our discussion of the activities of welfare to work agencies (Chapter 4), Byrne reminds us that sensible 'solutions [have] to be demand led' but:

> ... Welfare to work is supply side. The interpretation is that workers are defective, not morally or even rationally as was the understanding in the early 19th Century.... but in terms of personal deficits. The obligation on them is to redress

these personal deficits, as a condition of benefit, in order to make themselves fit for labour. There is no specification of the conditions of that labour as having to represent "good work". The logic of the employment form of much of post-industrial capitalism is that the work will not be good work. However, people have to be made to do it.... Welfare to Work is a constitutive process for this. (Byrne, 1999, p 99)

Another key text for our discussion here – introduced in Chapter 2 – is Guy Standing's *The precariat* (2011). While we see some significant disagreements between Standing and Byrne, particularly in how each pictures contemporary configurations of the class structure and the extent to which insecurity is a defining condition of a new 'dangerous class', as Standing would have it, there would seem to be some agreement that behind the emergence of the poor work that is central to Byrne's analysis of social exclusion and the precarious work that is fundamental to Standing's argument is a similar set of global economic and political processes. *The precariat* opens with this statement:

In the 1970s, a group of ideologically inspired economists captured the ears and minds of politicians. The central plank of their 'neo-liberal' model was that growth and development depended on market competitiveness; everything should be done to maximise competition and competitiveness, and to allow market principles to permeate all aspects of life. One theme was that countries should increase labour market flexibility, which came to mean an agenda for transferring risks and insecurity onto workers and their families. The result has been the creation of a global 'precariat', consisting of many millions around the world without an anchor of stability. (Standing, 2011, p 1)

Some 12 years earlier, Madanipour and colleagues (1998, pp 7-8) described exactly the same process as it unfolded in Europe:

Increased global competition leads employers to transfer risks onto the workforce wherever possible. As the balance of employment throughout Europe has shifted from manufacturing to the new service industries the transfer of risks breeds new forms of insecurity among large segments of the workforce, through increased part-time and temporary working and self-employment, and creates new pressures on household and kinship structures in providing support for their members. As global competitiveness has become the rallying cry of neo-liberal governments throughout Europe ... welfare state systems of support for households and individuals are being reconstructed in order to reduce public expenditure.

The outcomes of these globalisation processes at a European level have more recently been described by Frazer et al (2011a, p 2). These processes have produced significant 'structural changes in the organisation of economic and social models' with 'deep changes in economic, employment and social spheres' across many developed countries. The growth in the knowledge-based economy has been accompanied by the growth of structural unemployment. They go on:

The combination of all these different mutations in economic, social spheres has contributed to the recognition of a new form of poverty in Europe. The European labour markets have experienced across the last decades a growing segmentation and casualization or employment, with the relative expansion of lower quality jobs, characterised notably by low wages or limited hours or temporary duration or bad working conditions. (p 3)

Returning to Standing, while he describes many pressures towards 'precariatisation' – and the diversity and heterogeneity of the proposed membership, social conditions and social problems said to constitute the precariat as a class is one of the reasons we remain doubtful about his thesis *in toto* – there remains an emphasis on the neoliberal politics and free market thinking of governments from the 1970s in creating the conditions in which the precariat is said to have emerged. Thus:

One neo-liberal claim that crystallised in the 1980s was that countries needed to pursue 'labour market flexibility'. Unless labour markets were made more flexible, labour costs would rise and corporations would transfer production and investment to places where costs were lower; financial capital would be invested in those countries, rather than 'at home'... in essence, the flexibility advocated by the brash neo-classical economists meant systematically making employees more insecure, claimed to be a necessary price for retaining investment and jobs. (Standing, 2011, p 6)

In Chapter 2 we raised some questions about Standing's argument and its fit with our research, specifically the extent to which his depiction of the precariat captures the experiences of the research participants. There we drew attention to some apparent differences. Here we emphasise similarities. Standing (2011, p 10) says that the precariat consists of people who lack seven forms of labour-related security that were pursued by social democratic and labour parties and trades unions after the Second World War (labour market, employment, job, work, skill, income and representation security). Although he is at pains to point out that not all members of the precariat will share all these forms of insecurity, by our reading of Standing's definitions the participants experienced them all – in ways that have been documented in this book. According to Standing, then, they are archetypal members of the precariat. As noted, we are not certain that we agree with his thesis overall but nevertheless, it is one that has very successfully drawn attention to the growth of insecurity in the working lives of substantial sections of the populace. It has also served well our particular purpose here – along with the other sources in this section, particularly Byrne's investigation of 'social exclusion' – to demonstrate the economic and political processes that sit behind and help explain our qualitative story from Teesside of poverty, insecurity and the low-pay cycle. At the same time, these studies have shown that the experiences described in this book are not special or unique to Teesside; they have global provenance and resonance. As Byrne himself commented in respect of some of our earlier research, Teesside may be 'one of the most deindustrialised locales in the UK' but 'the trends are general' (Byrne, 1999, p 93).

This is confirmed by some further, recent research about the central subjects of our study that was published just as our book was going to press (in November 2012). We report this briefly, to conclude this section. These studies point to the growing scope and reach of poverty and insecurity in Britain caused by the factors described and analysed in this book. According to a comprehensive study of the finances of employed households commissioned by *The Guardian* (Hill, 2012a, 2012b), almost 7 million working-age adults are living in 'extreme financial stress', *despite being in employment and largely independent of state support*. These 3.6 million households have little or no savings or home equity and struggle to feed themselves and their children adequately. These findings challenge the political mantra of all three political parties that 'work is the route out of poverty' and the Work and Pensions Secretary Iain Duncan Smith's recent argument that 'parents should get a job to ensure their children are not brought up in poverty' (see *The Daily Telegraph*, 13 June 2012). Consistent with our study's findings, the head of Experian Public Sector, Bruno Rost, who conducted the research for *The Guardian*, using their own database and government research, described a 'new' emergent group of the 'most deprived' categories in British society, those who are working but are nevertheless suffering high levels of financial stress. Described by Rost as 'traditionally proud, self-reliant, working people ... these are the new working class – except the work they do no longer pays' (Experian, 2012).

Like our study, these more recent studies directly challenge the government's claim that employment straightforwardly lifts people away from poverty – 2.2 million children live on the edge of, or in, poverty, despite one or both adults earning low to middle incomes (Resolution Foundation, 2012). Those at risk of slipping into official poverty vary from region to region and cannot be described narrowly as exclusively northern or inner-city and are also found across large parts of South West England, outer London and East Anglia (Resolution Foundation, 2012). Meanwhile, Oxfam recently found that more people in poverty were working than were unemployed, and the number in work but claiming Housing Benefit had more than doubled since 2005 (Moussa, 2012). Overall, since the economic crisis of 2008, those already in poverty have seen their poverty deepen, and millions more have become increasingly vulnerable (Moussa, 2012).

Poverty, insecurity and poor work: what *should* be done?

In what follows we wish to reflect on what might be done about the poverty and poor work that our study described, and which the passages above have sought to explain. We are not in the business of saying nothing is possible, short of the full-scale dismantling of the late capitalist economy. Change is necessary, if we are to challenge the poverty and insecurity of the low-pay, no-pay cycle, and we believe it is possible. We do this in the full knowledge, of course, that, first, all of the policy suggestions we make in this chapter run directly counter to the current tide of prevailing policy and politics in the UK and, second, even if they were enacted, the sorts of suggestions we describe will do little to overturn the inherent inequalities of an economic and political system that generates poverty and poor work in the first place. So this chapter is about describing steps – reforms – to welfare and to work which are imaginable and which, if taken, would undoubtedly change the lives of the informants for the better. If we accept that welfare to work policies, as broadly understood, are ones that have been configured to *feed* poor work – a key argument of this book, begun in Chapter 2 and continued above – then it is not beyond our imagination to reflect on how they may be reconfigured to *tackle* poor work. Another key contention of the book has been that the eyes of politicians and policy makers have been too fixed on the supply side of the labour market. Let us take pronouncements about 'employment being the best route out of poverty' and 'making work pay' at face value as truly meant, and consider then how policy might better do this, given what we have learned from this study. This, as we have argued, necessarily means turning our eyes towards the demand side of the economy.

Making bad jobs better: routes away from poor work

In the UK, the US and elsewhere there is a growing body of research and policy practice that insists that 'bad jobs' can be made better. A key proponent here is the US academic, Paul Osterman, who, with colleagues, has examined in detail a range of approaches and measures that might 'make bad jobs good'. Osterman and Shulman (2011, p 4) comment that:

> It is both possible and desirable to address job quality directly and to encourage employers to provide better work for those at the bottom. There is a great deal of evidence that a combination of carrots and sticks can lead to considerable progress and we believe that the nation will be much better off for the effort.

In the US, Osterman (2011) reports 24 per cent of adult workers work for wages that pay two thirds of the median wage and 19 per cent are in jobs that pay below the poverty line. 'There will always be hotel room cleaners and food servers and medical assistants and the myriad of other low paid jobs', but that people are *trapped* in these jobs is the real policy problem: 'the evidence is clear that most adults holding these jobs will not escape from them over their working lives' (Osterman and Shulman, 2011, p 3). Osterman (2011) argues that the normal policy responses to the problem of low-paid jobs (for example, creating jobs and up-skilling the workforce) are necessary but not sufficient, arguing that, first, while moves towards full employment help, some people will still be left in poorly paid jobs and, second, that better qualifications and skills do not guarantee freedom from low-paid work (see Chapter 6). Thus, working with, and pressuring, firms and governments to improve jobs at the bottom is necessary.

There are different dimensions to the policy proposals that Osterman and Shulman set out in the key text *Good jobs America* (2011): creating more quality jobs, improving access to good jobs and, what we concentrate on here, making bad jobs better. Policy could enforce change through legislation (with the UK's National Minimum Wage being a good example, or alternately via tax incentives to improve pay), and Living Wage campaigns could pressure employers particularly, but not exclusively, in the public sector, to make low-paid jobs better paid (an idea we return to shortly). Local authorities could, for instance, develop 'contract compliance' arrangements where suppliers, sub-contractors or those seeking agreement for commercial property development are contracted to provide jobs at the Living Wage. Osterman (2008) points out that unionised jobs typically pay substantially more, highlighting the role a revived trades union movement might play in tackling bad jobs.

Not only can employers be 'pressured' to improve jobs via governments and trades unions, as with the examples above, they can be 'helped' along this route, Osterman argues. Examples given include human resources strategies that invest in training and the development of progression routes – or 'career ladders' – within firms (Osterman and Shulman, 2011). Sissons (2011) concludes from his discussion of the persistence and growth of low-waged work in the UK (discussed earlier in relation to the hollowing out of middle-range occupations in the UK) that policies need to be developed to increase the wage mobility of workers *within* the work that they do. He, too, draws attention to the potential for 'progression opportunities for low wage workers with the same employer' (2011, p 32), pointing to the value of 'career ladders'. He cites several examples from practice in the US in the healthcare and customer services sectors which chiefly involve investment in training that allows workers to gain the skills and qualifications necessary to moving up to higher grades and types of work in the same organisation (for example, the Jobs with a Future Partnership, based in Wisconsin, created a six-week training programme in phlebotomy which enabled low-paid nursing assistants to graduate to entry-level phlebotomist positions). Sometimes, Osterman (2011) argues, there is a role here for 'intermediary organisations' employed by the firm to provide training for employees and for US community colleges to become involved with employers in the provision of training to people while in employment. Sissons (2011) draws attention to research that shows that some industrial sectors and organisations are much better suited to the provision of career ladders than others (chiefly reflecting the proportion of good and bad jobs in the organisation or sector).

Schools, hospitals and banking, he says, offer better opportunities for advancement schemes than some sectors, as do larger rather than smaller organisations.

Some research has been able to demonstrate that investment in strategies to make bad jobs better need not run counter to the profit motive of private sector business. For instance, in the US retail industry, Zeynep (2012) recently concluded that 'good jobs' are actually good for employers as well as employees. Highly successful retail traders can invest in their workers while also keeping prices low and making strong profits: 'bad jobs are not a cost-driven necessity but a choice' (Zeynep, 2012, p 3). Our study identified a small number of interviewees who had been able to escape recurrent poverty and the low-pay, no-pay cycle via their engagement with better-quality employment (Chapter 7). As a counterpoint to the majority experience of churning around insecure jobs that offered little career progression, they worked for employers that offered jobs that retained them (for example, employers adopted a sympathetic or at least non-punitive attitude to employees' personal troubles) and helped them advance in work (for example, by investment in training and support for gaining qualifications that led to internal promotion). Given the right encouragement, we imagine that some of the larger employers for whom the interviewees worked could be persuaded to adopt better employment practices, that would help people advance from low-paid jobs, of the sort described in this section (the most obvious examples in Middlesbrough might be with the university, health service and local council employment but innovations such as 'career ladders' need not, of course, be restricted to public sector employment).

Osterman (2011) recognises the challenges facing policies and strategies to make bad jobs better. These include the necessity of sustainable state funding to support these efforts, the challenge of 'scaling up' local examples of good practice so as to seriously confront extensive low-paid work and, like Sissons, the difficulties presented by (or to) smaller employers who may lack the resources to make investments in their workforce and the necessary scope for internal career ladders. A key point Osterman makes is that the project of making bad jobs better can and needs to be 'sold' to employers in terms of their own interests, that is, that this can increase the performance and profitability of the firm. He is also clear that there might be limits to what could be done:

> We know that it is possible to design effective interventions that up-grade the quality of jobs and that improve the

> working experience of low wage employees. ... despite
> these accomplishments, however, it is not clear just how
> far it is possible to go with interventions of this kind.
> (Osterman, 2008, p 43)

He points out that problems may arise because progress can be very slow and there are also difficulties in working with employers, especially in difficult economic times, who may have more pressing issues and particularly with smaller-scale employers who have little experience of or scope for human resource initiatives (for example, it would be difficult to imagine some of the employers in our study, the corner shop, the local cafe or hairdresser salon, wanting or being able to consider the possibility of career ladders for employees; see Chapter 4).

A recent ESRC seminar in the UK, with international participants, drew together policy makers, employers, representatives of think-tanks and academics to investigate how to make 'bad jobs better'. As well as a discussion of strategies such as career ladders, it argued that better infrastructure such as transport and improved childcare opportunities could all help people to move towards better employment opportunities. A key conclusion of the seminar series, however, was that governments have a key and important role to play in facilitating improvement (Lloyd and Commander, 2011). So, while much can be done and is being done by local actors (such as community groups, trades unions, councils and employers), real impact and change is only possible if facilitated and encouraged by central government (Lloyd and Commander, 2011). For instance, within the ESRC seminar series Phillip Barron discussed the London Development Agency's Career Ladders Programme. This was an ambitious programme operating in the retail and hospitality sectors of the labour market to assist those like the interviewees to achieve job progression. Barron argued that the scheme had real potential to boost social mobility and produce benefits for the economy, but he also reported that the scheme was soon to fold because of government cutbacks (Lloyd and Commander, 2011).

Making bad jobs better: paying a Living Wage and improving conditions

We would strongly recommend the value of trying to improve progression opportunities for people in poor work, but we would also caution against assuming that such progression is necessarily desired by all of those who do poor work. Many of the interviewees spoke positively about the jobs they undertook; there was strong commitment expressed by some for working in the care sector, for example. As well as thinking of how we provide routes *away* from low-paid, low-status poor work, we need to address how to improve the quality of jobs that remain at the bottom of the occupational hierarchy. After all, they will always need doing and need people to do them. We turn to this question next. It seems to us that there are two key aspects here: raising the pay of poor work and improving its conditions.

Osterman (2008, p 44) argues that 'improving low wage work is the next frontier of labour market policy'. Low pay is only one facet of bad jobs and, of course, not all low-paid workers are poor (Solow, 2008), but for the interviewees the levels of pay that they earned was a key factor in their continued poverty (Chapter 9). Thus, we would concur with Solow that low pay is a '"social condition" which needs to be improved' (2008, p 2). There are no simple mechanisms to get employers to raise rates of pay. Osterman (1988) argues that unionisation is important in this respect (see earlier), although in the UK this is an area where much ground has been lost over the last three decades, with many of the lowest-paid occupations non-unionised.

One alternative strategy can be found in the emergence of Living Wage campaigns that, after some success in London, are taking shape in other parts of the UK, including North East England. In essence, these are campaigns that seek and then work with broad local support (for example, from faith and community groups, trades unions, charities) to lobby local employers to raise the pay of their low-paid staff (upwards from the statutory legal floor of the National Minimum Wage and taking into account the local cost of living). Living Wage campaigns had initial success with public sector employers but have also successfully worked with large, private sector firms. Hirsch and Moor (2012, p 4) point out that 'in the ten years since its launch, the Living Wage campaign has become a powerful force for change in London. Initially dismissed as impossible, it is now recognised as a compelling cause which offers benefits to workers, employers and to wider society.' Research suggests that over 10,000 families have been lifted out of poverty in London because of the impact of the Living Wage. Critically, Living Wage campaigners and researchers argue that benefits do not simply accrue to workers in their pay packets. For instance, Wills et al (2009, p 2), through research with cleaners at Queen Mary, University of London, found that 'the move [by the university] to be a living wage employer and bring the cleaning service in-house has stimulated improvements in job quality, productivity and service delivery, with very little increase in costs'. They argue that there can be 'very real business gains' for employers who pay the Living Wage (Wills et al, 2009, p 21).

This conclusion was shared by one of the projects within the wider Joseph Rowntree Foundation programme of research on recurrent poverty (see Chapter 2). Metcalf and Dhudwar (2010, p 1) found that paying above the National Minimum Wage also helped reduced job insecurity and improved staff retention; 'some employers could switch to offering higher paid, more secure jobs without damaging their business' (see also Goulden, 2010). The Fair Pay Network suggest that there is now a 'substantial amount of evidence that fair pay policies bring a string of unexpected benefits to the employer as well as to the individuals who feel their pay levels rising' (2012). These include increased efficiency and productivity as well as enhancing the company's reputation as a fair employer. For instance, Mark Constantine, Chief Executive of Lush (a chain of cosmetics stores and now 'a Living Wage employer'), is quoted as saying: 'if I am honest it makes business sense to pay a living wage because staff can deliver [sic] better service if they are not worrying about the rent' (quoted in Fair Pay Network, 2012). As more employers commit to paying the Living Wage, campaigns for it can pick up momentum; after all it does not make good public relations sense for a business to be known as one that prefers *not* to pay its workers a Living Wage.

More broadly, the campaign for a Living Wage has the potential to tap into apparent public support for the idea that income for workers should be 'fair'. While there may be rather less public appetite for policy agendas that seek to tackle 'poverty' or 'inequality', there is some evidence that 'fairness' is a discourse that holds more sway with the public. For instance, an interesting study by Lawton and Lanning (2011) examined the issue of 'fairer pay' for those caught up in 'bad jobs'. They examined attitudes to pay among people at different levels of the pay scale (very high earners to low to medium earners). Their findings included that while there was *some* concern about income inequality, there was relatively strong support for the status quo, with participants subscribing to a meritocratic philosophy that high pay was a legitimate reward and low pay reflected less effort by workers. Nevertheless – and this is the important point for our discussion here – the study uncovered concerns about the discrepancy between very high and very low pay. The theme of fairness – that everyone contributes, therefore everyone should be appropriately rewarded – was popular with the research participants. Lawton and Lanning suggest that greater workplace democracy is one avenue through which fairer pay could be achieved, but acknowledge that the political trend is currently not running in this direction in the UK. For us, the key point of their research is its demonstration (of at least the potential for) strong public support for the idea of a 'Living Wage'.

Tackling poor work is not just about creating workplace ladders to help people move away from it or paying people higher wages for doing it. Schmitt (2012, p 10) argues that 'the intense policy focus on low pay can obscure the reality that low pay is often among the least of the labour market problems facing low-wage workers.' Lack of access to basic employment rights, such as holiday pay and time off for sickness, mean that, particularly in countries like the US with weak welfare protection systems, 'low-wage workers face a host of problems beyond low wages' (Schmitt, 2012, p 10). Lloyd and Warhurst (2010) agree, noting that 'bad jobs' are not just characterised by low pay but also by limited benefits, sick pay, leave, pensions and lack of union representation through which to be able to exert their own influence over working conditions. Lloyd and Warhurst (2010) also point to lack of certainty around working hours (particularly for those with variable and 'zero hours' contracts). These descriptions of the poor conditions of employment were all ones described by the informants to our study (see Chapters 7 and 8). Bambra (2011) argues that providing better terms and conditions of employment, where workers have more control over their work, is likely to increase a sense of job security (for instance, by reducing the risk that crises in people's wider lives necessarily leads to the loss of a job) and to lead to better health outcomes for employees. In 2004, the Citizens' Advice Bureau argued that, as a result of extended workplace rights introduced by the New Labour government since 1997, millions of UK workers were benefiting from policies such as the right to apply for flexible, 'family-friendly' working and the right to paid paternity leave. They went on to give this important caveat:

> Hundreds of thousands of the most vulnerable and low paid workers in the UK economy, many of them performing unglamorous but essential tasks, have yet to benefit from the Government's strategy. They are nonunionised, and are working from home or in small workplaces such as care homes, hairdressers, bars, restaurant and hotels, shops and other retail centres, food processing factories, cleaning companies, and other low-skilled or 'service' jobs. (CAB, 2004, p 3)

It is worth noting that this description of the *sorts* of employment that are less likely to have benefited from government action, and therefore to have poorer conditions of employment, almost exactly matches the sorts of employment done by the informants in our study. The Joseph Rowntree Foundation programme as a whole reached the conclusion that employers can develop human resource and employment strategies that reduce the need for temporary and flexible jobs (ones that often have some of the worst conditions of employment) by moving away from core to periphery staffing models. Drawing on this research, Goulden (2010) argues that such improvements to employment conditions might be made relatively easily and at little cost. However, we echo Osterman's argument (above) that employers may need 'pressuring' as well as 'helping' to improve conditions of employment. There is a clear implication in the description given by the Citizens' Advice Bureau (above) – that the worst conditions of employment tend to be found in workplaces and jobs that are not unionised – about the role that trades unions need to play here.

Social security not insecurity

We have suggested some ways that poor work may be improved, via building ladders away from it, by increasing the pay that comes to it and by seeking ways to improve its conditions. While it is implied in some of the research and practice we have discussed that the insecurity of poor work will be lessened by such changes, none of them are directly concerned with or seem able to contend with the extent of the insecurity of the low-pay, no-pay cycle that our study uncovered.

This is one reason why we need to consider not just improvements to 'the low pay' side of this couplet but to the 'no pay' element of it too. Second, even if *were* able to reduce job insecurity substantially, we are a long way from a state of 'full employment'. As noted in Chapter 3, for instance, regardless of the booms and troughs of the national economy, Middlesbrough has generally suffered at least twice the national average rate of unemployment for three decades. Regardless of how many of the workless are able to find jobs, there will always be some individuals who have to rely on welfare, for shorter or longer periods. In this short section, then, we turn from work to welfare. What can be done to address the poverty and insecurity that typified the informants' lives?

The people in our study wanted jobs. As we have described, that they experienced spells when they did not have them was chiefly a function of the nature of local labour market opportunities (a conclusion not just of our study but of the Joseph Rowntree Foundation programme as a whole). In those periods, reliance on state welfare benefits that are designed only to provide for subsistence, and that follow the long-held principle of 'less eligibility' (Chapter 2), *made people poor*. For example, Kenway (2009) estimates that JSA (taking into account that other costs, such as housing, will be met by other benefits) provides around only half of the income necessary to avoid being in poverty, as officially measured. For the interviewees, this problem of 'below the poverty-line benefits' was worsened by failures in the administration and processing of benefits, by risks and costs of the transitions between welfare to work and back again, and by the long-term debts that this all necessitated. Because, as we have shown in this book (see Chapter 9), work does *not* always provide a route out of poverty, and because the exigencies of the current UK labour market, and attendant welfare to work policies, currently demand and encourage engagement in poor work that regularly returns workers back to unemployment, we believe there is an overwhelming *moral* case to raise people out of poverty by raising welfare benefit levels. Kenway's review of the arguments for and against raising JSA concludes the same: 'the balance of the argument is clearly in favour of an increase in JSA' (2009, p 6).

At the time of writing the UK Prime Minister, David Cameron, has declared that 'we *can* make British poverty history and we *will* make British poverty history' (HM Government, 2012a, p 3; emphasis added). Later, we refer to questions of logic. For the time being, the only logical conclusion that can be drawn from this statement — and given the argument above — is that if we share ambitions to 'make poverty history', then we must raise the level of welfare that unemployed workers receive. While welfare benefits remain at subsistence levels, poverty will never become history.

Poverty, insecurity and poor work: what *is* being done?

In the second part of this chapter we turn our attention from what should, in our view, be done to tackle problems of recurrent poverty and the low-pay cycle to what is being done, as manifested in current UK government policy. It is important to record that the Coalition government is not ignorant of the problem of low pay churning. One of the earliest documents it published discussed poverty, worklessness and welfare dependency in the UK. It contained this statement:

> Even before the recent recession too many people experienced 'churn' between low-paid jobs and out-of-work benefits. The usual snapshot unemployment data miss this issue. Almost one million people made five or more claims for Job Seeker's Allowance between October

> 2000 and March 2010. While a high churn rate can reflect
> a system that is working well in encouraging people to
> accept temporary jobs instead of benefits, the prevalence
> of repeated claims over a period of years suggests that
> more could be done to help people turn an employment
> opportunity into sustained employment. (HM Government,
> 2010, p 28)

As far as we can see, however, this early recognition of the problem of
the low-pay, no-pay cycle has not been followed by significant policy
initiatives to tackle it (for example, of the sort described in the previous
section). Instead, the Coalition government has undertaken a major
programme of reform of the welfare system. Although there would
appear to be agreement between the major UK political parties that
this is needed (so as to simplify benefits and to ensure 'work pays', so
that people are not 'better off on benefits'), a major spur to undertake
it has been because of the government's perceived need to tackle the
UK's fiscal deficit via major cuts to public expenditure. The welfare
budget has been targeted for cuts of at least £15 billion. According
to the Welfare Reform Act 2012, reforms were aimed at making the
tax credits and benefits system fairer (to the taxpayer and to claimants)
and less complex, and at incentivising employment while protecting
the vulnerable. The key changes were the introduction of the Work
Programme (in 2011) and of Universal Credit (in 2013). Evidence
from our research shows that the benefit system often failed to meet
people's needs, either quickly or adequately, so any moves to address
these deficiencies must be welcomed.

Universal Credit

Because of its complexity and the extent of changes we are only able
to make partial comments about Universal Credit here. Means-tested
benefits for working families have been in existence for over 30 years
(Frazer, 2011) but were given extra impetus by the New Labour
government's desire to tackle child poverty and to 'make work pay'
(for example, with the introduction of Working Families Tax Credit,
which later split into Working Tax Credit and Child Tax Credit, both
of which provided weekly MIS for working families). These measures
have met with some success (see Chapter 2) and have been credited
with taking some children out of poverty (Cooke and Lawton, 2008).
Hills et al (2009) also argue that these measures have helped to keep
in-work poverty rates lower than they might have been. There are signs

that Universal Credit will have some positive impacts on lower earners. It aims to make it easier for people to take jobs and to keep more of their income, as it will be withdrawn more slowly than existing means-tested benefits, thus arguably 'eliminating the scope for claimants to face very weak work incentives' (Brewer et al, 2012, p 2). The government's recent raising of the income tax threshold will also mean that lower earners keep more of their wages (Osborne, 2012).

Yet research shows that there will be 'winners' and 'losers' with Universal Credit. Brewer et al (2012, p 4) argue that although it will 'strengthen' the incentive to work for many, it will also 'weaken incentives to work for (potential) second earners in couples, who will see Universal Credit withdrawn more quickly if they enter work than currently happens with tax credits'. Raising the tax threshold for low earners (in the 2012 Budget) may have been a step in the right direction towards raising the wages of low-paid earners, but many are forecasting minimal gains for the lowest earners as these have to be offset against the withdrawal or reduction of other benefits (CPAG, 2012). As the Resolution Foundation (2012) argue, 'couples with children are set to lose £479 a year on average as a result of the tax credit cuts, more than double the £203 gain they can expect from changes to the income tax and National Insurance Contributions system'. Changes to Working Tax Credits and the time lag between the implementation of these changes (April 2012) and the introduction of the Universal Credit in 2013, have resulted in significant income loses for poorer working families. Bell and Brewer (2012) point to one of the most detrimental aspects of this aspect of government welfare reforms:

> A change in the tax credit rules, announced in the 2010 Spending Review, means that a couple claiming Working Tax Credits, will now be eligible only if at least one of them works 24 or more hours a week, rather than, as used to be the case, if at least one of them works 16 hours or more a week. Some of the couples affected by the change will find that, if they are unable to increase their hours (and 78% of those affected families surveyed by USDAW said they would not be able to find additional hours) then they will hardly be any better off in work – and in some cases, actually worse off – than they would if they were not working instead of receiving benefits.

As Polly Toynbee (2012b) has put it, bizarrely for a government so committed to 'making work pay', changes to Working Tax Credits appear to be targeted *against* exactly those 'hard working families' that politicians love to praise. Estimated by the Treasury to come to a saving of £2 billion over four years, CPAG calculates that around 200,000 working families will typically each lose £3,870 per year in Working Tax Credits unless they can find extra part-time hours to work, and that the effect of this one change alone could be to push 35,000 families into poverty (Davies and Butler, 2012). In Middlesbrough 560 families containing 1,325 children stand to be negatively affected by this change (CPAG, 2012).

Moving away from the issue of tax credits, we can reflect on an apparent hardening of welfare policy under the Coalition government. Its emphasis on tackling 'welfare dependency' and 'making work pay' is by no means new and, most recently, was also a characteristic of the New Labour government's mixture of carrots and sticks to encourage the workless from welfare to work (see Chapter 2). However, cuts in welfare and in-work benefits (as with the Working Tax Credit, a general cap on benefits to households, the linking of benefits to the Consumer Price Index rather than Retail Price Index and so forth) signal a turn towards a more punitive approach to the poor, justified, they argue, by the need to reduce overall government spending. 'Making work pay' appears to be more about constraining or removing benefits than improvements in jobs or wages: 'less eligibility' reigns (see Chapter 2). Wright (2012, p 1) sums up these welfare reforms as follows:

> Receiving financial support from the state when unemployed or unable to work (because of ill health, disability or caring commitments) is harder now than at any time in the last 60 years. Driven by unequivocal cost-cutting and an ideological drive to tackle 'welfare dependency', eligibility criteria for a range of benefits have been tightened, and claiming benefits is more conditional on actively seeking work – backed by harsh penalties for non-compliance. Furthermore, benefits are paid at low (often inadequate) rates, which are set to devalue over time.

Thus, according to commentators like CPAG (2012), the claim that Universal Credit will improve work incentives and reduce complexity in the benefits system are not only unproven, but are predicated on a major extension of conditionality running in tandem with a harsher sanctions regime. Thus, at the time of writing, the Coalition is steaming ahead with some of the most punitive policies towards the workless that this country has ever seen, with the Universal Credit alleged to create an unprecedented increase in sanctions and conditionality, imposing work-related requirements on virtually all adult claimants.

Part of the ideological justification for this is the continuing insistence by government (and not restricted to this one) that labour market behaviour is governed by financial incentives alone (see Chapter 2), that benefit levels are sufficient to inculcate 'dependency' and that, therefore, for many, unemployment may be a 'lifestyle choice' (Osborne, 2010). In other words, a fundamental assumption of the reforms remains that the problem of unemployment and poverty is a supply-side one of the personal characteristics, behaviours and lack of work incentives of the unemployed. Thus, according to the Department for Work and Pensions (DWP, 2011a), 'many people on benefits perceive the financial risks of moving into work as too great. For some groups the gains to work, particularly at low hours, are small, and any gain can easily be wiped out altogether by in-work costs such as transport' (an argument that was popular with the welfare to work agency staff that we interviewed; see Chapter 4). Thus, policies around welfare and work still operate from the position that the workless need to be 'activated' and encouraged to embrace 'positive attitudes to work' and to understand that work should be 'the norm', with such attitudinal changes claimed to be notoriously hard to achieve (Marangozov and Dewson, 2011, p 3).

The Work Programme

This interpretation of unemployment and the view of the unemployed informs the second main policy avenue that the Coalition government has instituted to tackle worklessness. This is the Work Programme. Replacing a host of other programmes set up by New Labour, the Work Programme is the flagship programme intended to assist the workless into jobs. Via contracts set up with major private sector welfare to work providers (who then sub-contract with smaller, often voluntary sector agencies), a key aim is to provide quicker and more long-term support to the workless (with a strong focus on retaining people in work, not just the initial movement into a job) (DWP, 2011a). Given a key finding of our study, that a main problem for many was not getting work but getting work that lasted, these are aims that we applaud. There is a strong emphasis in the Work Programme on 'sustained job outcomes', which, in the case of those deemed furthest from the labour market, means remaining in a job for two years. For other groups this is interpreted as 12 or 18 months. Welfare to work providers are paid by results, to a maximum payment of £13,700 for placing one unemployed person in a job for two years (if he or she is deemed to be in the 'hardest to help' category).

Although evaluations of this programme were not available at the time of writing, it had come in for considerable criticism by this point (April 2012). In particular, voluntary sector organisations have described difficulties in the funding and working arrangements of the programme. Holt (2011), for instance, reports findings from a survey undertaken by ACEVO (Association of Chief Executives of Voluntary Organisations) which found serious concerns about the likely success of the Work Programme in meeting its targets and particular concerns about the way that voluntary sector organisations were being funded and supported to work with those most disadvantaged in the labour market. The report warned of 'systemic failure' unless some of these problems could be addressed (see also BBC News, 2011c, which raises similar concerns over the viability of the programme).

We would add three further criticisms. First, the presumption again is the age-old one: the unemployed are so because of their deficits. Intensive support from welfare to work providers will enable their movement into jobs. Perhaps the fundamental problem, that employability schemes of this sort do not create employment, is why only 8 per cent of the voluntary sector organisations that responded to the ACEVO survey felt that the Work Programme was likely to hit its targets. An early report on the Work Programme by the National Audit Office (2012, p 4), while positive in some respects, also noted that 'there is a significant risk that they [the DWP] are over-optimistic' in respect of the potential of the programme to place clients into jobs, in part at least because of the state of the national economy. Second, while emphasising sustainability in employment, the Work Programme does not appear to recognise the problem of the low-pay, no-pay cycle. Overall, the programme is mainly geared towards those 'at risk of *long-term* unemployment' (DWP, 2011, p 5, our emphasis), with help also available for those with disabilities and other labour market disadvantages (who can qualify more quickly for support). People on JSA and over the age of 25 are only eligible for the programme after they have been unemployed for a year. Thus, given their relatively short periods of worklessness – and their churning around jobs and unemployment – many of the participants in our study would be ineligible for the Work Programme; they would remain 'the missing workless'. A key conclusion of our study is that better support should be extended to the short-term unemployed in order to help them access better-quality, lasting jobs and to make progress through employment. In addition, the introduction and wide availability of a careers guidance service for adults could play a role in reaching 'the missing workless' and in helping people escape the cycle of low-paid and insecure work. Third, there is another sense in which the Work Programme appears to ignore the low-pay, no-pay cycle. There is an admirable emphasis on lasting employment but this is not matched by any apparent interest in moving unemployed people into *better-paid work*. Gentleman (2012) provides a journalistic account of the experience of one Work Programme scheme in Hull (as noted, however, formal evaluations are not yet available). The sort of work that the 'success stories' from this programme were getting was typical of the sort of work done by informants to our own study: work as security guards, shelf stacking in supermarkets, care workers, factory cleaning. Much of this work was part time and all was low paid (agencies receive their government payments so long as participants withdraw from benefits, regardless of whether the job is full or part time). Given the history of welfare to work schemes in feeding poor work (see Chapters 2 and 11), we would support the suggestion from Sissons (2011, p 47; emphasis added) that:

> ... Work Programme providers offer not just a route into work, but a route into work that offers the chance for progression – something which is of critical importance in addressing the low-wage/no-wage cycle between work and benefits. In this context it may be appropriate for policymakers to look at ways to set incentives that encourage and *reward progression in-work as well as sustainability*.

To conclude this discussion of the Work Programme mention needs to be made of its introduction of much greater conditionality and sanctioning of benefits. As we have seen with Universal Credit, unemployed people face greater threats and risks than previously in their engagement with government welfare to work programmes. Although the 'right' to benefits has long been conditional on the 'responsibility', for instance, to 'actively seek work', recent work experience schemes for young adults under the Work Programme have finally ushered in a more complete version of 'workfare' (that is, that the receipt of benefits is dependent on undertaking work). There are several work experience programmes available to jobseekers, including the Mandatory Work Activity scheme, which, as its name implies, is a compulsory scheme officially aimed at inculcating work behaviours in those regarded as lacking them. This scheme requires six to eight weeks unpaid work for up to 30 hours a week. 'Customers' who fail to participate in or complete the scheme (or are dismissed from it) lose their unemployment benefits for 13 weeks. If a second 'failure' is recorded within the same year, 'customers' stand to lose their benefits for six months. This is welfare to work with a big stick. Not only has this aspect of the Work Programme come under heavy fire for apparently forcing unemployed people to work unpaid in low-quality jobs that offer little chance of permanent recruitment, it also has been challenged for seemingly offering employers a steady stream of free labour, thus substituting the need to offer these work experience positions as jobs. As *The Guardian* journalist Deborah Orr (2012) explains: 'the trouble with the work programme as it operates at the moment is that it puts out fire with gasoline. It offers companies a steady stream of free labour, just at a time when the emphasis should be on creating stable and lasting employment.'

Public services and the poor

The lives that the informants led were not just ones that centred on work and welfare and they were not just affected by government policy in respect of work and welfare. One outcome of Coalition government spending cuts will be that already disadvantaged people and places will be disadvantaged further (Giles, 2010). Evidence for this comes from the think-tank, the Institute for Fiscal Studies (IFS). Arguments following the government's first Budget in 2010 centred on whether it was progressive or regressive. The IFS argued that the government was only able to make claims for a progressive budget if measures announced by the previous government, omitting large welfare cuts to the poor and ignoring cuts to public services (of which the poor are the heaviest users), were ignored. The IFS Director, Robert Chote, said at the time: 'perhaps the most important omission in any distributional analysis of this sort is the impact of the looming cuts to public services, which are likely to hit poorer households significantly harder than richer households' (quoted in Giles, 2010). In one of the first, in-depth analyses of the early effects of government cuts to local authority spending, research for the Joseph Rowntree Foundation (Hastings et al, 2012, p 7) concludes that 'the national evidence clearly suggests that the biggest impacts will be felt in the most disadvantaged local authorities.' Surveys by Voluntary Organisations Network North East (VONNE) demonstrate the effect of public sector cutbacks on charities and other voluntary sector groups that provide services for disadvantaged groups in North East England (see Butler, 2011). Based on responses from 120 charities in the region, it shows many to be battling for survival as a result of cuts. Demands for their services are rising substantially at the same time as 73 per cent have seen a reduction in funding and 40 per cent a loss of staff. One in five organisations reported that they will or may close. More focused research on the same topic by Clayton et al (2012) comes to similar conclusions, albeit stressing the professional commitment of staff to continue to deliver services under these austere circumstances. There is a 'double whammy' here. Not only do we see a threat to organisations that work successfully with disadvantaged people (Chapter 6 showed how some of the better employment support services experienced by the informants were ones located in the voluntary sector); they can also offer better-quality employment. Chapter 7 noted how the three people in our study who had managed to 'escape' recurrent poverty and poor work had all done so by securing employment in exactly the sort of not-for-profit, voluntary sector organisations that are now faring so badly under government austerity drives. Our own research locality has fared badly already (see Chapter 3). The first round of cuts made by Middlesbrough Council included the closure of a range of public services, with associated redundancies (for example, four libraries, eight youth and community centres, various services for the disabled, subsidised bus services, dial-a-ride schemes and some local sports and leisure facilities). Many of the libraries and community centres in which we met and talked to research participants are now closed, at the time of writing. As bad as these early hits from the government's austerity measures may be, writing in February 2012, the journalist Polly Toynbee warns us, however, that at this stage it is impossible to see the full effects of cutback to public services because: 'only 6% of public service cuts have happened yet. Another 94% are still to come, with cascades of more public servants sacked. In benefits, 88% of cuts are still to come' (Toynbee, 2012c).

Conclusions: the great myth and the great illogic

To end this book we briefly dwell on two themes, what we call 'the great myth' and 'the great illogic'.

In this book, particularly in Chapter 2 and this one, we sketched out how the poor and unemployed are located and seen, not just in the history and contemporary examples of public policy, but in the popular view too. Returning to the opening of the book we are reminded of Polly Toynbee's comment that the real lives of ordinary people living in poverty usually remains invisible. Part of our objective – during the empirical middle part of this book – was to make them visible. In doing so we believe we have provided enough evidence to declare that much of the way that the poor and workless are described is false. In other words, much that claims to speak of the poor and workless are myths (see Shildrick et al, 2012). These are old, powerful and widely held myths, but myths nonetheless (Welshman, 2007; PSE, 2011). They tell us that people are poor because of their own behaviour (if they really are poor at all), that – now in the name of social justice – the unemployed need to 'change the way they think about work and its wider benefits' and need encouragement 'to take the leap into employment' (HM Government, 2012b, p 39), that the problem of young adults being unemployed can be resolved by coercing them into unpaid 'work experience' in supermarkets and budget shops. These myths are also peddled by the tabloid press in their campaigns against 'benefit scroungers' and by humorous television programmes about 'shameless' benefit cultures. These myths are *increasingly* believed by the general public, over half of whom, to repeat from Chapter 7, believe that 'unemployment benefits are too high', and that this 'discourages the unemployed from finding jobs'. Nearly two thirds think lazy parents help explain child poverty (NatCen, 2011). This shows the reach and power that these myths hold. Indeed, they find great support among the poor and the workless themselves, as they, too, reject the stigma and shame of these labels, pointing to 'others' who they imagine better fit the bill (MacDonald and Marsh, 2005). This is a great myth indeed.

We know of no evidence that might make these viewpoints other than myth (see MacDonald and Marsh, 2005, for a fuller discussion). And, we suggest, the key findings with which we began this chapter demonstrate the disconnection of these ideological standpoints and myths from the lived experiences of the interviewees. Unemployment was not 'a lifestyle choice'. Living on benefits meant poverty and insecurity. It was to be avoided if possible, not embraced in a culture of dependency. People wanted decent, lasting jobs; they got low-paid, low-skilled and low-quality poor work. Certainly work was often not a route out of poverty, but it seems pernicious to seek to 'solve' this problem by deepening the poverty of those on welfare benefits (so as to 'incentivise' employment) and illogical to cut assistance to families experiencing in-work poverty (as with cuts to Working Tax Credits) rather than rewarding recurrent engagement with employment with policies to improve the pay and conditions of that employment. This book, we hope, has helped to expose these mythologies of the workless and in doing so, the fallacies of welfare reforms, at least as they refer to those caught up in the low-pay, no-pay cycle (which, after all, is a problem recognised as substantial by this Coalition government in its first days in office).

Of course, myths usually have a purpose. They can distract attention, cover up realities and justify actions. Following Byrne and Standing, it is easy to understand contemporary mythologies of the workless and the welfare dependent as a cover for the new, more punitive and 'active' turn in government welfare policy described in this chapter. These are policies that punish the poor, that feed the workless into poor work and that do nothing to tackle the most significant form of social exclusion in contemporary society, the low-pay, no-pay cycle.

This great myth is exposed for what it is by the great illogic. The welfare reforms discussed in this chapter – with their emphasis on greater conditionality and sanctions to hasten the move from welfare to work – are being instituted in economically inauspicious times. *Where is the work, for those on welfare?* Locally to our study, according to central government statistics for February 2012, there were nearly 24 people on JSA in Middlesbrough chasing every vacancy reported by Jobcentre Plus (ONS, 2012) (with the Great Britain average being 5.7 jobseekers for every notified vacancy). Polly Toynbee (2012a) puts it very nicely: 'with dole claimants rising towards 3 million, and 6.3 million in all seeking work or longer hours, the government has devised a strange sociology suggesting an epidemic of laziness, ignoring the worst depression since the 1930s.'

What might be done about all of this? In this chapter we have argued that things can be done differently. Exposing the myth of 'the welfare scrounger' is the first step towards better-informed debate and policy. Improving the quality and pay of those important and necessary jobs at the bottom of the labour market is a step in the right direction (and ladders of progression away from them, for those who want that). As Knight (2011, p 125) argues: 'if reasonably paid work were a feature of people's lives, most other problems would disappear.' Certainly better-paid and more lasting jobs – and a welfare system that promised social security not greater insecurity – would have done much to improve the interviewees' lives. They needed neither educating about the value or importance of work, nor chiding or coercing into jobs. What they needed most was better jobs.

References

Abraham, K. (1988) 'Flexible staffing arrangements and employers' short-term adjustment strategies', in R.A. Hart (ed) *Employment, unemployment and labour utilisation*, Boston, MA: Unwin Hyman.

Alcock, P. (2003) 'The benefits system', in P. Alcock, C. Beatty, S. Fothergill, R. Macmillan and S. Yeandle (eds) *Work to welfare: How men become detached from the labour market*, Cambridge: Cambridge University Press.

Alcock, P. (2006) *Understanding poverty*, Basingstoke: Palgrave MacMillan.

Allen, C. (2007) *Crime, drugs and social theory*, Aldershot: Ashgate.

Arnett, J.J. (2004) *Emerging adulthood: The winding road from late teens through the twenties*, Oxford: Oxford University Press.

Arnett, J.J. (2006) 'Emerging adulthood in Britain: a response to Bynner', *Journal of Youth Studies*, vol 9, no 1, pp 111-23.

Atkinson, J. (1984) *Flexibility, uncertainty and manpower management*, IMS Report no 89, Brighton: Institute of Manpower Studies.

Atkinson, J. and Williams, M. (2003) *Employer perspectives on the recruitment, retention and advancement of low-pay, low-status employees*, London: Government Chief Social Researcher's Office.

Auer, P. and Cazes, S. (2003) *Employment stability in an age of flexibility*, Geneva: International Labour Organization.

Baker, A. and Billinge, M. (2004) *Geographies of England: The North–South divide, material and imagined*, Cambridge: Cambridge University Press.

Bambra, C. (2011) 'Work, worklessness and the political economy of health inequalities', *Journal of Epidemiology and Community Health*, vol 65, no 9, pp 746-50.

Bambra, C., Whitehead, M. and Hamilton, V. (2005) 'Does "welfare to work" work? A systematic review of the effectiveness of the UK's Welfare to Work programmes for people with a chronic illness or disability', *Social Science & Medicine*, vol 60, no 9, pp 1905-18.

Barber, B. (2012) 'Incapacity Benefit tests are failing disabled people, say TUC', Blog, 15 March, TUC (www.tuc.org.uk/equality/tuc-20786-f0.cfm).

Barnard, M. (2005) *Drugs in the family: The impact on parents and siblings*, York: Joseph Rowntree Foundation.

Barnardo's (2012) *Priced out. The plight of low income families and young people living in fuel poverty*, London: Barnardo's.

Bates, I., Clark, J., Cohen, B., Finn, D., Moore, R. and Willis, P. (1984) *Schooling for the dole? The new vocationalism*, Basingstoke: Palgrave.

Batty, E., Cole, I. and Green, S. (2011) *Low-income neighbourhoods in Britain: The gap between policy ideas and residents' realities*, York: Joseph Rowntree Foundation (www.jrf.org.uk/sites/files/jrf/poverty-neighbourhood-resident-experienceEBOOK.pdf).

Bauman, Z. (1998) *Work, consumerism and the new poor*, Buckingham: Open University Press.

Baumberg, B. (2011) 'Fit for work, securing the health of the working age population', *Employment Studies*, vol 13, pp 3-5, Brighton: Institute for Employment Studies.

BBC News (2010a) 'Spending cuts to hit north harder' (www.bbc.co.uk/news/uk-england-11141264).

BBC News (2010b) 'Jobs blow for Garland North East call centre staff' (http://news.bbc.co.uk/1/hi/england/tees/8687770.stm).

BBC News (2011a) 'Up to 550 jobs to go at Middlesbrough Council' (www.bbc.co.uk/news/uk-england-tees-12673268).

BBC News (2011b) 'More than 4,500 apply for SSI steel jobs in Redcar' (www.bbc.co.uk/news/uk-england-tees-14464021).

BBC News (2011c) 'The report: the Work Programme', Radio 4, 15 September (www.bbc.co.uk/programmes/b014ggh3).

Beatty, C. and Fothergill, S. (2011) *Incapacity benefit reform: The local, regional and national impact*, Sheffield: Centre for Regional Economic and Social Research.

Beck, U. (1992) *Risk society*, London: Sage Publications.

Bell, F. (1907) *At the works: A study of a manufacturing town*, London: Virago.

Bell, K. and Brewer, M. (2012) 'Changes to the Working Tax Credit may not always make work pay and raise serious questions about fairness', London School of Economics blog posting, 20 March (http://blogs.lse.ac.uk/politicsandpolicy/2012/03/20/house-rules-and-tax-credits/).

Bellis, A., Sigala, M. and Dewson, S. (2011a) *Identifying claimants' needs: Research into the capability of Jobcentre Plus advisers*, London: Department for Business, Innovation and Skills.

Bellis, A., Sigala, M. and Dewson, S. (2011b) *Employer engagement and Jobcentre Plus*, DWP Research Report 742, London: The Stationery Office.

Benati, L. (2001) 'Some empirical evidence on the discouraged worker effect', *Economics Letters*, vol 70, no 3, pp 387-95.

Ben-Galim, D. and Lanning, T. (2010) *Strengths against shocks: Low-income families and debt*, London: Institute for Public Policy Research.

Beynon, H. (1997) 'The changing practices of work,' in R.K. Brown (ed) *The changing shape of work*, Basingstoke: Macmillan.

Beynon, H., Hudson, R. and Sadler, D. (1994) *A place called Teesside: A locality in a global economy*, Edinburgh: Edinburgh University Press.

Beynon, H., Grimshaw, D., Rubery, J. and Ward, K. (2002) *Managing employment change: The new realities of work*, Oxford: Oxford University Press.

Birdwell, J., Grist, M. and Margo, J. (2011) *The forgotten half*, London: Demos/Private Equity Foundation.

Blair, T. (1998) 'Building a modern welfare state', Prime Minister's speech to a meeting of Labour Party members in Dudley Town Hall, West Midlands, 15 January (reported in *The Independent*, 16 January 1998 at www.independent.co.uk/news/blair-well-build-a-welfare-state-for-the-21st-century-1138878.html).

Bradshaw, J., Cusworth, L., Oldfield, N., Middleton, S., Kallard, K., Smith, N. and Davis, A. (2008) *A minimum income standard for Britain*, York: Joseph Rowntree Foundation.

Brady, D. (2009) *Rich democracies, poor people: How politics explain poverty*, Oxford: Oxford University Press.

Brewer, M., Browne, J. and Jin, W. (2012) *Universal Credit: A preliminary analysis*, Briefing Note 116, London: Institute for Fiscal Studies.

Briggs, A. (1963) *Victorian cities*, Harmondsworth: Penguin.

Brooke-Kelly, E. (2005) 'Leaving and losing jobs: resistance of rural low-income mothers', *Journal of Poverty*, vol 9, no 1, pp 83-103.

Broughton, A. (2010) *UK: Flexible forms of work: 'Very atypical' contractual arrangements*, European Working Conditions Observatory (www.eurofound.europa.eu/ewco/studies/tn0812019s/uk0812019q.htm).

Brown, P. and Scase, R. (eds) (1991) *Poor work: Disadvantage and the division of labour*, Milton Keynes: Open University Press.

Brown, P., Lauder, H. and Ashton, D. (2011) *The global auction: The broken promises of education, jobs, and incomes*, Oxford: Oxford University Press.

Bunt, K., McAndrew, F. and Kuechel, A. (2005) *Jobcentre Plus Employer (Market View) Survey 2004*, London: Department for Work and Pensions.

Butler, P. (2011) 'Charity cuts: it's grim up north', *The Guardian*, 1 September.

Butler, R. and Bauld, L. (2005) 'The parents' experience: coping with drug use in the family', *Drugs: Education, Prevention and Policy*, vol 12, no 1, February, pp 35-45.

Butler, T. and Watt, P. (2007) *Understanding social inequality*, London: Sage.

Butterworth, P., Leach, L., Strazdins, L., Olesen, S., Rodgers, B. and Broom, D. (2011) 'The psychosocial quality of work determines whether employment has benefits for mental health: results from a longitudinal national household panel survey', *Occupational & Environmental Medicine*, vol 68, pp 806-12.

Bynner, J. (2005) 'Rethinking the youth phase: the case for emerging adulthood?', *Journal of Youth Studies*, vol 8, no 4, pp 367-84.

Byrne, D. (1999) *Social exclusion*, Milton Keynes: Open University Press.

CAB (Citizens' Advice Bureau) (2004) *Somewhere to turn*, London: CAB.

Cam, S., Purcell, J. and Tailby, S. (2003) 'Contingent employment in the UK', in O. Bergstrom and D. Storrie (eds) *Contingent employment in Europe and the United States*, Cheltenham: Edward Elgar.

Campbell, M. and Meadows, P. (2001) *What works locally?*, York: Joseph Rowntree Foundation.

Canny, A. (2004) 'What employers want and what employers do: Cumbrian employers: recruitment, assessment and provision of education/learning opportunities for their young workers', *Journal of Education and Work*, vol 17, no 4, pp 495-513.

Cassidy, J. (2009) *How markets fail: The logic of economic calamities*, London: Penguin Books.

Castell, S. and Thompson, J. (2007) *Understanding attitudes to poverty in the UK*, York: Joseph Rowntree Foundation.

Chzhen, Y. and Middleton, S. (2007) *The impact of tax credits on mothers' employment*, York: Joseph Rowntree Foundation.

Citizens' Advice Scotland (2011) 'Employers "exploiting workers and breaking the law" on minimum wage' (www.cas.org.uk/news/2011-news/September/Employers+exploiting+workers+and+breaking+t he+law+on+minimum+wage).

Clayton, J., Donovan, C., Ballantyne, N. and Merchant, J. (2012) *An exploration of the impact of the Coalition government's Spending Review on the North East Region*, Sunderland: University of Sunderland.

Clayton, N. and Brinkley, I. (2011) *Welfare to what? Prospects and challenges for employment recovery*, London: The Work Foundation.

Cleveland County Council Research and Intelligence Unit (1988) *Cleveland statistics in brief*, Middlesbrough: Cleveland County Council.

Coates, D. and Lekhi, R. (2008) *'Good work': Job quality in a changing economy*, London: The Work Foundation.

Coates, D. with Johnson, N. and Hackett, P. (2012) *From the Poor Law to welfare to work: What have we learned from a century of anti-poverty policies?*, London: The Smith Institute and Webb Memorial Trust.

Collini, S. (2012) *What are universities for?*, London: Penguin Books.

Cook, G. and Lawton, K. (2008) *Working out of poverty: A study of the low-paid and working poor,* London: IPPR.

CPAG (Child Poverty Action Group) (nd) *CPAG POVERTY in the UK: A summary of facts and figures* (www.cpag.org.uk/povertyfacts/#causes).

CPAG (2012) *Welfare Reform Bill: Second reading briefing from CPAG,* London: CPAG.

Crisp, R. and Nixon, D. (2010) 'Class, culture and the economic marginalisation of working-class men', CRESR Research Seminar, Sheffield: Sheffield Hallam University.

Crisp, R., Batty, E., Cole, I. and Robinson, D. (2009) *Work and worklessness in deprived neighbourhoods: Policy assumptions and personal experiences,* York: Joseph Rowntree Foundation.

Crossley, S. (2011) *Poverty factsheet,* Durham: Institute for Local Governance.

Cunningham-Burley, S., Backett-Milburn, K. and Kemmer, D. (2006) 'Constructing health and sickness in the context of motherhood and paid work', *Sociology of Health and Illness,* vol 24, no 4, pp 385-409.

Danziger, S., Heflin, C., Corcoran, M., Otlmans, E. and Wang, H. (2002) 'Does it pay to move from welfare to work?', *Journal of the Association for Policy Analysis and Management,* vol 21, Fall, pp 671-92.

Davies, C. and Butler, P. (2012) 'Ticking time bomb placed under the poorest families', *The Guardian,* 31 March.

Daycare Trust and Save the Children (2011) *Making work Pay: The childcare trap,* London: Daycare Trust and Save the Children.

Deacon, A. (2002) *Perspectives on welfare,* Buckingham: Open University Press.

Dean, H. and Mitchell, G. (2011) *Wage top-ups and work incentives: The implications of the UK's Working Tax Credit scheme,* London: London School of Economics and Political Science.

DETR (Department for the Environment, Transport and the Regions) (2000) *Index of multiple deprivation,* London: DETR.

Devicienti, F. (2000) *Poverty persistence in Britain: A multivariate analysis using the BHPS, 1991–1997,* Colchester: Institute for Social & Economic Research, University of Essex.

Devins, D. and Hogarth, T. (2005) 'Employing the unemployed: some case study evidence on the role and practice of employers', *Urban Studies,* vol 42, no 2, pp 245-56.

Dex, S. and Smith, C. (1992) *The nature and pattern of family friendly employment policies in Britain,* York: Joseph Rowntree Fund.

DH (Department of Health) (1999) *National Service Framework for mental health,* London: DH.

Dickens, W. (1999) 'Rebuilding urban labour markets: what can community development accomplish?', in R. Ferguson and W. Dickens (eds) *Urban problems and community development*, Washington, DC: Brookings Institute Press.

Dooley, D. (2003) 'Unemployment, underemployment, and mental health: conceptualizing employment status as a continuum', *American Journal of Community Psychology*, vol 32, nos 1-2, pp 9-20.

Dorling, D. (2010) *Injustice*, Bristol: The Policy Press.

Dorling, D. (2012) *Fair play: A Daniel Dorling reader on social justice*, Bristol: The Policy Press.

Dorsett, R., Campbell-Barr, V., Hamilton, G., Hoggart, L., Marsh, A., Miller, C., Phillips, J., Ray, K., Riccio, J.A., Rich, S. and Vegeris, S. (2007) *Implementation and first year impacts of the UK Employment Retention and Advancement (ERA) demonstration*, DWP Research Report No 412, Leeds: Corporate Document Services.

Duncan Smith, I. (2010) Press Release accompanying *Government response to Households Below Average Income figures*, London: Department for Work and Pensions (www.dwp.gov.uk/newsroom/press-releases/2010/may-2010/dwp067-10-200510.shtml).

DWP (Department for Work and Pensions) (2010) 'Biggest back to work programme in decades will be built on payment by results' (www.dwp.gov.uk/newsroom/press-releases/2010/dec-2010/dwp184-10-221210.shtml).

DWP (2011a) *The Work Programme*, London: DWP (www.dwp.gov.uk/docs/the-work-programme.pdf).

DWP (2011b) *Welfare reform* (www.dwp.gov.uk/policy/welfare-reform/).

Edwards, P.K. (2006) 'Non-standard work and labour market re-structuring in the UK', Paper for Associazione Nuovi Lavori Conference, 'The Latest in the Labour Market', Rome, 23 February (www2.warwick.ac.uk/fac/soc/wbs/research/irru/publications/recentconf/pe_rome.pdf).

EHRC (Equality and Human Rights Commission) (2010) *Inquiry into recruitment and employment in the meat and poultry processing sector*, London: EHRC.

Ehrenreich, B. (2002) *Nickel and dimed: Undercover in low wage USA*, London: Granta.

Ellwood, D. (1988) *Poor support*, New York: Basic Books.

Emslie, C., Ridge, D., Zeibland, S. and Hunt, K. (2006) 'Men's accounts of depression: reconstructing or resisting hegemonic accounts of masculinity', *Sociology of Health and Illness*, vol 62, pp 2446-57.

Engstrom, M. (2009) 'Involving care-giving grandmothers in family interventions when mothers with substance use problems are incarcerated', *Family Process*, September, vol 47, no 3, pp 357-71.

Evans, G. (2007) *Educational failure and white working class children in Britain*, Basingstoke: Palgrave.

Evening Gazette (2010) 'Garland workers in payout victory at tribunal', 26 October (www.gazettelive.co.uk/news/teesside-news/tm_headline=garland-workers-in-payout-victory-at-tribunal%26meth od=full%26objectid=27543997%26siteid=84229-name_page.html).

Exeter, D., Boyle, P., and Norman, P. (2011) 'Deprivation, (im)mobility and cause-specific premature mortality in Scotland', *Social Science and Medicine*, vol 72, pp 389–97.

Experian (2012) *BBC local growth research* (http://news.bbc.co.uk/1/shared/bsp/hi/pdfs/15_03_12experian.pdf).

Experian Public Sector (2012) 'At risk Britain' (http://publicsector.experian.co.uk/).

Fagg, A. (2012) 'Ministers admit to sickness benefits backlog', BBC News, 8 February (www.bbc.co.uk/news/uk-16937742).

Fair Pay Network (2012) *Face the difference: The impact of low pay in national supermarket chains*, London: Fair Pay Network.

Farrall, S. and Calverley, A. (2006) *Understanding desistance from crime: Theoretical directions in resettlement and rehabilitation*, Maidenhead: Open University Press.

Farrell, S. et al (eds) (2011) *Escape attempts: Contemporary perspectives in later life punishment*, London: Routledge.

Felstead, A. and Jewson, N. (1999) 'Flexible labour and non-standard employment', in A. Felstead and N. Jewson (eds) *Global trends in flexible labour*, Basingstoke: Macmillan.

Fenton, S. and Dermott, E. (2006) 'Fragmented careers', *Work, Employment & Society*, vol 20, no 2, pp 205-21.

Fevre, R. (2007) 'Employment insecurity and social theory: the power of nightmares', *Work, Employment & Society*, vol 21, no 3, pp 517-35.

Finn, D., Mason, D., Rahim, N. and Casebourne, J. (2008) *Problems in the delivery of benefits, tax credits and employment services*, York: Joseph Rowntree Foundation.

Foord, J. et al (1985) 'The quiet revolution: social and economic change on Teesside 1965 to 1985', Special Report for BBC North East, Newcastle: BBC.

Forde, C. (2001) 'Temporary arrangements: the activities of employment agencies in the UK', *Work, Employment & Society*, vol 15, pp 631-44.

Foster, D. and Hoggett, P. (1999) 'Change in the Benefits Agency: empowering the exhausted worker', *Work, Employment & Society*, vol 13, no 1, pp 19-39.

Fraser, D. (2009) *The evolution of the British welfare state*, Basingstoke: Palgrave.

Frazer, N., Gutierrrez, R. and Pena-Casas, R. (2011a) 'Introduction', in N. Frazer, R. Gutierrrez and R. Pena-Casas (eds) *Working poverty in Europe: A comparative approach*, Basingstoke: Palgrave Macmillan.

Frazer, N., Gutierrrez, R. and Pena-Casas, R. (eds) (2011b) *Working poverty in Europe: A comparative approach*, Basingstoke: Palgrave Macmillan.

Frazer, N. (2011) 'United Kingdom: tackling poverty in a flexible labour market' in N. Frazer, R. Gutierrrez and R. Pena-Casas (eds) *Working poverty in Europe: A comparative approach*, Basingstoke: Palgrave Macmillan.

Frosh, S., Phoenix, A. and Pattman, R. (2002) *Young masculinities*, Cambridge: Polity Press.

Furlong, A. (1992) *Growing up in a classless society?*, Edinburgh: Edinburgh University Press.

Furlong, A. (2006) 'Not a very NEET solution: representing problematic labour market transition among early school-leavers', *Work, Employment & Society*, vol 20, pp 553-69.

Furlong, A. and Cartmel, F. (2004) *Vulnerable young men in fragile labour markets*, York: Joseph Rowntree Foundation.

Furlong, A. and Cartmel, F. (2007) *Young people and social change*, Maidenhead: McGraw Hill.

Furlong, A. and Kelly, P. (2005) 'The Brazilianisation of youth transitions in Australia and the UK', *Australian Journal of Social Studies*, vol 40, pp 207-25.

Galbraith, J. (2008) *The predator state: How Conservatives abandoned the free market and why Liberals should too*, New York: Free Press.

Gardiner, K. (1997) *Bridges from benefit to work*, York: Joseph Rowntree Foundation.

Garnham, A. (2012) 'Local figures for children and families losing Working Tax Credit in April', CPAG Press Release, 20 March (www.cpag.org.uk/content/local-figures-children-and-families-losing-working-tax-credit-april).

Garthwaite, K. (2012) 'Incapacitated? Exploring the health and illness narratives of long term Incapacity Benefit recipients', PhD thesis, Durham University.

Gentleman, A. (2012) 'Rising unemployment puts Cameron's work programme in the spotlight', *The Guardian*, 31 January (www.guardian.co.uk/society/2012/jan/31/unemployment-cameron-work-programme).

Giles, C. (2010) 'Poor to be hit most by service cuts', *Financial Times*, 23 June (www.ft.com/cms/s/0/47b05ac2-7efe-11df-8398-00144feabdc0.html#axzz1quImGrxe).

Glyn, A. (2006) *Capitalism unleashed: Finance, globalization, and welfare*, Oxford: Oxford University Press.

Golding, P. and Middleton, S. (1982) *Images of welfare: Press and public attitudes to poverty*, Oxford: Martin Robinson and Co Limited.

Goode, J. (2010) 'The role of gender dynamics on credit and debt in low income families', *Critical Social Policy*, vol 30, no 1, pp 99-119.

Goodwin, J. and O'Connor, H. (2005) 'Exploring complex transitions: looking back at the "golden age" of from school to work', *Sociology*, vol 39, no 2, pp 201-20.

Goulden, C. (2010) *Cycles of poverty, unemployment and low pay*, York: Joseph Rowntree Foundation.

Graham, H. (ed) (2000) *Understanding health inequalities*, Milton Keynes: Open University Press.

Grandparents Plus (http://grandparentsplus.org.uk)

Grant, A. (2011) 'New Labour, welfare reform and conditionality: pathways to work for Incapacity Benefit claimants', Unpublished PhD thesis, Cardiff University.

Grant, L. (2009) 'Women's disconnection from local labour markets: real lives and policy failures', *Critical Social Policy*, vol 29, no 3, pp 330-50.

Gray, A. (2002) 'Jobseekers and gatekeepers: the role of the private employment agency in the placement of the unemployed', *Work, Employment & Society*, vol 16, no 4, pp 655-74.

Griggs, J. (2010) *Protect, support and provide: Examining the role of grandparents in families at risk of poverty*, London: Equality and Human Rights Commission.

Hamilton, K. (2012) 'Low income families and coping through brands', *Sociology*, vol 46, no 1, pp 74-90.

Hammen, C. (1997) *Depression*, London: Psychology Press.

Hasluck, C. (1999) *Employers, young people and the unemployed: A review of research*, Research Report ESR 12, Sheffield: Employment Service.

Hastings, A., Bramley, G., Bailey, N. and Watkins, D. (2012) *Serving deprived communities in a recession*, York: Joseph Rowntree Foundation (www.jrf.org.uk/sites/files/jrf/communities-recession-services-full.pdf).

Hendra, R., Riccio, J., Dorsett, R., Greenberg, D., Knight, G., Phillips, J., Robins, P., Vegeris, S., Walter, J., Hill, A., Ray, K. and Smith, J. (2011) *Breaking the low-pay, no-pay cycle: Final evidence from the UK Employment Retention and Advancement (ERA) demonstration*, DWP Research Report No 765, London: The Stationery Office.

Hill, A. (2012a) 'Millions of working families one push from penury', *The Guardian*, 18 June.

Hill, A. (2012b) 'Breadline Britain: 7m adults just one bill away from disaster', *The Guardian*, 19 June.

Hills, J., Le Grand, J. and Piachaud, D. (2002) *Understanding social exclusion*, Oxford: Oxford University Press.

Hills, J., Sefton, T. and Stewart, K. (2009) *Towards a more equal society? Poverty, inequality and policy since 1997*, Bristol: The Policy Press.

Hirsch, D. (2011) *A minimum income standard for the UK in 2011*, York: Joseph Rowntree Foundation.

Hirsch, D. and Moore, R. (2012) *The living wage in the United Kingdom*, London, Living Wage Foundation.

HM Government (2010) *Coalition agreement*, London: The Stationery Office.

HM Government (2012a) *Ministerial foreword*, Social Mobility and Child Poverty Commission, information pack for Chair and Members, London: Child Poverty Unit.

HM Government (2012b) *Social justice: Transforming lives*, London: Department for Work and Pensions.

HM Treasury (1997) *The modernisation of Britain's tax benefit system*, London: HM Government.

Holmes, C. and Mayhew, K. (2012) *The changing shape of the UK job market and its implications for the bottom half of earners*, London: Resolution Foundation.

Holt, A. (2011) 'Sector fears over Work Programme "failures"', *Charity Times*, 11 October (www.charitytimes.com/ct/Sector_fears_over_Work_Programme_failures.php%20.php).

Holzer, H. (1998) *Will employers hire welfare recipients? Research survey evidence from Michigan*, Institute for Research on Poverty Discussion Paper No 1177-98, Madison, WI: Institute for Research on Poverty.

Hooper, C., Gorin, S., Cabral, C. and Dyson, C. (2006) *Living with hardship 24/7: The diverse experiences of families in poverty in England*, London: The Frank Buttle Trust.

Houseman, S., Kalleberg, A. and Erickcek, G. (2003) 'The role of temporary employment agency employment in tight labour markets', *Industrial and Labor Relations Review*, vol 57, pp 105-27.

Hudson, R. (1986) 'Sunset over the Tees', *New Socialist*, September, p 13.

Hudson, R. (1989a) *Wrecking a region: State policy, party politics and regional change in North-east England*, London: Pion Press.

Hudson, R. (1989b) 'Labour market changes and new forms of work in old industrial regions', *Environment and Planning D: Society and Space*, vol 7, pp 5-30.

IFS (Institute for Fiscal Studies) (2012) 'Households with children to lose the most from tax and benefit changes in the coming year', Press Release, 8 March (www.ifs.org.uk/pr/taxben_080312.pdf).

ILO (International Labour Organisation) (nd) *Underemployment*, Geneva: ILO (www.ilo.org/global/statistics-and-databases/statistics-overview-and-topics/underemployment/lang--en/index.htm).

IMD (2004) *Index of multiple deprivation*, London: Department of Communities and Local Government.

Ingham, G. (2008) *Capitalism*, Cambridge: Polity Press.

Inui, A. (2009) 'NEETs, freeters and flexibility: reflecting precarious situations in the new labour market', in A. Furlong (ed) *Handbook of youth and young adulthood: New perspectives and agendas*, Abingdon: Routledge.

IPPR (Institute for Public Policy Research) (2010a) *Rebalancing local economies: Widening economic opportunities for people in deprived communities*, Newcastle: IPPR (www.ippr.org/images/media/files/publication/2011/05/Rebalancing%20Local%20Economies%20Report%20Oct2010_1801.pdf).

IPPR (2010b) 'New analysis reveals record numbers unable to find full-time work', Press Release, London: IPPR (www.ippr.org/pressreleases/?id=3994).

Jackson, B. (1968) *Working class community*, London: RKP.

Jahoda, M. (1979) 'The impact of unemployment in the 1930s and the 1970s', *Bulletin of the British Psychological Society*, vol 32, pp 309-14.

Jahoda, M. (1982) *Employment and unemployment: A social psychological analysis*, Cambridge: Cambridge University Press.

Jenkins, S.P. (2011) *Changing fortunes: Income mobility and poverty dynamics in Britain*, Oxford: Oxford University Press.

Johnston, L., MacDonald, R., Mason, P., Ridley, L. and Webster, C. (2000) *Snakes and ladders: Young people, transitions and social exclusion*, Bristol: The Policy Press.

Jones, G. (2002) *The youth divide*, York: Joseph Rowntree Foundation/York Publishing Services.

Jones, O. (2011) *Chavs: The demonization of the working class*, London: Verso.

Joshi, H., Wiggins, R., Bartley, M., Mitchell, R., Gleave, S. and Lynch, K. (2000) 'Putting health inequalities on the map' in Graham, H. (ed) *Understanding health inequalities*, Milton Keynes: Open University Press.

Joyce, R. (2012) 'Tax and benefit reforms due in 2012-13, and the outlook for household incomes', IFS Briefing note BN126, London: Institute for Fiscal Studies.

Kearns, A. and Parkinson, M. (2001) 'The significance of neighbourhood', *Urban Studies*, vol 38, no 12, pp 2103-10.

Keen, S. (2011) *Debunking economics: The naked emperor dethroned?*, London: Zed Books.

Keep, E. (2004) 'High performance working', SSDA Expert Panel Meeting, 8/9 June (www.ssda.org.uk/ssda/default.aspx?page=520).

Keep, E. and Mayhew, K. (2010) 'Moving beyond skills as a social and economic panacea', *Work, Employment & Society*, vol 24, no 3, pp 565-77.

Kelvin, P. and Jarrett, J. (1985) *Unemployment: Its social psychological effects*, Cambridge: Cambridge University Press.

Kenway, P. (2009) *Should adult unemployment benefits now be raised?*, York: Joseph Rowntree Foundation.

Kingfisher, C.P. (1998) 'How providers make policy: an analysis of everyday conversation in a welfare office', *Journal of Community and Applied Psychology*, vol 8, no 2, pp 119-36.

Klee, H., Jackson, M. and Lewis, S. (2002) *Drug misuse and motherhood*, London: Routledge.

Knight, B. (2011) 'What is to be done?', in *What Beatrice Webb would say now*, London: Webb Memorial Trust.

Knight, G. and Kasparova, D. (2006) *Lone parents: In work benefit calculations – Work and benefit outcomes*, DWP Research Report No 367, London: The Stationery Office.

Lash, S. and Urry, J. (1994) *Economics of signs and space,* London: Sage.

Lawless, P. (1995) 'Inner-city and suburban labour markets in a major English conurbation: processes and policy implications', *Urban Studies*, vol 32, no 7, pp 1097-125.

Lawton, K. (2009) *Nice work if you can get it: Achieving a sustainable solution to low pay and in work poverty*, London: Institute for Public Policy Research.

Lawton, K. and Lanning, T. (2011) 'The role of workplace democracy in promoting fairer pay and job quality. What policy interventions might bad jobs better?', ESRC Seminar Series: Making Bad Jobs Better, London.

Lemos, S. and Portes, J. (2008) *The impact of migration from the new European Union member states on native workers*, DWP Working Paper No 52, London: The Stationery Office.

Lindsay, C. (2010) 'In a lonely place? Social networks, job seeking and the experience of long-term unemployment', *Social Policy and Society*, vol 9, no 1, pp 25-37.

Lindsay, C. and McQuaid, R.W. (2004) 'Avoiding the "McJobs": unemployed job seekers and attitudes to service work', *Work, Employment & Society*, vol 18, no 2, pp 296-319.

Lindsay, C. and McQuaid, R.W. (2005) 'The concept of employability', *Urban Studies*, vol 42, no 2, pp 197-219.

Lipsky, M. (1980) *Street-level bureaucracy: Dilemmas of the individual in public services*, New York: Russell Sage Foundation.

Lister, R. (2004) *Poverty*, Chichester: Wiley.

Lloyd, C. and Commander, J. (2011) 'Making bad jobs better', ESRC Seminar Series, Notes from Seminar 4.

Lloyd, C. and Warhurst, C. (2010) 'Bad jobs practice, policy and effects', Presentation given at 'Making Bad Jobs Better' seminar, Glasgow.

Lloyd, C., Mason, G. and Mayhew, K. (eds) (2008) *Low-wage work in the United Kingdom*, New York: Russell Sage Foundation.

Lucas, K., Tyler, S. and Christodolou, G. (2008) *The value of new public transport in deprived areas: Who benefits, how and why?*, York: Joseph Rowntree Foundation.

Lupton, R. (2003) *Poverty street: The dynamics of neighbourhood decline and renewal*, Bristol: The Policy Press.

Lupton, R. (2012) *Postcode discrimination in employment: An investigation of job search for young people from disadvantaged neighbourhoods in three local labour markets, including a test for 'postcode discrimination'*, York: Joseph Rowntree Foundation.

Lupton, R. and Power, A. (2002) 'Social exclusion and neighbourhoods' in Hills, J. et al (eds) *Understanding social exclusion*, Oxford: Oxford University Press.

MacDonald, R. (1994) 'Fiddly jobs, undeclared working and the something for nothing society', *Work, Employment & Society*, vol 8, no 4, pp 507-30.

MacDonald, R. (1996) 'Welfare dependency, the enterprise culture and self-employed survival', *Work, Employment & Society*, vol 10, no 3, pp 431-47.

MacDonald, R. (ed) (1997) *Youth, the 'underclass' and social exclusion*, London: Routledge.

MacDonald, R. (2009) 'Precarious work: risk, choice and poverty traps', in A. Furlong (ed) *Handbook of youth and young adulthood: New perspectives and agendas*, Abingdon: Routledge.

MacDonald, R. (2010) 'Essentially barbarians?', in Davies, P., Francis, P. and Jupp, V. (eds) *Doing criminological research*, London: Sage.

MacDonald, R. (2011) 'Youth transitions, unemployment and underemployment: plus ça change, plus c'est la même chose?', *Journal of Sociology*, vol 47, no 4, pp 427-44.

MacDonald, R. and Coffield, F. (1991) *Risky business? Youth and the enterprise culture*, Lewes: Falmer Press.

MacDonald, R. and Marsh, J. (2005) *Disconnected youth? Growing up in Britain's poor neighbourhoods*, London: Palgrave.

MacDonald, R. and Shildrick, T. (2010) 'The view from below: criminally involved young men's biographical encounters with criminal justice agencies', *Child and Family Law Quarterly*, vol 22, no 2, pp 186-99.

MacDonald, R. and Shildrick, T. (2012) 'Youth and wellbeing: experiencing bereavement and ill health in marginalised young people's transitions', *The Sociology of Health and Illness*, DOI: 10.1111/j.1476-9566.2012.01488.x (early view).

MacDonald, R., Shildrick, T., Webster, C. and Simpson, D. (2005) 'Growing up in poor neighbourhoods: the significance of class and place in the extended transitions of "socially excluded" young adults' *Sociology*, vol 39, no 5, pp 837–91.

MacDonald, R., Webster, C., Shildrick, T. and Simpson, M. (2011) 'Paths of exclusion, inclusion and desistance: understanding marginalized young people's criminal careers', in S. Farrell et al (eds) *Escape attempts: Contemporary perspectives on life after punishment*, London: Routledge.

McCormick, B. (1990) 'A theory of signalling during job search, employment efficiency and "stigmatised" jobs', *Review of Economic Studies*, vol 57, pp 299-313.

McDowell, L. (2001) *Young men leaving school: White working class masculinity*, Leicester: National Youth Agency.

McDowell, L. (2003) 'Masculine identities and low paid work: young men in urban labour markets', *International Journal of Urban and Regional Research*, vol 27, no 4, pp 828-48.

McDowell, L., Batnitzky, A. and Dyer, S. (2009) 'Precarious work and economic migration: emerging divisions of labour in Greater London's service sector', *International Journal of Urban and Regional Research*, vol 33, no 1, pp 3-25.

McKnight, A. (2002) 'Low paid work: drip-feeding the poor', in J. Hills, J. Le Grand and D. Piachaud (eds) *Understanding social exclusion*, Oxford: Oxford University Press.

McQuaid, R. and Lindsay, C. (2005) 'The concept of employability', *Urban Studies*, vol 42, no 2, pp 197-219.

McQuaid, R., Fuertes, V. and Richard, A. (2010) *How can parents escape from recurrent poverty?*, York: Joseph Rowntree Foundation.

Madanipour, A., Cars, G. and Allen, J. (eds) (1998) *Social exclusion in European cities*, London: Jessica Kingsley Publishers.

Marangozov, R. and Dewson, S. (2011) *Study of the School Gates Employment Support Initiative*, DWP Research Report, no 747

Marmot, M. (2010) *Fair society, healthy lives: The Marmot Review* (www.marmotreview.org).

Marsden, D. and Duff, E. (1975) *Workless*, Harmondsworth: Pelican.

Mason, G., Mayhew, K. and Osborne, M. (2008) 'Low-paid work in the United Kingdom: an overview', in C. Lloyd, M. Mason and K. Mayhew, *Low-waged work in the United Kingdom*, New York: Russell Sage Foundation.

Maruna, S. (2001) *Making good: How ex-convicts reform and rebuild their lives*, Washington, DC: American Psychological Association Books.

Metcalf, H. and Dhudwar, A. (2010) *Employers' role in the low-pay/no-pay cycle*, York: Joseph Rowntree Foundation.

Middlesbrough Council (nd) *Regeneration and resilience in Middlesbrough* (www.middlesbrough.gov.uk/ccm/navigation/children-and-family-care/strategic-needs-assessment/general-information-about-middlesbrough/economic-resilience/).

Middlesborough PCT (Primary Care Trust) and Middlesborough Council (2006) *Public health strategy*, Middlesborough PCT/ Council.

Morris, L. (1995) *Social divisions*, London: UCL Press.

Moussa, H. (2012) *The perfect storm: Economic stagnation, the rising cost of living, public spending cuts, and the impact on UK poverty*, Oxfam Briefing Paper, June, Oxfam (http://policy-practice.oxfam.org.uk/publications/the-perfect-storm-economic-stagnation-the-rising-cost-of-living-public-spending-228591).

Murad, N. (2002) 'The shortest way out of work', in P. Chamberlayne, M. Rustin and T. Wengraf (eds) *Biography and social exclusion in Europe*, Bristol: The Policy Press.

Murray, C. (1994) *Underclass: The crisis deepens*, London: Institute of Economic Affairs.

NAO (National Audit Office) (2012) *The introduction of the Work Programme*, London: NAO (www.nao.org.uk/publications/1012/dwp_work_programme.aspx).

NatCen (2011) 'BSA 28: in it together or just for ourselves?' (www. natcen.ac.uk/media-centre/press-releases/2011-press-releases/bsa-28-in-it-together-or-just-for-ourselves).

Newman, K. and Tan Chen, V. (2007) *The missing class: Portraits of the near poor in America*, Boston, MA: Beacon Press.

Newton, B., Hurstfield, J., Miller, L., Page, L. and Akroyd, K. (2005) *What employers look for when recruiting the unemployed and inactive: Skills, characteristics and qualifications*, DWP Research Report No 295, London: Department for Work and Pensions (www.bcmeurope.com/openspace/documents/4_12_5_What%20employers%20are%20looking%20for.pdf).

Nicholas, K. (1986) *The social effects of unemployment on Teesside, 1919-39*, Manchester: Manchester University Press.

Nickson, D., Warhurst, C., Commander, J., Hurrell, S.A. and Cullen, A. (2012) 'Soft skills and employability: evidence from UK retail', *Economic and Industrial Democracy*, vol 33, no 1, pp 62-81.

Nixon, D. (2006) '"I just like working with my hands": employment aspirations and the meaning of work for low skilled unemployed men in Britain's service economy', *Journal of Education and Work*, vol 19, no 2, pp 201-17.

Nunn, A., Bickerstaffe, T., Hogarth, T., Bosworth, D., Green, A.E. and Owen, D. (2010) *Postcode selection? Employers' use of area- and address-based information shortcuts in recruitment decisions*, DWP Research Report No 664, London: The Stationery Office.

OECD (Organisation for Economic Co-operation and Development) (2005) *Employment outlook 2005*, Paris: OECD.

Offe, C. (1984) *Contradictions of the welfare state*, London: Hutchinson.

Offe, C. (1985) *Disorganised capitalism*, Cambridge: Polity Press.

ONS (Office for National Statistics) (2009) *Social Trends*, London: ONS

ONS (2012) *Nomis official labour market statistics: Labour market profile, Middlesbrough* (www.nomisweb.co.uk/reports/lmp/la/2038432077/report.aspx?town=Middlesbrough).

Orr, D. (2012) 'The workfare debate is now a slanging match. But I have my own proposal...', *The Guardian*, 25 February.

Osborne, G. (2010) Speech by the Chancellor of the Exchequer, the Rt Hon George Osborne MP, on the spending announcements, 17 May.

Osborne, G. (2012) *Budget 2012*, London: HM Treasury.

Osterman, P. (2008) 'Improving job quality: policies aimed at the demand side of the low wage labour market', in T.J. Bartik and S.A. Houseman (eds) *A future of good jobs? America's challenge in the global economy*, Kalamazoo, MI: Upjohn Institute for Employment Studies.

Osterman, P. (2011) 'Making bad jobs good', Presentation at Making Bad Jobs Better seminar, London (www.makingbadjobsbetter.org.uk).

Osterman, P. and Shulman, B. (2011) *Good jobs America: Making work better for everyone*, New York: Russell Sage Foundation.

Park, R., McKenzie, R. and Burgess, E. (1925) *The city: Suggestions for the study of human nature in the urban environment*, Chicago, IL: University of Chicago Press.

Parker, H., Bury, C. and Eggington, R. (1998) *New heroin outbreaks amongst young people in England and Wales*, Police Research Group, Paper 92, London: Home Office.

Perry, J. (2010) *Paying over the odds? Real life experiences of the poverty premium*, Manchester: Church Action on Poverty.

Polanyi, K. (1944) *The great transformation: The political and economic origins of our time*, Boston, MA: Beacon Press.

Pollert, A. and Charlwood, A. (2009) 'The vulnerable worker in Britain and problems at work', *Work, Employment & Society*, vol 23, no 2, pp 346-62.

PSE (Poverty and Social Exclusion Group) (2011) *Consultation response: Social mobility and child poverty review*, Swindon: Economic and Social Research Council (www.poverty.ac.uk/sites/default/files/consultationresponse.doc).

Purcell, J., Purcell, K. and Tailby, S. (2004) 'Temporary work agencies: here today, gone tomorrow?', *British Journal of Industrial Relations*, vol 42, no 4, pp 705-25.

Quintini, G., Martin, P. and Martin, S. (2007) *The changing nature of the school to work transition process in OECD countries*, Discussion paper 2582, Bonn: Institute for the Study of Labor.

Raffe, D. and Willms, J.D. (1989) 'Schooling the discouraged worker', *Sociology*, vol 23, pp 559-81.

Ray, K., Hoggart, L., Vegaris, S. and Taylor, R. (2010) *Better off working: Work, poverty and benefit cycling*, York: JRF findings.

Resolution Foundation (2012) *The economic decline of low to middle income Britain*, London: Commission on Living Standards (www.resolutionfoundation.org/).

Ribbens McCarthy, J., with Jessop, J. (2005) *Young people, bereavement and loss: Disruptive transitions?*, London: National Children's Bureau/ JRF.

Ritchie, H., Casebourne, J. and Rick, J. (2005) *Understanding workless people and communities: A literature review*, DWP Research Report No 255, Leeds: Corporate Document Services.

Roberts, K. (2009) *Youth in transition: Eastern Europe and the West*, London: Palgrave.

Roberts, K. and Parsell, G. (1992) 'The stratification of youth training', *British Journal of Education and Work*, vol 5, pp 65-83.

Roberts, S. (2011) 'Beyond "NEET" and "tidy" pathways: considering the "missing" middle of youth studies', *Journal of Youth Studies*, vol 14, no 1, pp 21-39.

Ross, A. (2009) *Nice work if you can get it: Life and labour in precarious times*, New York: New York University Press.

Rowlingson, K., Orton, M. and Taylor, E. (2010) *Do we still care about inequality?, British Social Attitudes Survey 2011-2011*, London: NatCen.

Santayana, G. (1905) *Reason in common sense*, vol 1, *The life of reason*, Charles Scribner's Sons.

Saraceno, S. (2011) 'Childcare needs and childcare policies: a multidimensional issue', *Current Sociology*, vol 59, pp 78-96.

Savage, L. (2011) *Low pay Britain*, London: Resolution Foundation.

Schmitt, J. (2012) *Low wage lessons*, Washington, DC: Centre for Economic and Policy Research.

Scambler, G. (2002) *Health and social change*, Buckingham: Open University Press.

Scurry, T. and Blenkinsopp, J. (2011) 'What is graduate underemployment? A review of the literature', *Personnel Review*, vol 40, no 5, pp 643-59.

Shaw, A., Egan, J. and Gillespie, M. (2007) *Drugs and poverty: A literature review*, Glasgow: Scottish Drugs Forum.

Shildrick, T., MacDonald, R., Furlong, A., Roden, J. and Crow, R. (2012) *Intergenerational cultures of worklessness? A qualitative exploration in Glasgow and Middlesbrough*, York: Joseph Rowntree Foundation.

Sianesi, B. (2011) *Employment Retention and Advancement (ERA) demonstration: The impact on workers' outcomes*, DWP Research Report No 759, London: The Stationery Office.

Sissons, P. (2011) *The hourglass and the escalator: Labour market change and mobility*, London: The Work Foundation.

Sixsmith, J., Boneham, M. and Goldring, J.E. (2003) 'Accessing the community: gaining insider perspectives from the outside', *Qualitative Health Research*, vol 13, pp 4578-89.

Skeggs, B. (1997) *Formations of class and gender*, London: Sage Publications.

Smith, D. (2005) *On the margins of inclusion*, Bristol: The Policy Press.

Smith, N. and Middleton, S. (2007) *A review of poverty dynamics research in the UK*, York: Joseph Rowntree Foundation.

Smithies, R. (2007) 'Making a case for flat tax credits: income fluctuation amongst low income families benefits', *The Journal of Poverty and Social Justice*, vol 15, no 1, pp 3-16.

Solow, R. (2008) 'The United Kingdom story', in C. Lloyd, M. Mason and K. Mayhew (eds) *Low-waged work in the United Kingdom*, New York: Russell Sage Foundation.

Song, J., Floyd, F., Seltzer, M., Greenberg, J. and Hong, J. (2010) 'Long-term effects of child death on parents' health-related quality of life: a dyadic analysis', *Family Relations*, July, pp 269-82.

Speak, S. (2000) 'Barriers to lone parents' employment: looking beyond the obvious', *Local Economy*, vol 15, no 1, pp 32-44.

Spicker, P. (2007) *The idea of poverty*, Bristol: The Policy Press.

Standing, G. (2011) *The precariat: The new dangerous class*, London: Bloomsbury.

Stewart, M. (2007) 'The interrelated dynamics of unemployment and low-wage employment', *Journal of Applied Econometrics*, vol 22, pp 511-31.

Strathdee, R. (2001) 'Change in social capital and "risk" in school to work transitions', Work, Employment & Society, vol 15, no 2, pp 1-16.

Sunley, P., Martin, R. and Nativel, C. (2006) *Putting workfare in place: Local labour markets and the New Deal*, Oxford: Blackwell.

Syrett, S. (nd) *Area effects: A review of the evidence prepared for CLG by Professor Stephen Syrett* (www.ljmu.ac.uk/EIUA/EIUA_Docs/Area_Effects_Syrett.pdf).

Tees Valley Unlimited (2010a) *Interim worklessness assessment*, Middlesbrough: Tees Valley Unlimited.

Tees Valley Unlimited (2010b) *Economic statistics for boroughs in the Tees Valley*, Middlesbrough: Tees Valley Unlimited.

Tees Valley Joint Strategy Unit (2010) *Unemployment, worklessness and vacancies in the Tees Valley* (www.teesvalleyunlimited.gov.uk/).

Thomson, R., Bell, R., Holland, J., Henderson, S., McGrellis, S. and Sharpe, S. (2002) 'Critical moments: choice, chance and opportunity in young people's narratives of transition to adulthood', *Sociology*, vol 6, no 2, pp 335–54,

Tomlinson, M. and Walker, R. (2010) *Recurrent poverty: The impact of family and labour market changes*, York: Joseph Rowntree Foundation.

Toynbee, P. (2003) *Hard work: Life in low-pay Britain*, London: Bloomsbury.

Toynbee, P. (2012a) 'Families that want to work will suffer, not "scroungers"', *The Guardian*, 2 March.

Toynbee, P. (2012b) 'Tax credit cut will hit hardest those the Tories love to praise – working families', *The Guardian*, 1 March.

Toynbee, P. (2012c) 'The welfare reform bill will incentivise people: to turn on David Cameron', *The Guardian*, 2 February.

TUC (Trades Union Congress) (2007) *Hard work, hidden lives*, London: Commission on Vulnerable Employment (www.vulnerableworkers.org.uk/files/CoVE_full_report.pdf).

van Ham, M., Mulder, C.H. and Hooimeijer, P. (2001) 'Local underemployment and the discouraged worker effect', *Urban Studies*, vol 38, no 10, pp 1733-51.

Veit-Wilson, J. (1998) *Setting adequacy standards. How governments define minimum incomes*, Bristol: The Policy Press.

Vickerstaff, S. (2003) 'Apprenticeship in the "golden age": were youth transitions really smooth and unproblematic back then?', *Work Employment & Society*, vol 17, no 2, pp 269-87.

Vosko, L. (2006) 'Precarious employment', in L. Vosko (ed) *Precarious employment*, Montreal: McGill-Queen's University Press.

Waddell, G and Burton, K.A (2006) *Is work good for your health and well-being?*, London: The Stationery Office.

Waldfogel, J. (2010) *Britain's war on poverty*, New York: Russell Sage.

Warren, T., Fox, E. and Pascall, G. (2009) 'Innovative social policies: implications for work–life balance amongst low-waged women in England', *Gender, Work and Organisation*, vol 16, no 1, pp 126-50.

Watt, P. (2003) 'Urban marginality and labour market restructuring: local authority tenants and employment in an inner London Borough', *Urban Studies*, vol 40, no 9, pp 1769-89.

Webster, D. (2006) 'Welfare reform: facing up to the geographies of worklessness', *Local Economy*, vol 21, no 2, pp 107-16.

Webster, C., Simpson, D., MacDonald, R., Abbas, A., Cieslik, M., Shildrick, T. and Simpson, M. (2004) *Poor transitions: Social exclusion and young adults*, Bristol: The Policy Press.

Welshman, J. (2007) *From transmitted deprivation to social exclusion*, Bristol: The Policy Press.

Welshman, J. (2011) 'Supporting poor children in working families' in B. Knight (ed), *A minority view: What Beatrice Webb would say now*, Beatrice Webb Memorial Series on Poverty, vol 1, London: Alliance Publishing Trust.

Williams, S. (2011) *Poverty, gender and life-cycle under the English Poor Law, 1760–1834*, Woodbridge: The Boydell Press.

Willis, P. (1977) *Learning to labour: How working class kids get working class jobs*, London: Saxon House.

Wills, J., Kakpo, N. and Begum, R. (2009) *The business case for the living wage: The story of the cleaning service at Queen Mary, University of London*, London: Queen Mary, University of London.

Wills, J., May, J., Datta, K., Evans, Y., Herbert, J. and McIlwaine, C. (2008) *London's changing migrant division of labour*, London: Queen Mary University of London (www.geog.qmul.ac.uk/globalcities/reports/docs/workingpaper10.pdf).

Wintour, P. (2011) 'Payment by results scheme to help long-term unemployed launched', *The Guardian*, 9 June (www.guardian.co.uk/society/2011/jun/09/payment-results-longterm-unemployed).

Wirth, W. (1991) 'Responding to citizen needs: from bureaucratic accountability to individual coproduction in the public sector', in F.X. Kaufmann et al (eds) *The public sector: Challenges for coordination and learning*, Berlin and New York: De Gruyter.

Wolf, A. (2011) *Review of vocational education: The Wolf Report*, London: Department for Education.

Wright, S. (2003) 'Confronting unemployment in a street-level bureaucracy: Jobcentre staff and client perspectives', PhD thesis: University of Stirling.

Wright, S. (2012) 'Can welfare reform work?' *Poverty*, no 139, summer 2011, CPAG.

Zeynep, T. (2012) 'Why good jobs are good for retailers', *Harvard Business Review*, Jan/Feb, vol 90, issue 1/2.

Index

Note: Page numbers in italics refer to figures and boxes.